GEORGE A. ROMERO'S

LAND
OF THE
DEAD

IDW Publishing • San Diego, CA

GEORGE A. ROMERO'S

LAND OF THE DEAD™

Special thanks to George A. Romero, Mark Canton, Peter Grunwald, Bernie Goldman

Special thanks to Al Newman

Special thanks to Cindy Chang and Dawn Rosenquist for their invaluable assistance.

IDW Publishing is: Robbie Robbins, President • Chris Ryall, Publisher/Editor-in-Chief • Ted Adams, Vice President • Kris Oprisko, Vice President
Neil Uyetake, Art Director • Dan Taylor, Editor • Aaron Myers, Distribution Manager • Tom B. Long, Designer • Chance Boren, Editorial Assistant
Matthew Ruzicka, CPA, Controller • Alex Garner, Creative Director • Yumiko Miyano, Business Development • Rick Privman, Business development

www.IDWPUBLISHING.com

Based on the motion picture screenplay written by **George A. Romero**

Adapted by **Chris Ryall**

Art by **Gabriel Rodriguez**

Colors by **Jay Fotos**

Covers by **Chris Bolton**

Designed by **Neil Uyetake**

Lettered by **Robbie Robbins**

Edited by **Dan Taylor**

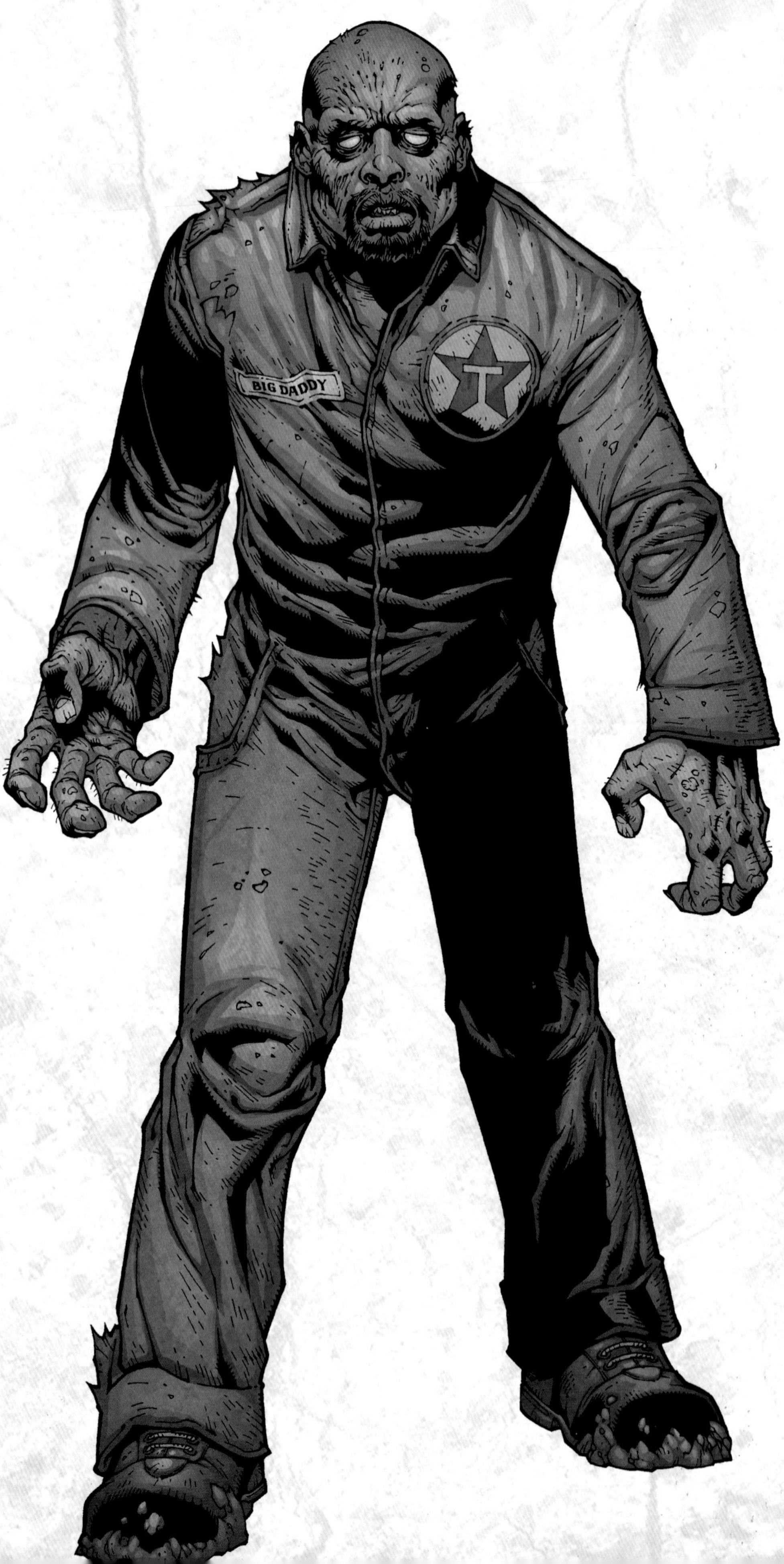
BIG DADDY

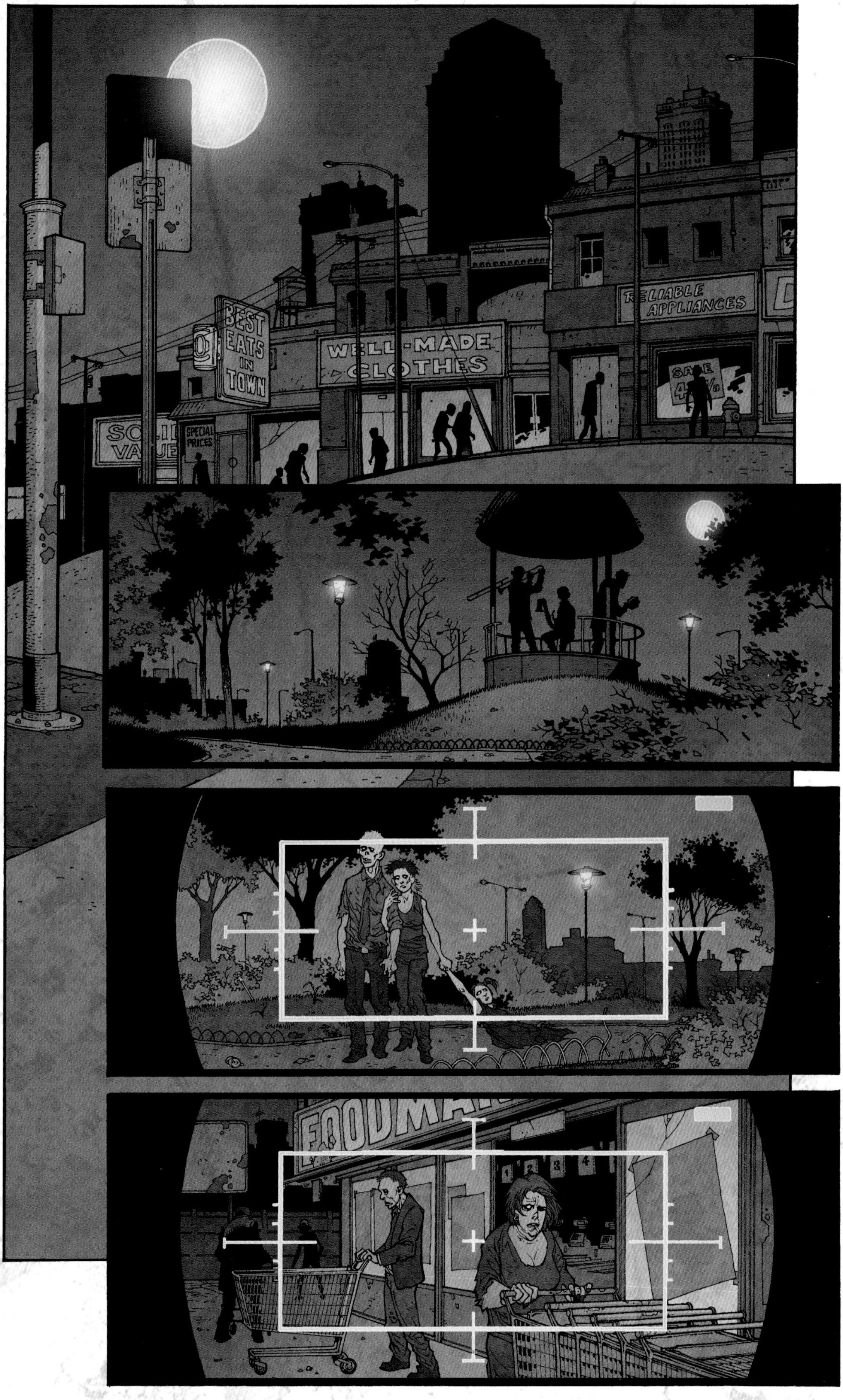

BEST EATS IN TOWN
WELL-MADE CLOTHES
RELIABLE APPLIANCES
SPECIAL PRICES

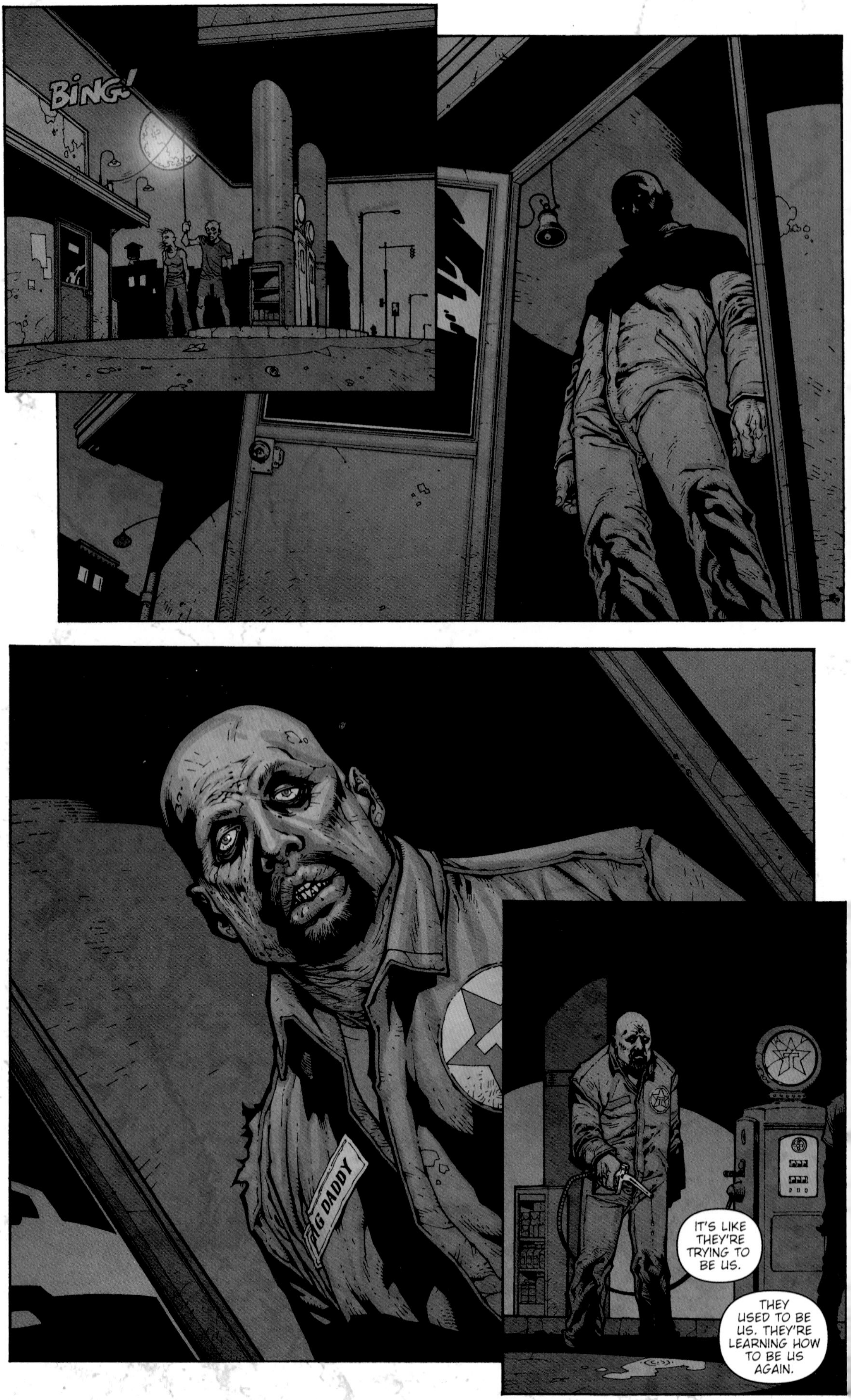
BING!
IT'S LIKE THEY'RE TRYING TO BE US.
THEY USED TO BE US. THEY'RE LEARNING HOW TO BE US AGAIN.

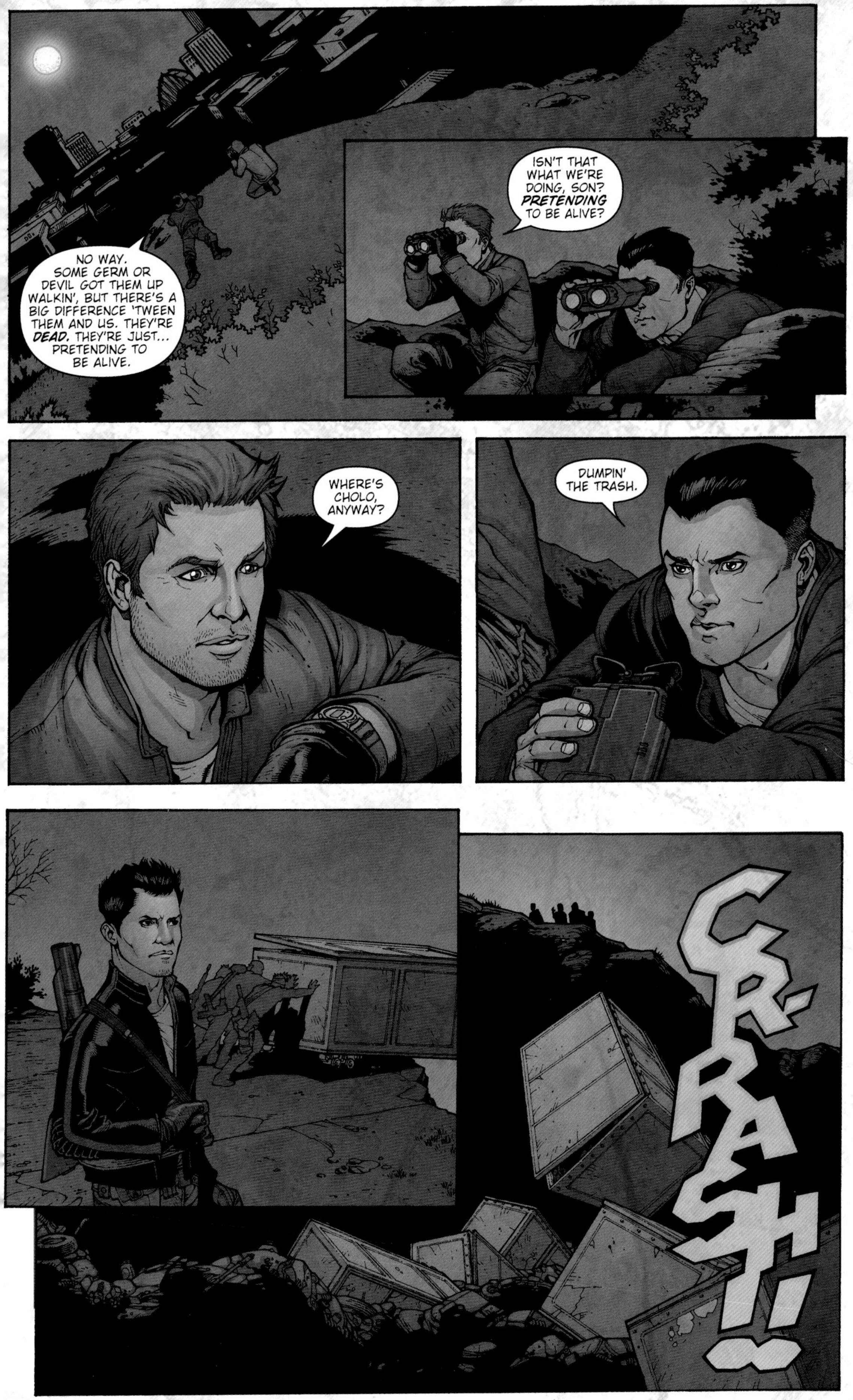
NO WAY. SOME GERM OR DEVIL GOT THEM UP WALKIN', BUT THERE'S A BIG DIFFERENCE 'TWEEN THEM AND US. THEY'RE DEAD. THEY'RE JUST... PRETENDING TO BE ALIVE.
ISN'T THAT WHAT WE'RE DOING, SON? PRETENDING TO BE ALIVE?
WHERE'S CHOLO, ANYWAY?
DUMPIN' THE TRASH.
CR-RASH!!

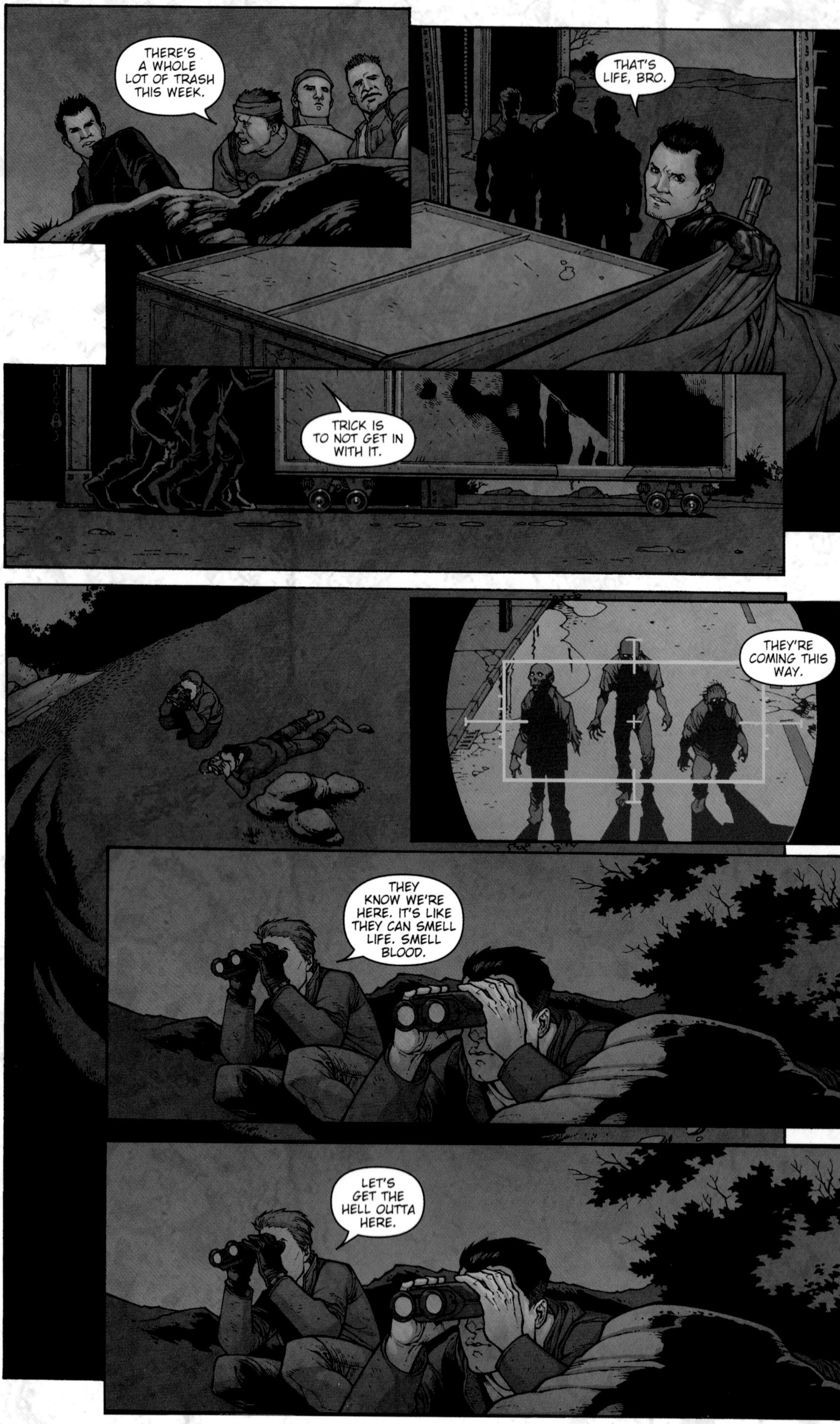
THERE'S A WHOLE LOT OF TRASH THIS WEEK.
THAT'S LIFE, BRO.
TRICK IS TO NOT GET IN WITH IT.
THEY'RE COMING THIS WAY.
THEY KNOW WE'RE HERE. IT'S LIKE THEY CAN SMELL LIFE. SMELL BLOOD.
LET'S GET THE HELL OUTTA HERE.

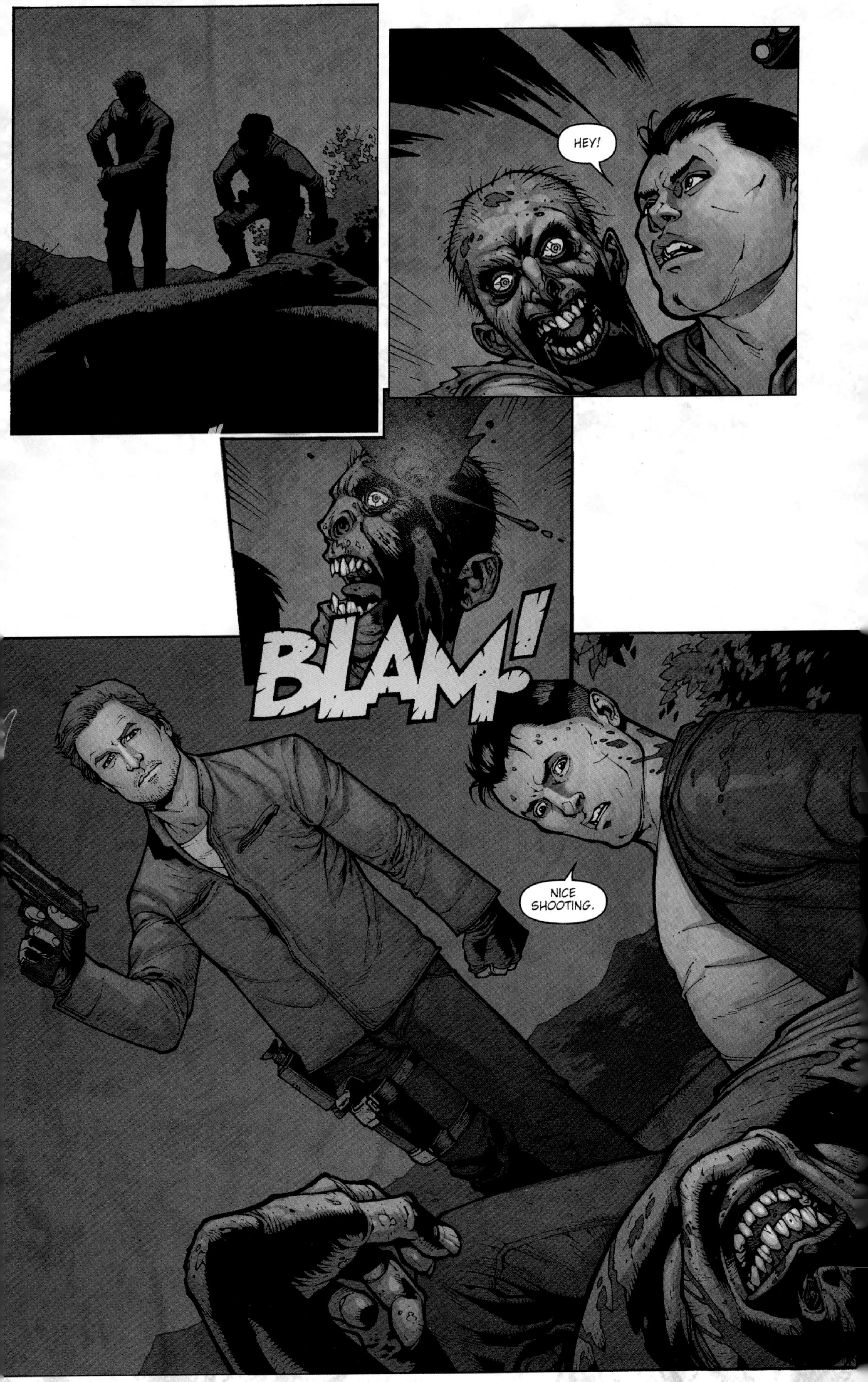
HEY!
BLAM!
NICE SHOOTING.

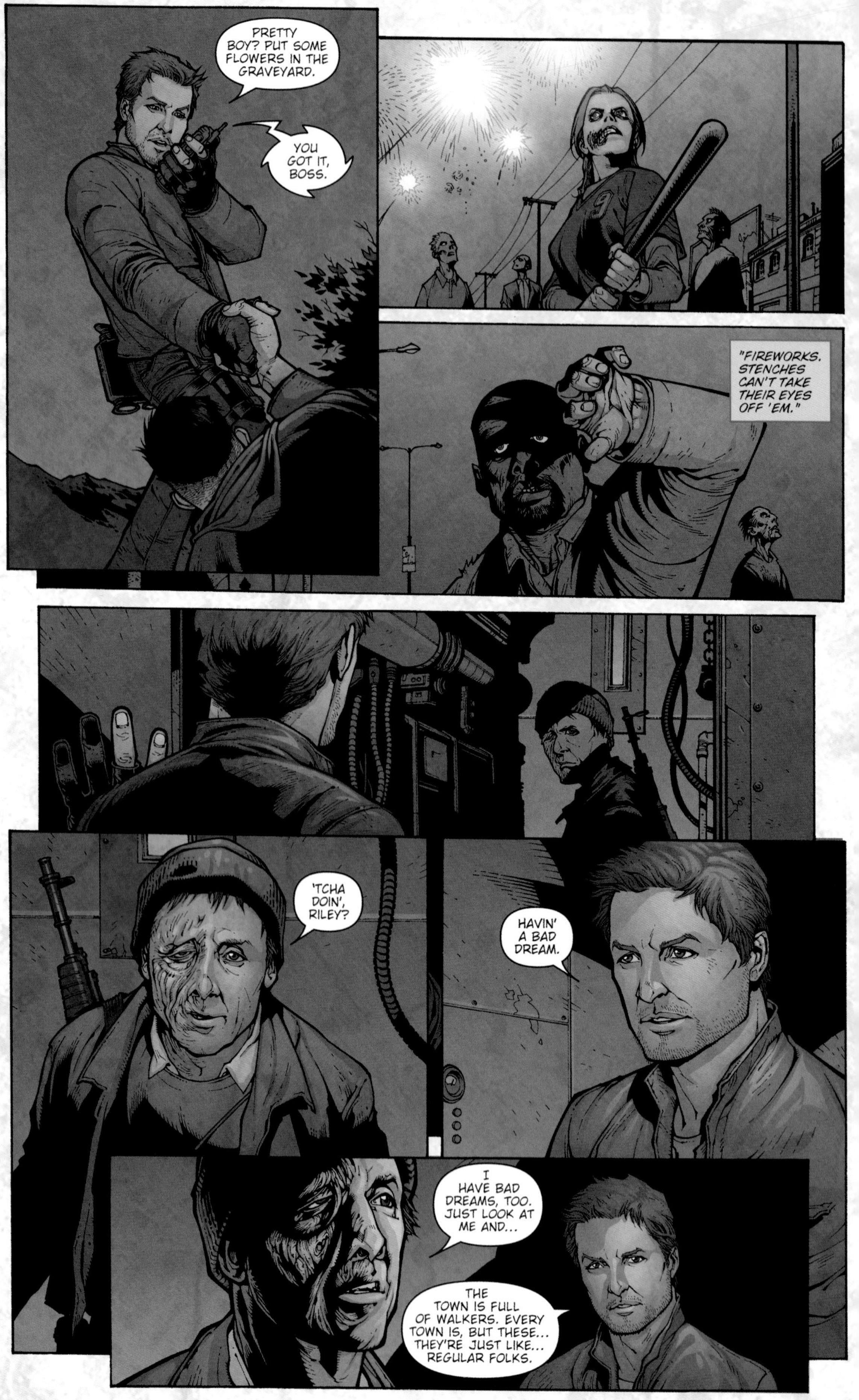
PRETTY BOY? PUT SOME FLOWERS IN THE GRAVEYARD.
YOU GOT IT, BOSS.
"FIREWORKS. STENCHES CAN'T TAKE THEIR EYES OFF 'EM."
'TCHA DOIN', RILEY?
HAVIN' A BAD DREAM.
I HAVE BAD DREAMS, TOO. JUST LOOK AT ME AND...
THE TOWN IS FULL OF WALKERS. EVERY TOWN IS, BUT THESE... THEY'RE JUST LIKE... REGULAR FOLKS.

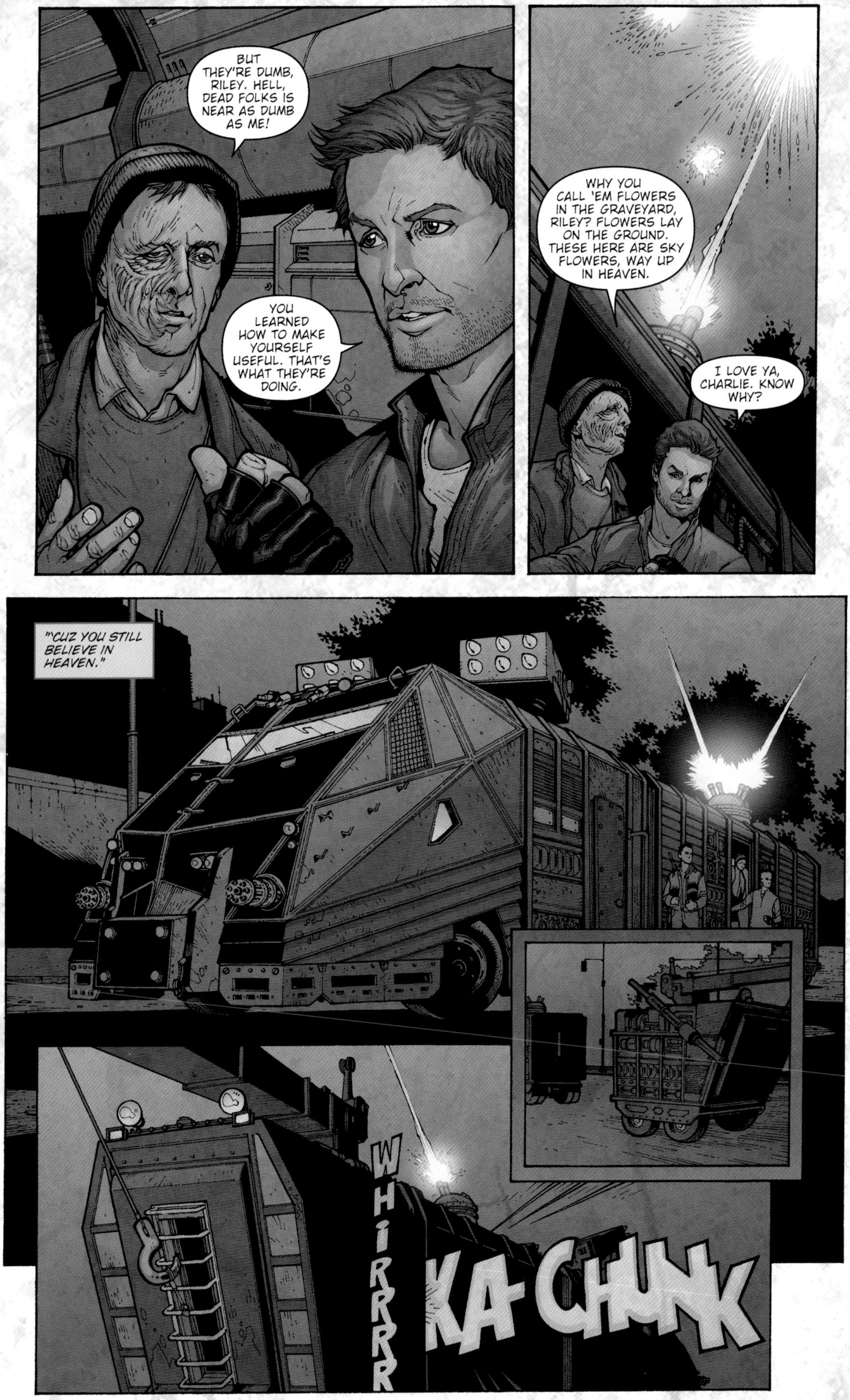
BUT THEY'RE DUMB, RILEY. HELL, DEAD FOLKS IS NEAR AS DUMB AS ME!
YOU LEARNED HOW TO MAKE YOURSELF USEFUL. THAT'S WHAT THEY'RE DOING.
WHY YOU CALL 'EM FLOWERS IN THE GRAVEYARD, RILEY? FLOWERS LAY ON THE GROUND. THESE HERE ARE SKY FLOWERS, WAY UP IN HEAVEN.
I LOVE YA, CHARLIE. KNOW WHY?
"CUZ YOU STILL BELIEVE IN HEAVEN."
WHIRRR
KA CHUNK

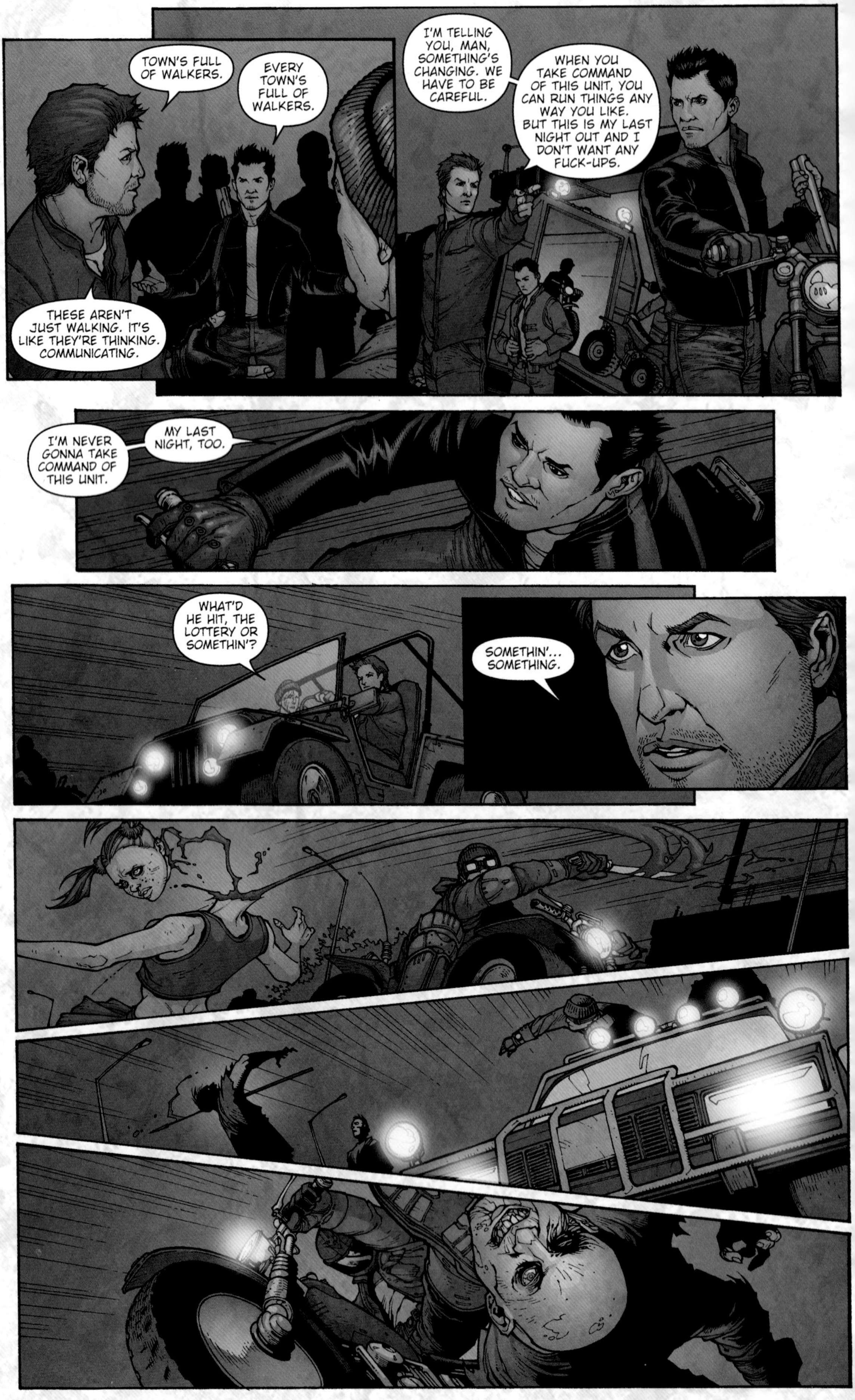
TOWN'S FULL OF WALKERS.
EVERY TOWN'S FULL OF WALKERS.
THESE AREN'T JUST WALKING. IT'S LIKE THEY'RE THINKING. COMMUNICATING.
I'M TELLING YOU, MAN, SOMETHING'S CHANGING. WE HAVE TO BE CAREFUL.
WHEN YOU TAKE COMMAND OF THIS UNIT, YOU CAN RUN THINGS ANY WAY YOU LIKE. BUT THIS IS MY LAST NIGHT OUT AND I DON'T WANT ANY FUCK-UPS.
I'M NEVER GONNA TAKE COMMAND OF THIS UNIT.
MY LAST NIGHT, TOO.
WHAT'D HE HIT, THE LOTTERY OR SOMETHIN'?
SOMETHIN'... SOMETHING.

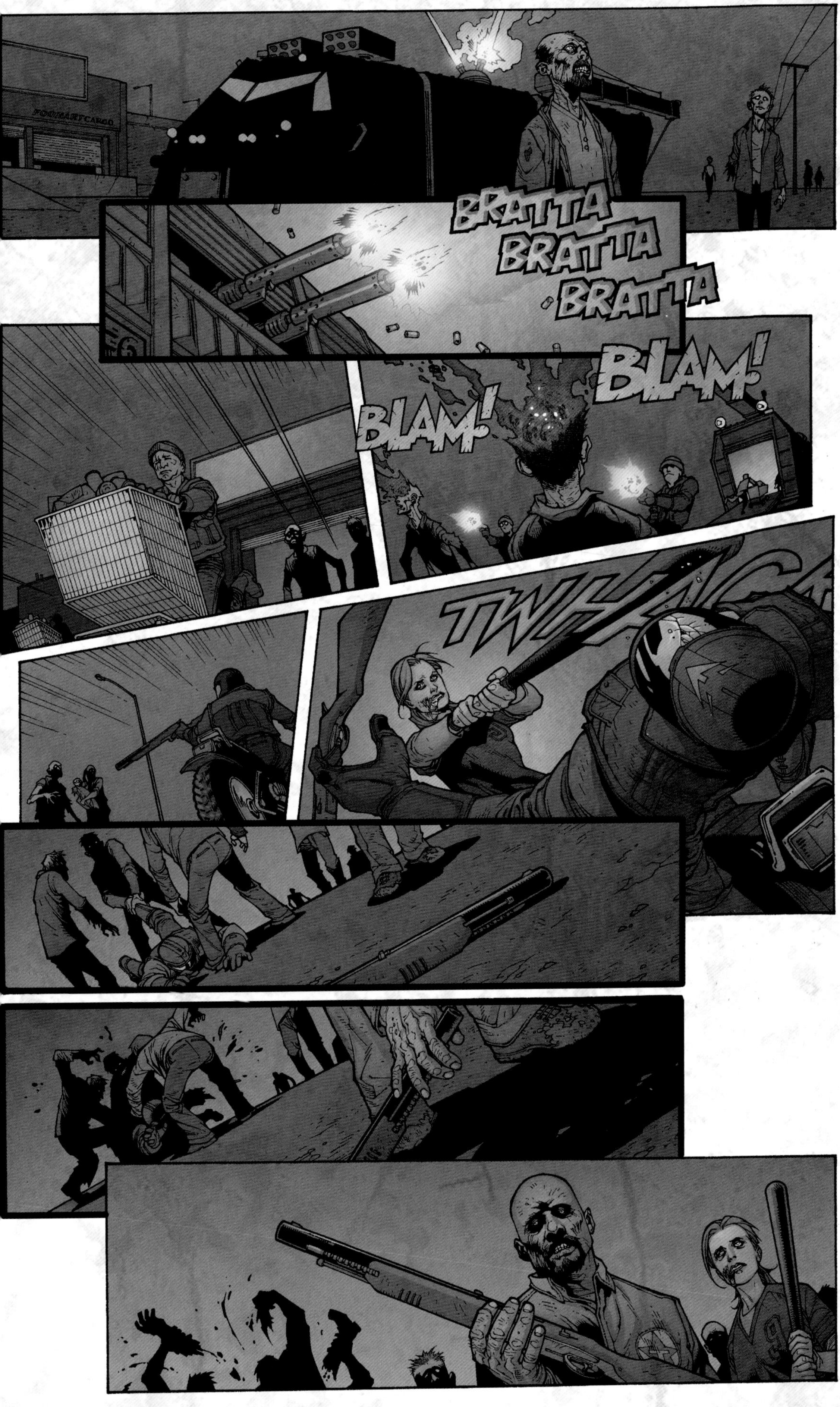
FOODMART CARGO
BRATTA
BRATTA
BRATTA
BLAM!
BLAM!
TWHACK

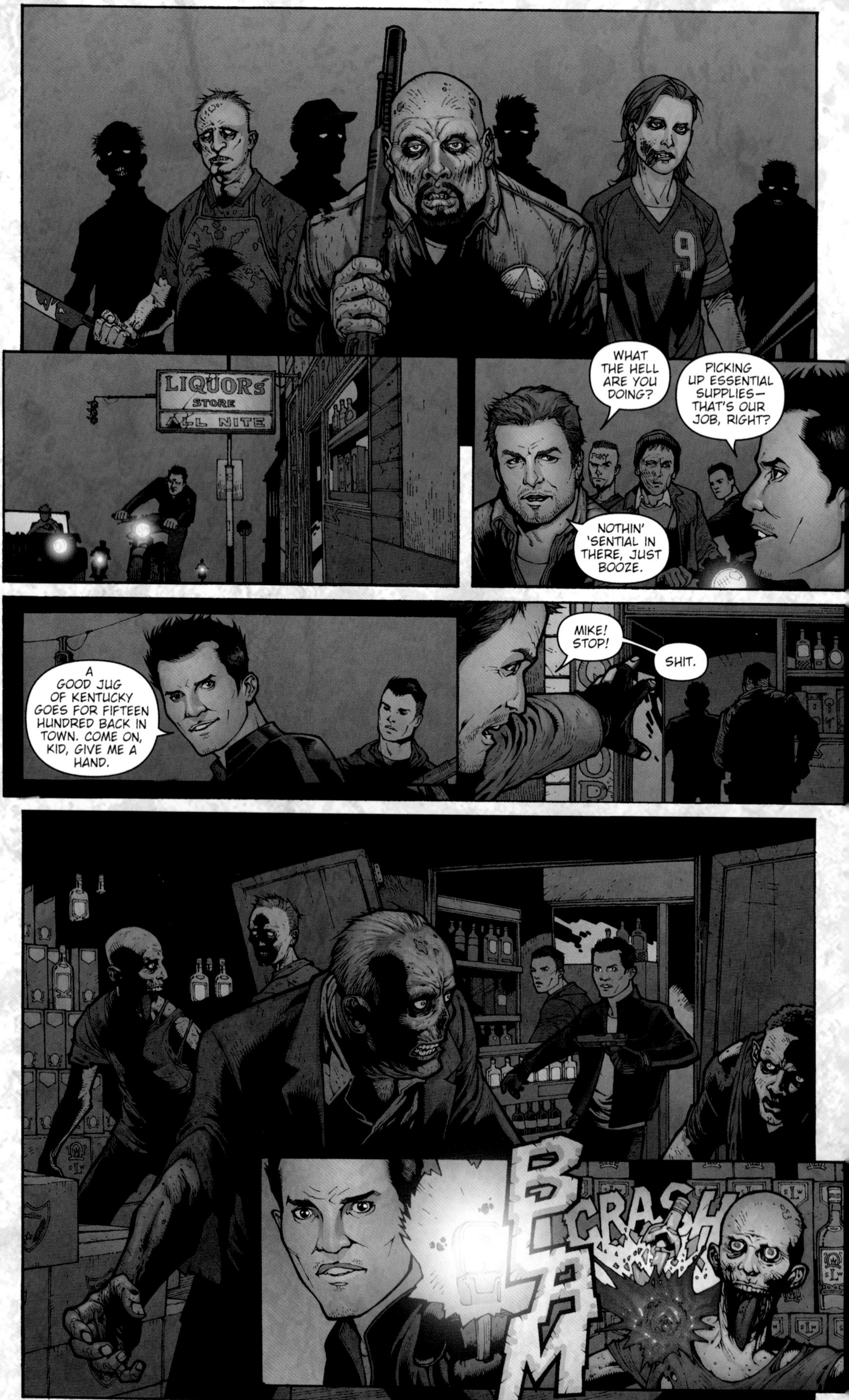
LIQUORS STORE
ALL NITE
WHAT THE HELL ARE YOU DOING?
PICKING UP ESSENTIAL SUPPLIES— THAT'S OUR JOB, RIGHT?
NOTHIN' 'SENTIAL IN THERE, JUST BOOZE.
A GOOD JUG OF KENTUCKY GOES FOR FIFTEEN HUNDRED BACK IN TOWN. COME ON, KID, GIVE ME A HAND.
MIKE! STOP!
SHIT.
BLAM
CRASH

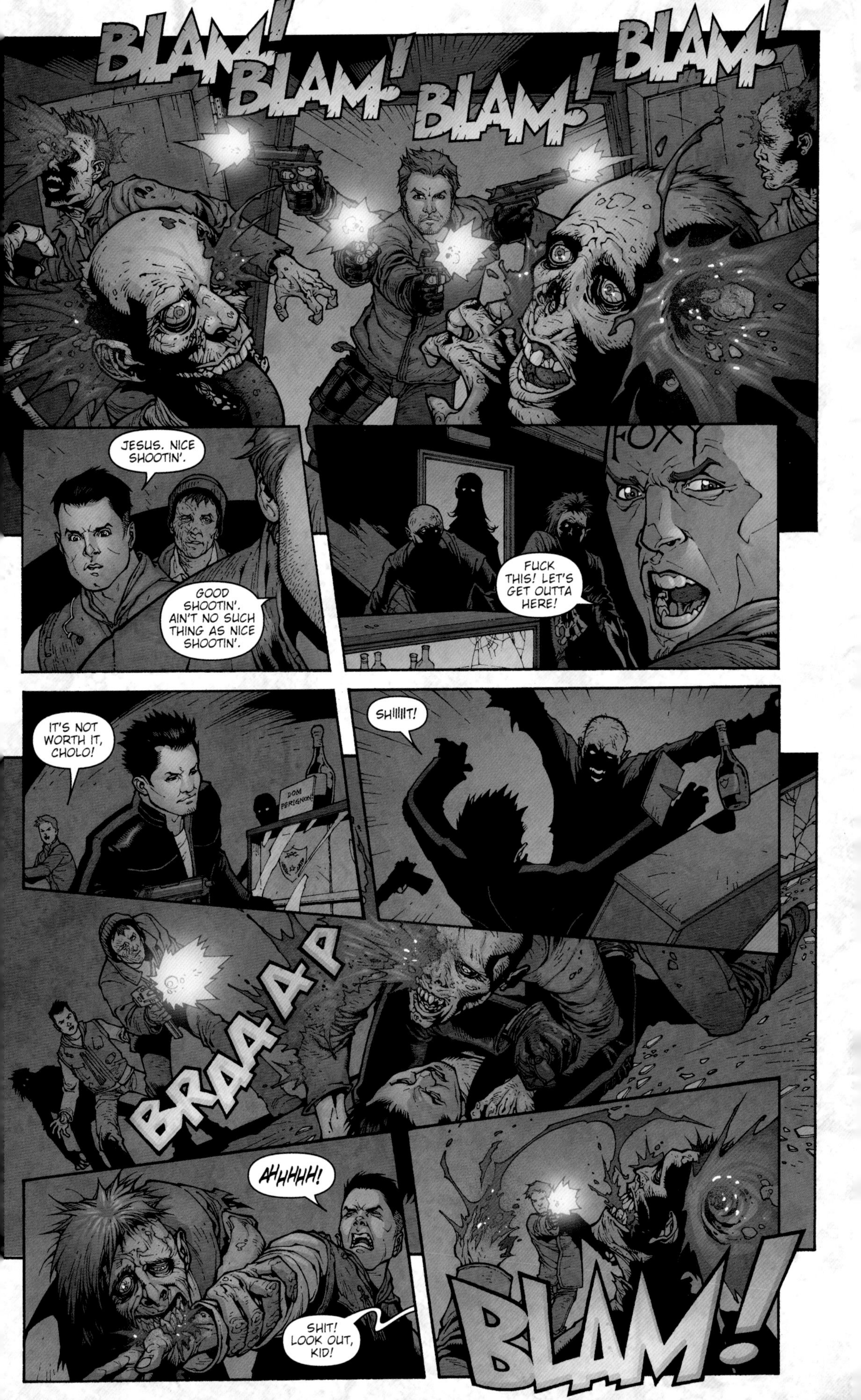
BLAM! BLAM! BLAM! BLAM!
JESUS. NICE SHOOTIN'.
GOOD SHOOTIN'. AIN'T NO SUCH THING AS NICE SHOOTIN'.
FOXY
FUCK THIS! LET'S GET OUTTA HERE!
IT'S NOT WORTH IT, CHOLO!
DOM PERIGNON
SHIIIIIT!
BRAAAP
AHHHHH!
SHIT! LOOK OUT, KID!
BLAM!

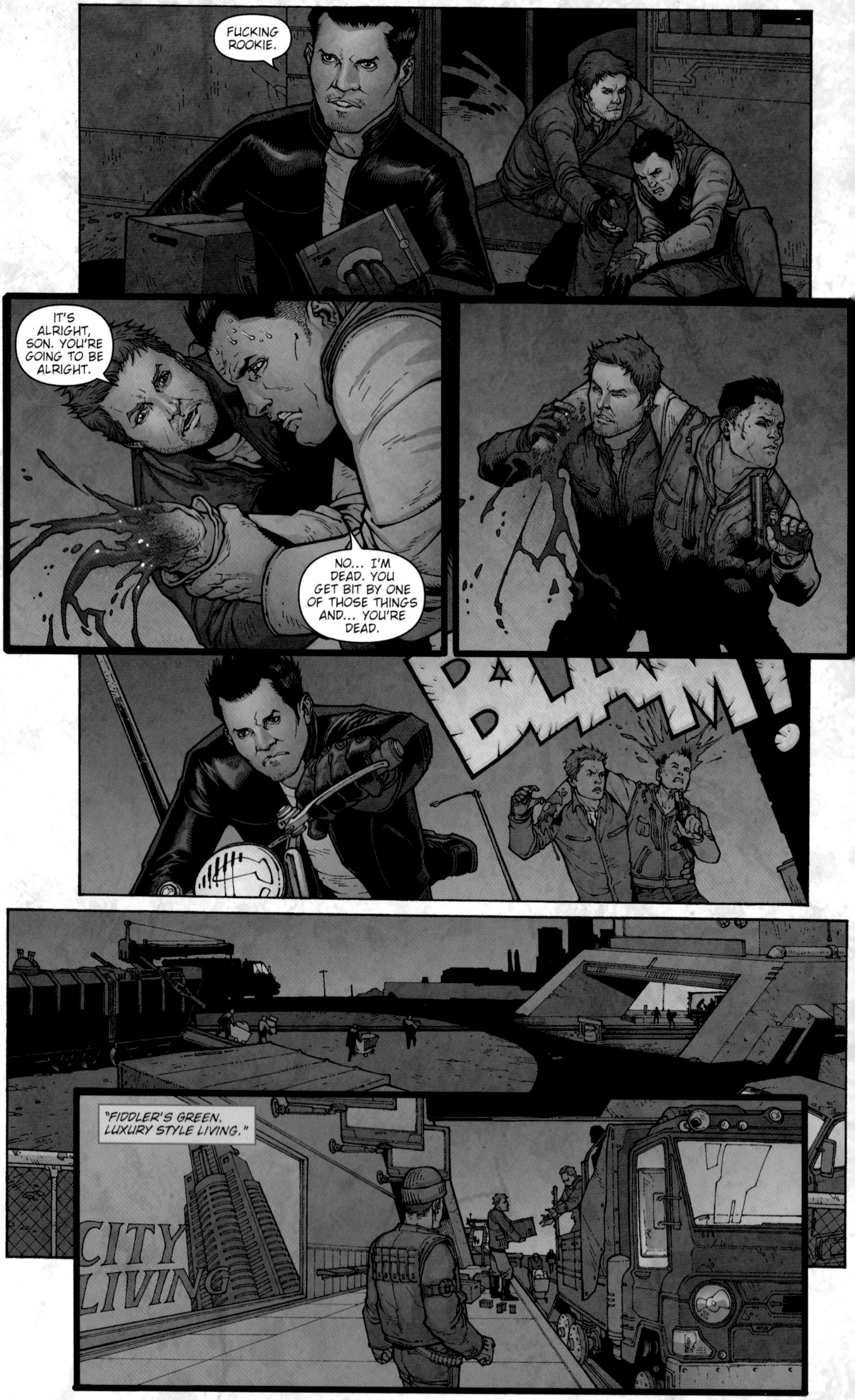
FUCKING ROOKIE.
IT'S ALRIGHT, SON. YOU'RE GOING TO BE ALRIGHT.
NO... I'M DEAD. YOU GET BIT BY ONE OF THOSE THINGS AND... YOU'RE DEAD.
BLAM!
"FIDDLER'S GREEN. LUXURY STYLE LIVING."
CITY LIVING

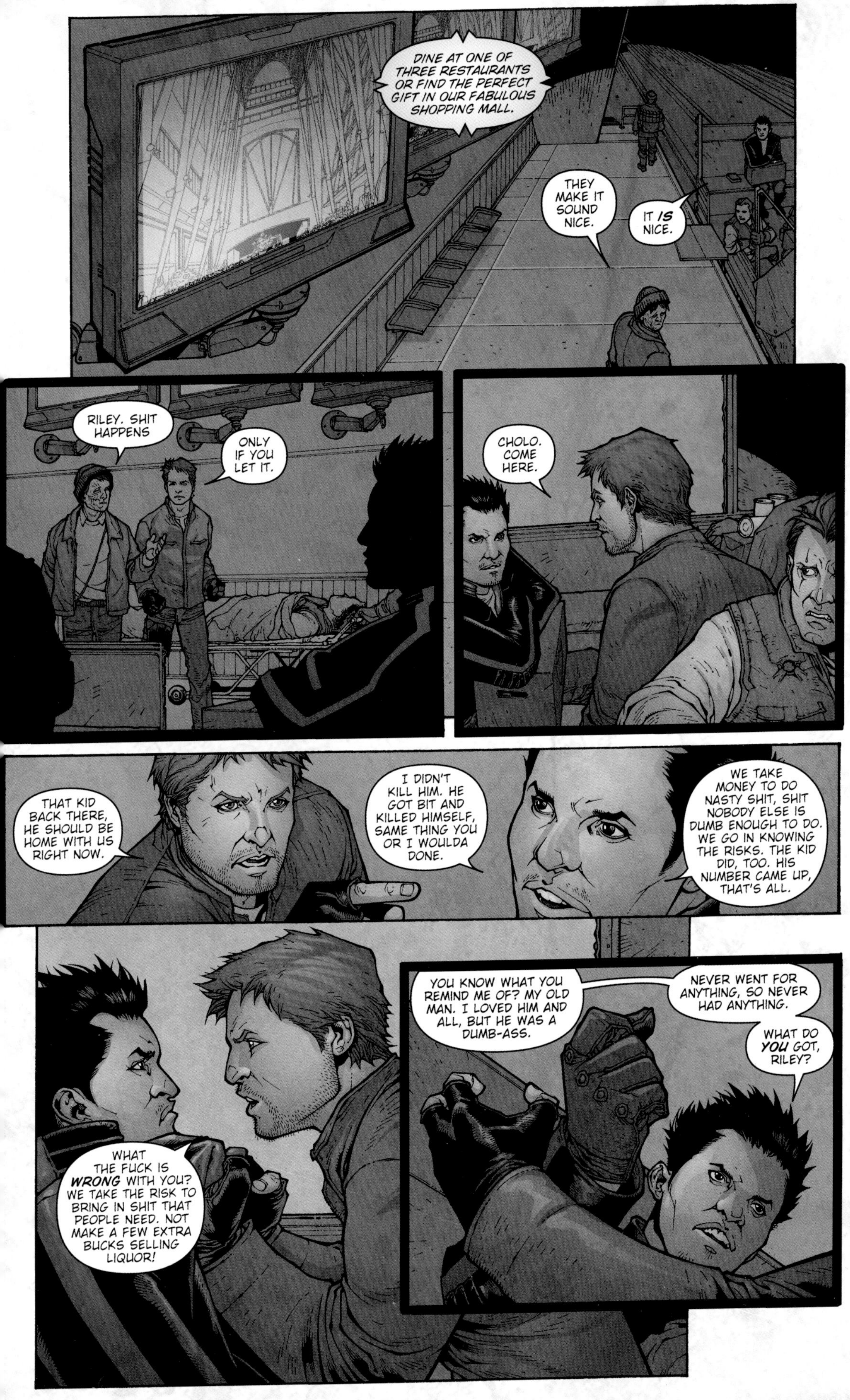
DINE AT ONE OF THREE RESTAURANTS OR FIND THE PERFECT GIFT IN OUR FABULOUS SHOPPING MALL.
THEY MAKE IT SOUND NICE.
IT *IS* NICE.
RILEY. SHIT HAPPENS
ONLY IF YOU LET IT.
CHOLO. COME HERE.
THAT KID BACK THERE, HE SHOULD BE HOME WITH US RIGHT NOW.
I DIDN'T KILL HIM. HE GOT BIT AND KILLED HIMSELF, SAME THING YOU OR I WOULDA DONE.
WE TAKE MONEY TO DO NASTY SHIT, SHIT NOBODY ELSE IS DUMB ENOUGH TO DO. WE GO IN KNOWING THE RISKS. THE KID DID, TOO. HIS NUMBER CAME UP, THAT'S ALL.
WHAT THE FUCK IS *WRONG* WITH YOU? WE TAKE THE RISK TO BRING IN SHIT THAT PEOPLE NEED. NOT MAKE A FEW EXTRA BUCKS SELLING LIQUOR!
YOU KNOW WHAT YOU REMIND ME OF? MY OLD MAN. I LOVED HIM AND ALL, BUT HE WAS A DUMB-ASS.
NEVER WENT FOR ANYTHING, SO NEVER HAD ANYTHING.
WHAT DO *YOU* GOT, RILEY?

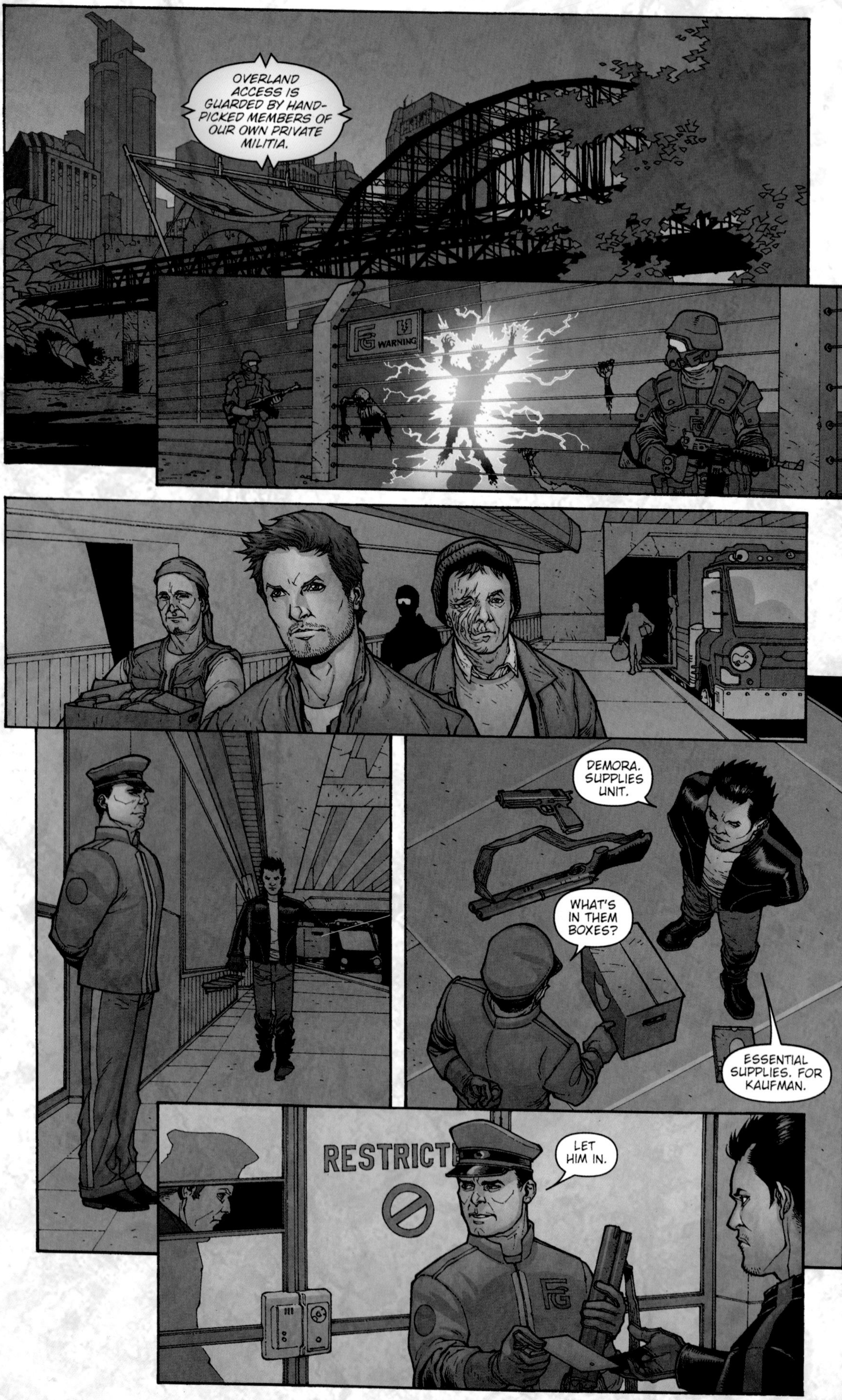

OVERLAND ACCESS IS GUARDED BY HAND-PICKED MEMBERS OF OUR OWN PRIVATE MILITIA.
WARNING
DEMORA. SUPPLIES UNIT.
WHAT'S IN THEM BOXES?
ESSENTIAL SUPPLIES. FOR KAUFMAN.
RESTRICTE
LET HIM IN.

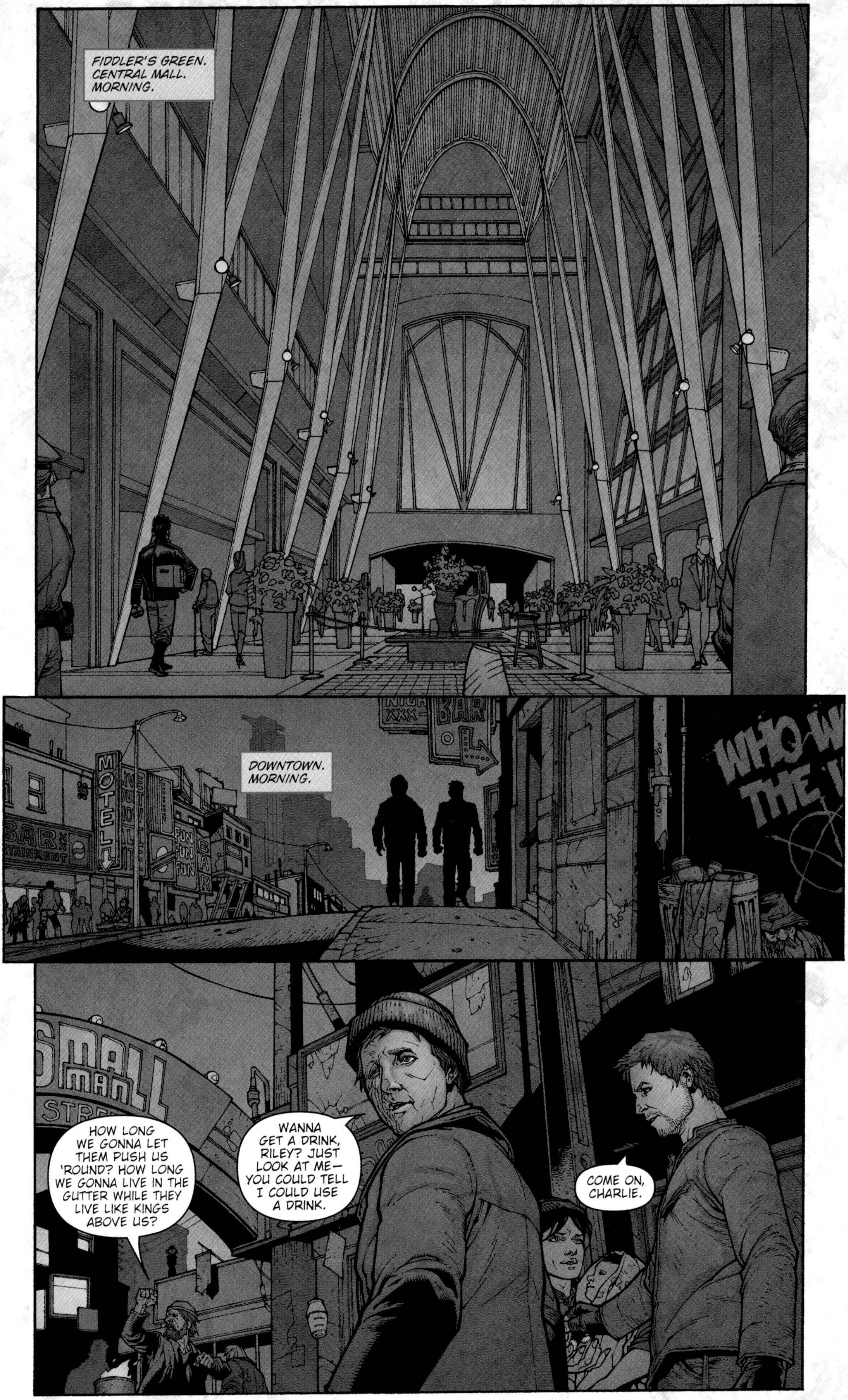
FIDDLER'S GREEN. CENTRAL MALL. MORNING.
DOWNTOWN. MORNING.
MOTEL
BAR
HOW LONG WE GONNA LET THEM PUSH US 'ROUND? HOW LONG WE GONNA LIVE IN THE GUTTER WHILE THEY LIVE LIKE KINGS ABOVE US?
WANNA GET A DRINK, RILEY? JUST LOOK AT ME— YOU COULD TELL I COULD USE A DRINK.
COME ON, CHARLIE.

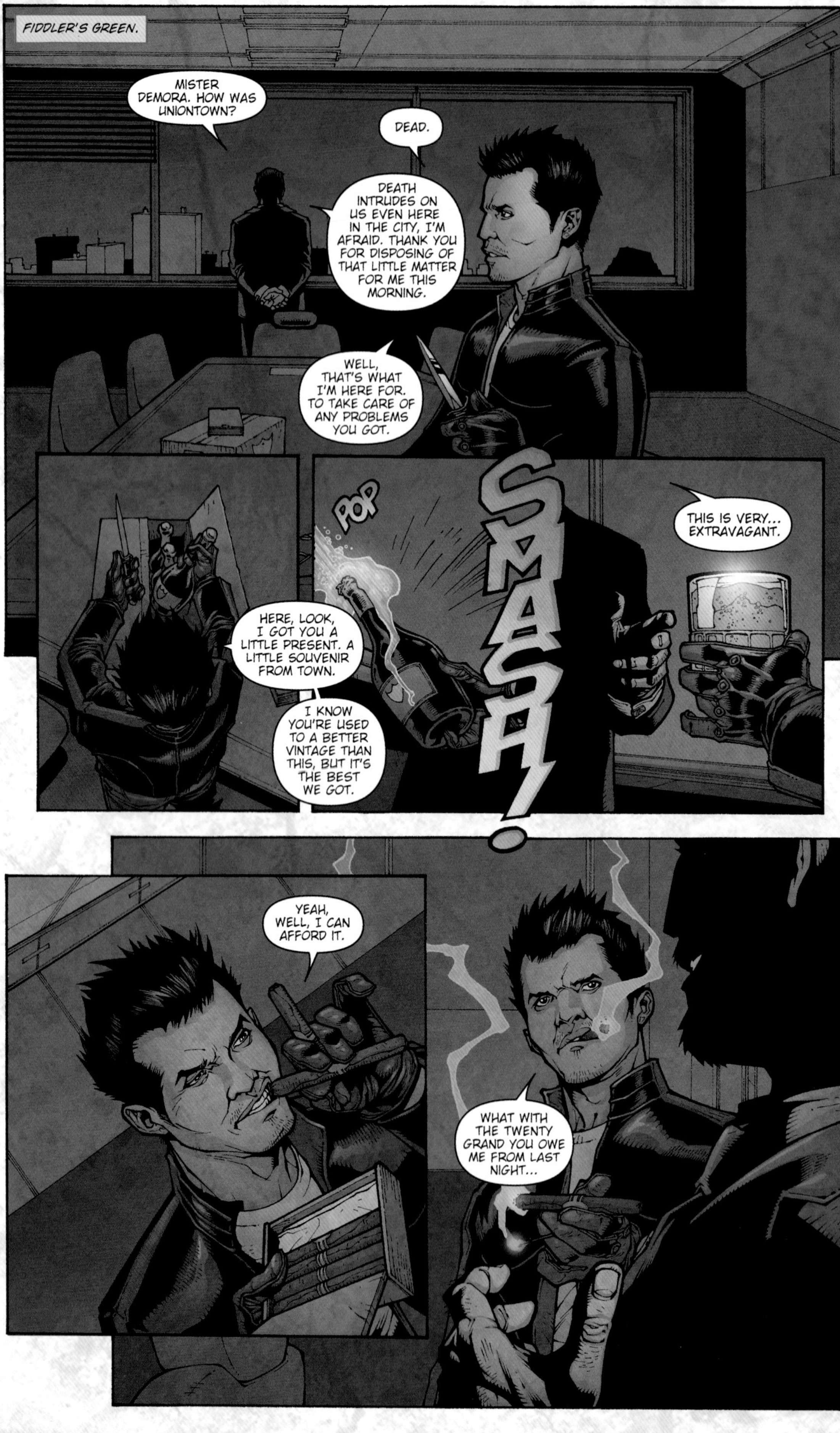
FIDDLER'S GREEN.
MISTER DEMORA. HOW WAS UNIONTOWN?
DEAD.
DEATH INTRUDES ON US EVEN HERE IN THE CITY, I'M AFRAID. THANK YOU FOR DISPOSING OF THAT LITTLE MATTER FOR ME THIS MORNING.
WELL, THAT'S WHAT I'M HERE FOR. TO TAKE CARE OF ANY PROBLEMS YOU GOT.
HERE, LOOK, I GOT YOU A LITTLE PRESENT. A LITTLE SOUVENIR FROM TOWN.
I KNOW YOU'RE USED TO A BETTER VINTAGE THAN THIS, BUT IT'S THE BEST WE GOT.
POP
SMASH!
THIS IS VERY... EXTRAVAGANT.
YEAH, WELL, I CAN AFFORD IT.
WHAT WITH THE TWENTY GRAND YOU OWE ME FROM LAST NIGHT...

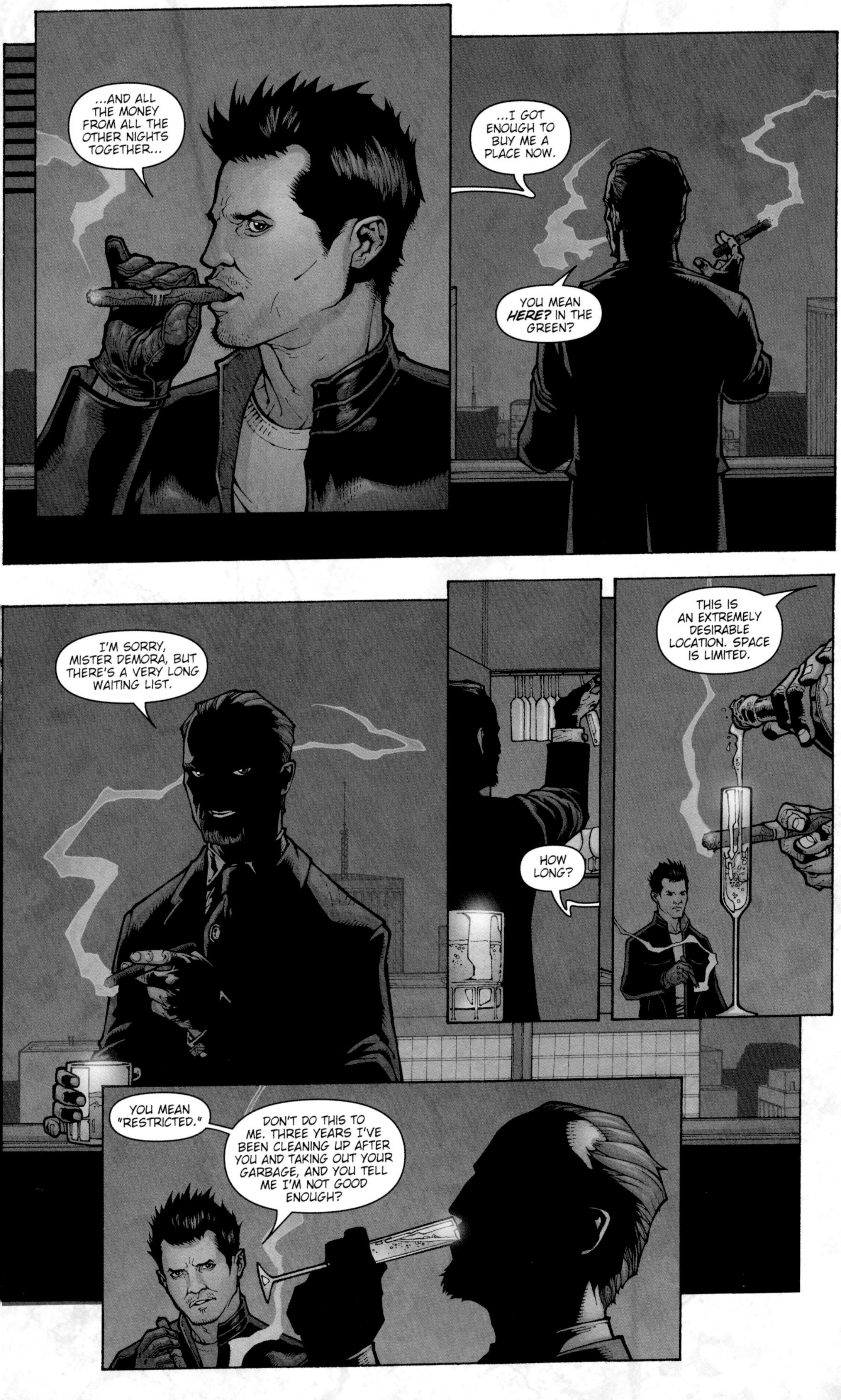
...AND ALL THE MONEY FROM ALL THE OTHER NIGHTS TOGETHER...
...I GOT ENOUGH TO BUY ME A PLACE NOW.
YOU MEAN *HERE?* IN THE GREEN?
I'M SORRY, MISTER DEMORA, BUT THERE'S A VERY LONG WAITING LIST.
HOW LONG?
THIS IS AN EXTREMELY DESIRABLE LOCATION. SPACE IS LIMITED.
YOU MEAN "RESTRICTED."
DON'T DO THIS TO ME. THREE YEARS I'VE BEEN CLEANING UP AFTER YOU AND TAKING OUT YOUR GARBAGE, AND YOU TELL ME I'M NOT GOOD ENOUGH?

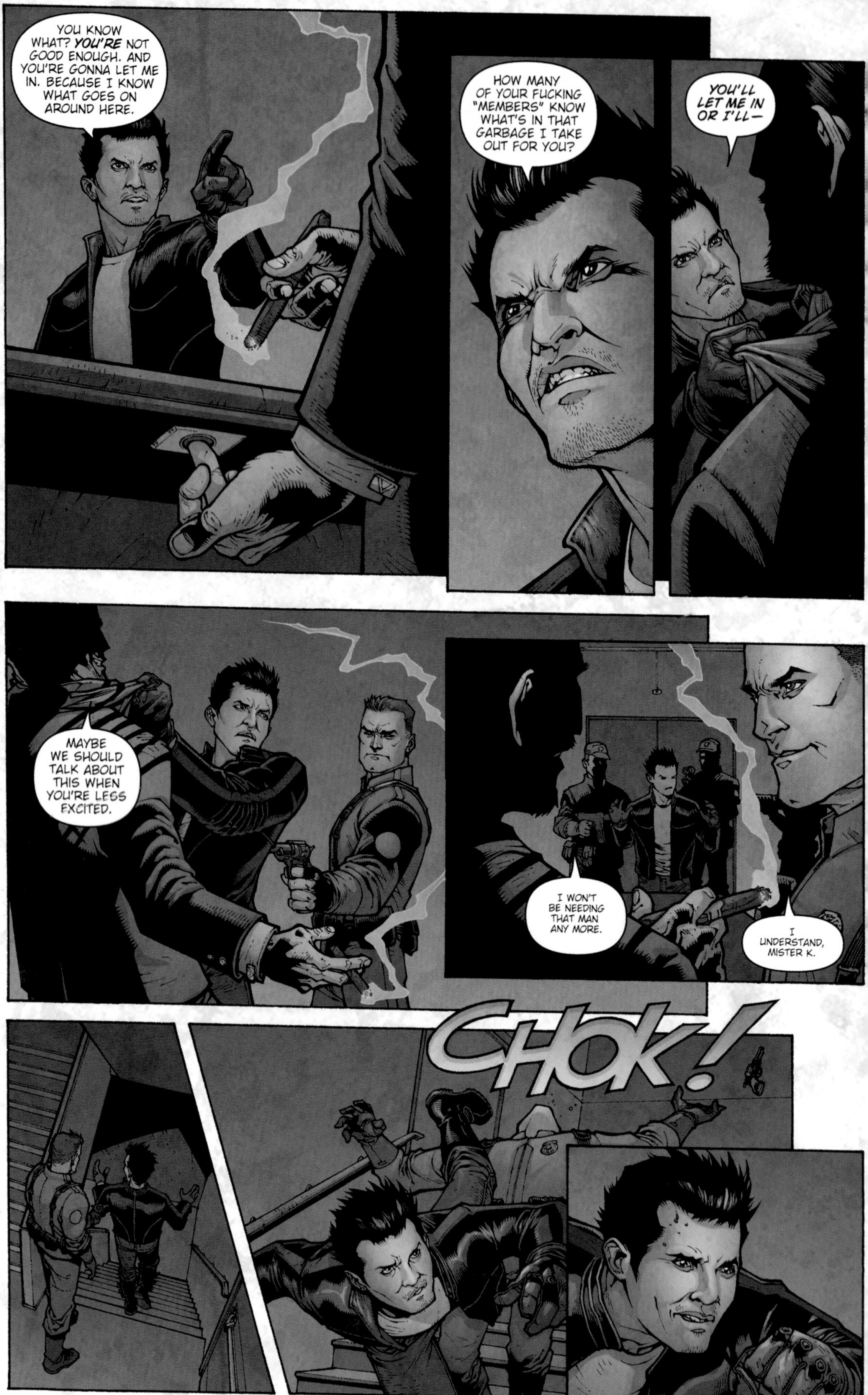
YOU KNOW WHAT? *YOU'RE* NOT GOOD ENOUGH. AND YOU'RE GONNA LET ME IN. BECAUSE I KNOW WHAT GOES ON AROUND HERE.
HOW MANY OF YOUR FUCKING "MEMBERS" KNOW WHAT'S IN THAT GARBAGE I TAKE OUT FOR YOU?
YOU'LL LET ME IN OR I'LL—
MAYBE WE SHOULD TALK ABOUT THIS WHEN YOU'RE LESS EXCITED.
I WON'T BE NEEDING THAT MAN ANY MORE.
I UNDERSTAND, MISTER K.
CHOK!

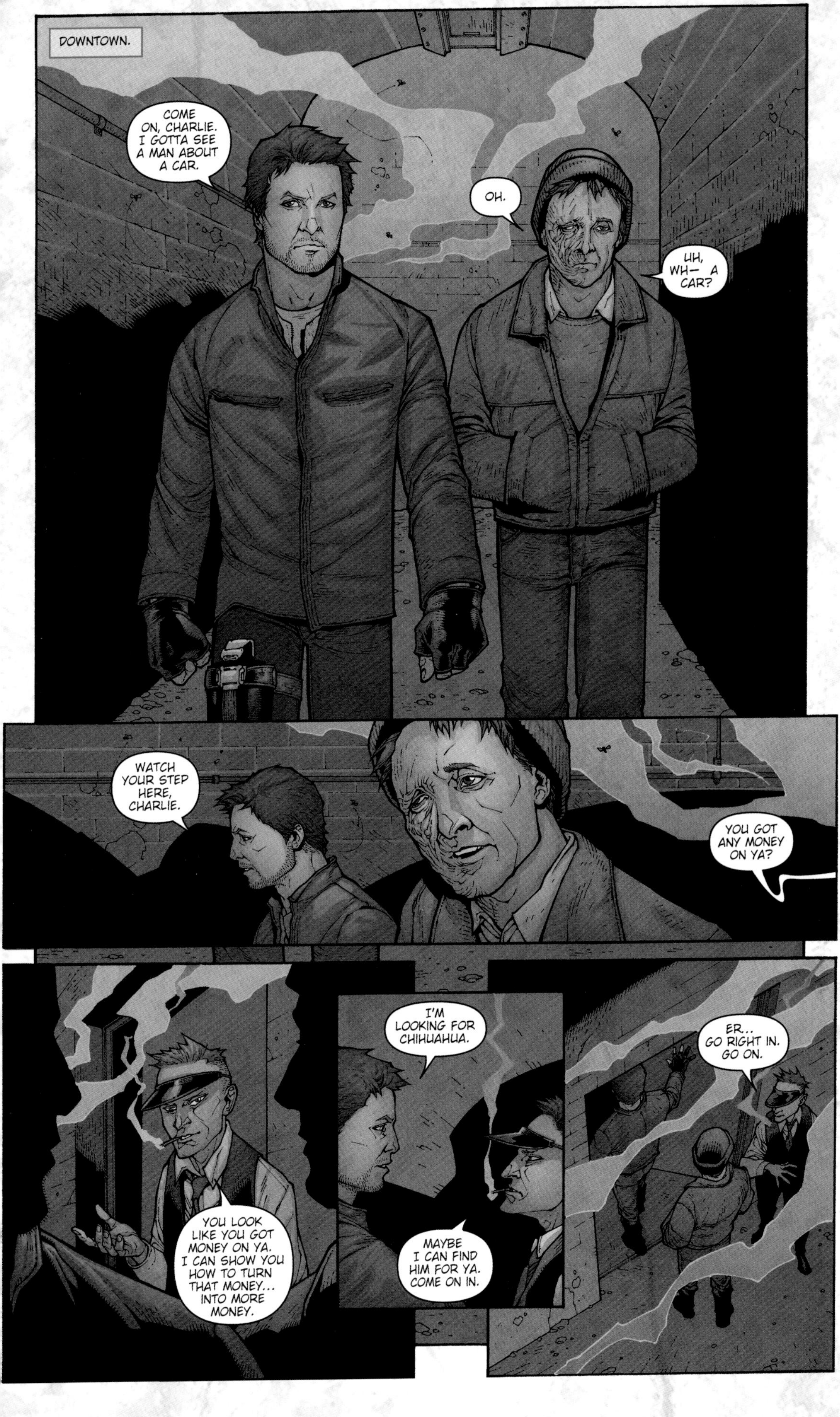
DOWNTOWN.
COME ON, CHARLIE. I GOTTA SEE A MAN ABOUT A CAR.
OH.
UH, WH— A CAR?
WATCH YOUR STEP HERE, CHARLIE.
YOU GOT ANY MONEY ON YA?
YOU LOOK LIKE YOU GOT MONEY ON YA. I CAN SHOW YOU HOW TO TURN THAT MONEY... INTO MORE MONEY.
I'M LOOKING FOR CHIHUAHUA.
MAYBE I CAN FIND HIM FOR YA. COME ON IN.
ER... GO RIGHT IN. GO ON.

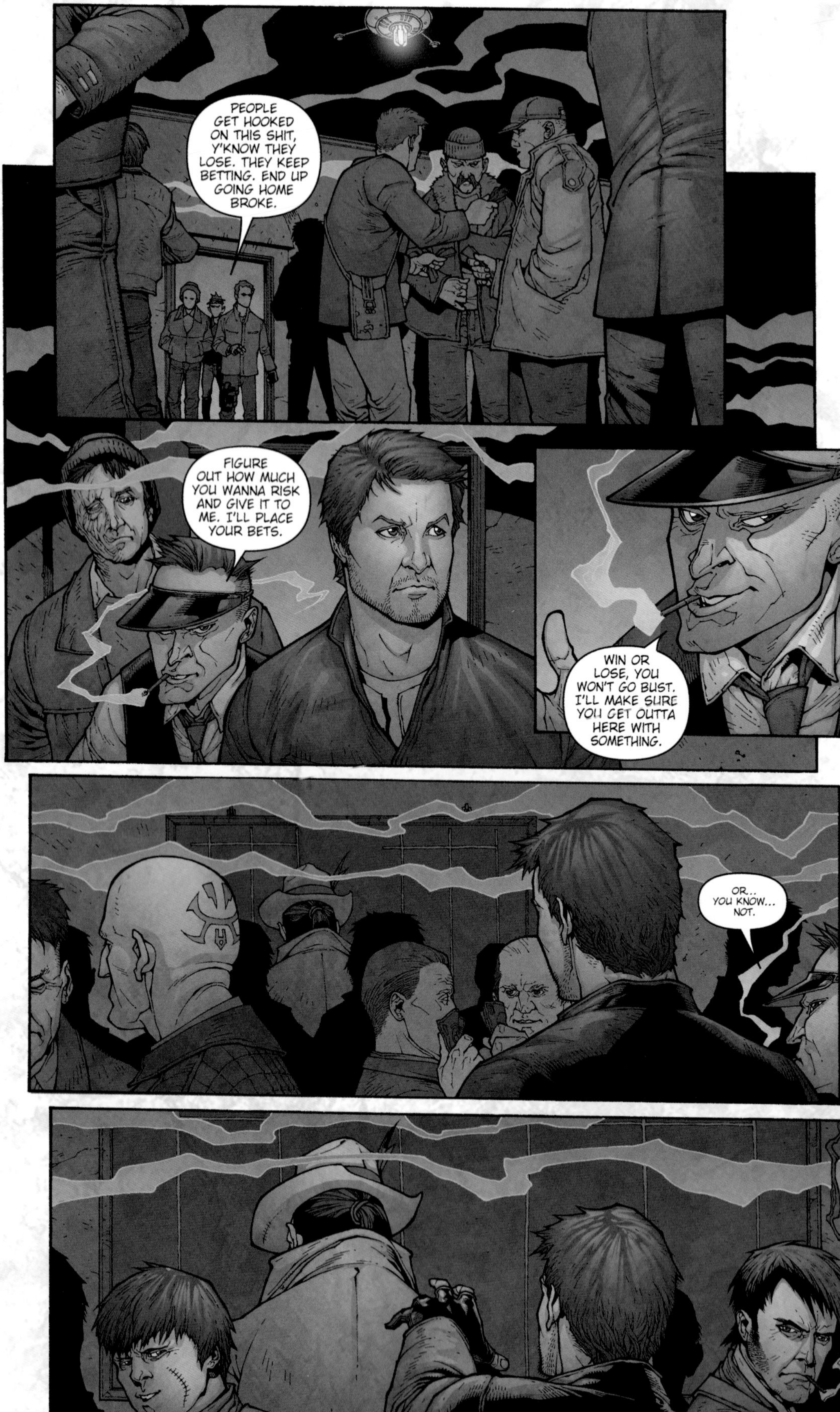
PEOPLE GET HOOKED ON THIS SHIT, Y'KNOW THEY LOSE. THEY KEEP BETTING. END UP GOING HOME BROKE.
FIGURE OUT HOW MUCH YOU WANNA RISK AND GIVE IT TO ME. I'LL PLACE YOUR BETS.
WIN OR LOSE, YOU WON'T GO BUST. I'LL MAKE SURE YOU GET OUTTA HERE WITH SOMETHING.
OR... YOU KNOW... NOT.

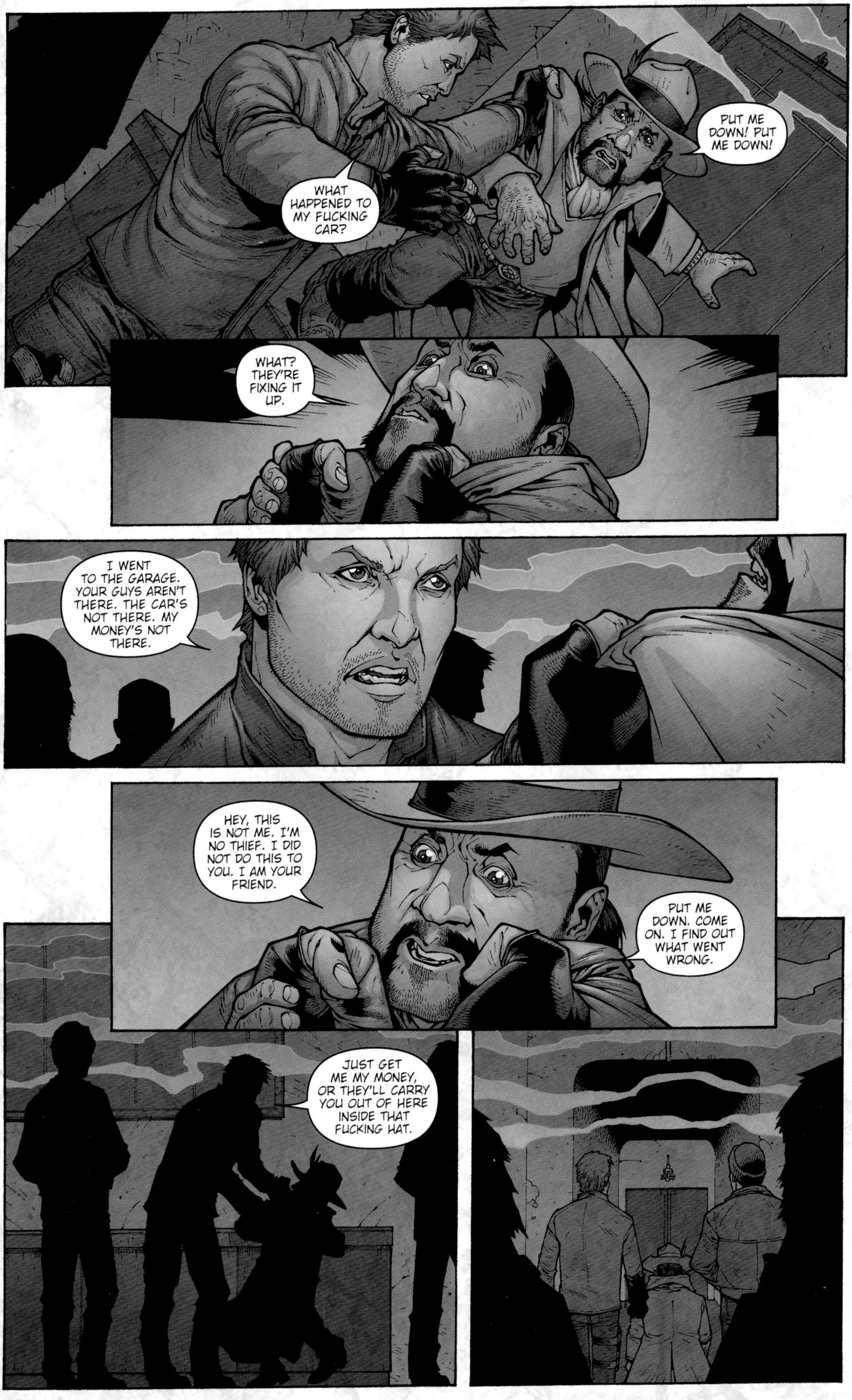
WHAT HAPPENED TO MY FUCKING CAR?
PUT ME DOWN! PUT ME DOWN!
WHAT? THEY'RE FIXING IT UP.
I WENT TO THE GARAGE. YOUR GUYS AREN'T THERE. THE CAR'S NOT THERE. MY MONEY'S NOT THERE.
HEY, THIS IS NOT ME. I'M NO THIEF. I DID NOT DO THIS TO YOU. I AM YOUR FRIEND.
PUT ME DOWN. COME ON. I FIND OUT WHAT WENT WRONG.
JUST GET ME MY MONEY, OR THEY'LL CARRY YOU OUT OF HERE INSIDE THAT FUCKING HAT.

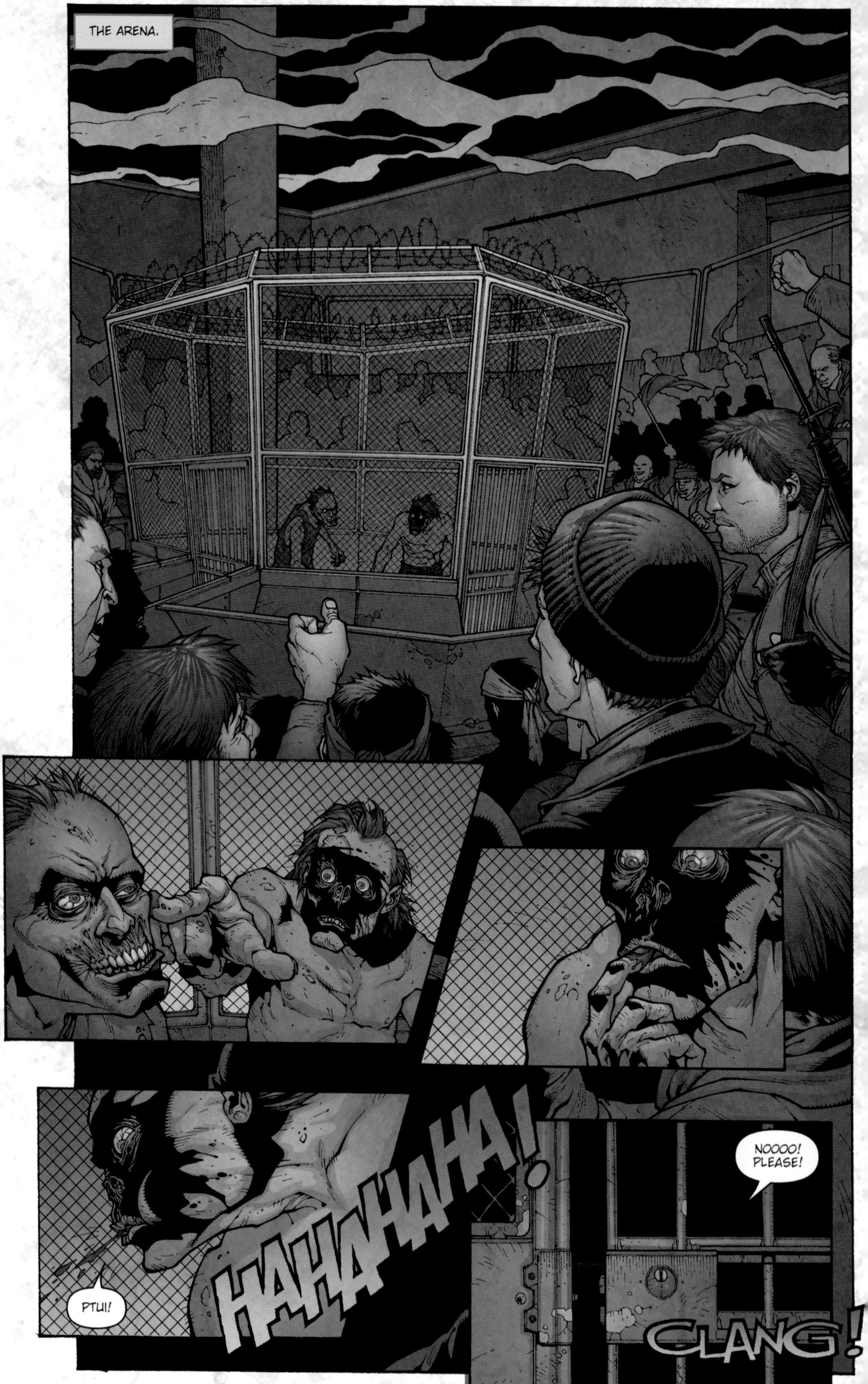
THE ARENA.
PTUI!
HAHAHAHA!
NOOOO! PLEASE!
CLANG!

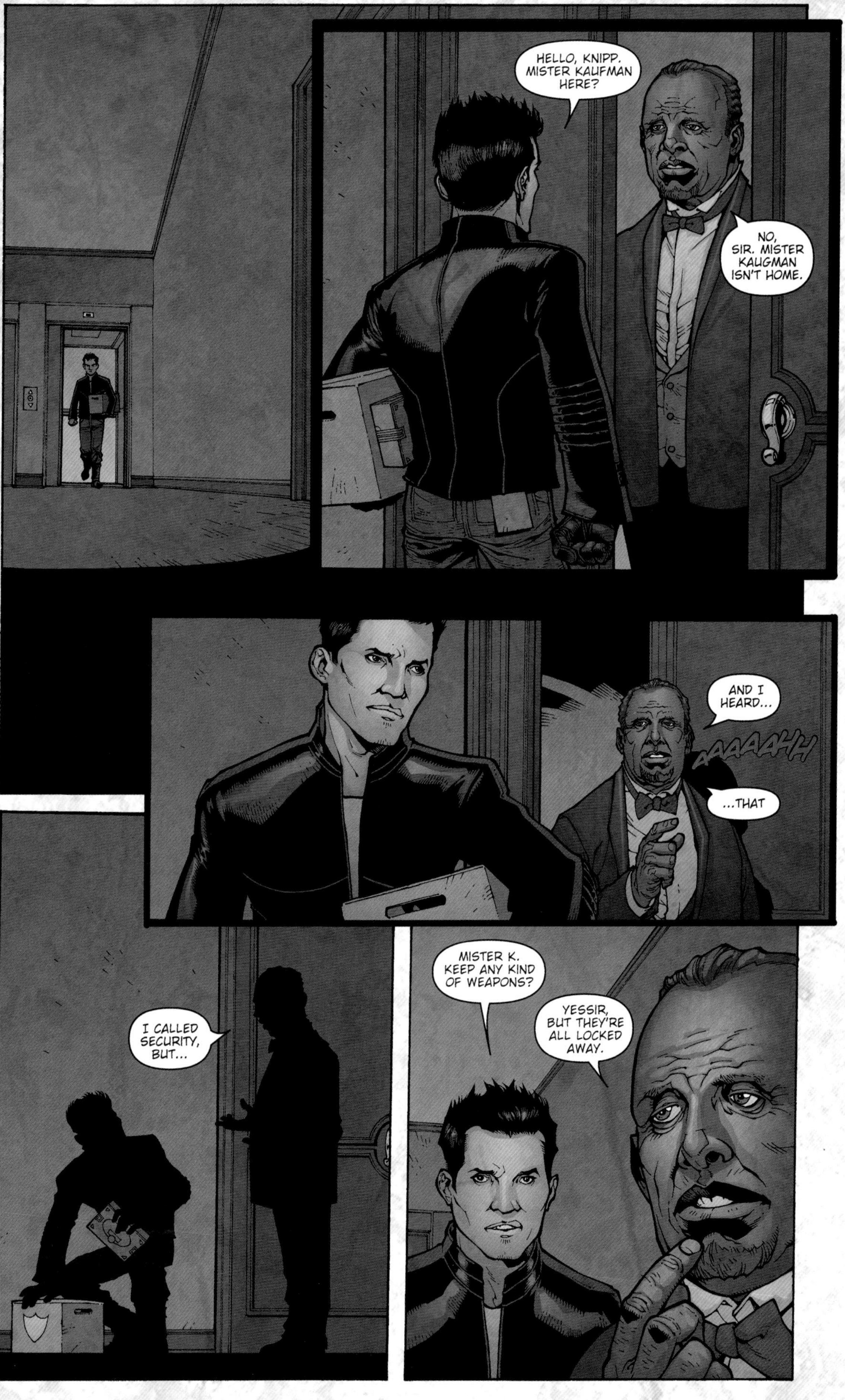
HELLO, KNIPP. MISTER KAUFMAN HERE?
NO, SIR. MISTER KAUGMAN ISN'T HOME.
AND I HEARD...
AAAAAHH
...THAT
I CALLED SECURITY, BUT...
MISTER K. KEEP ANY KIND OF WEAPONS?
YESSIR, BUT THEY'RE ALL LOCKED AWAY.

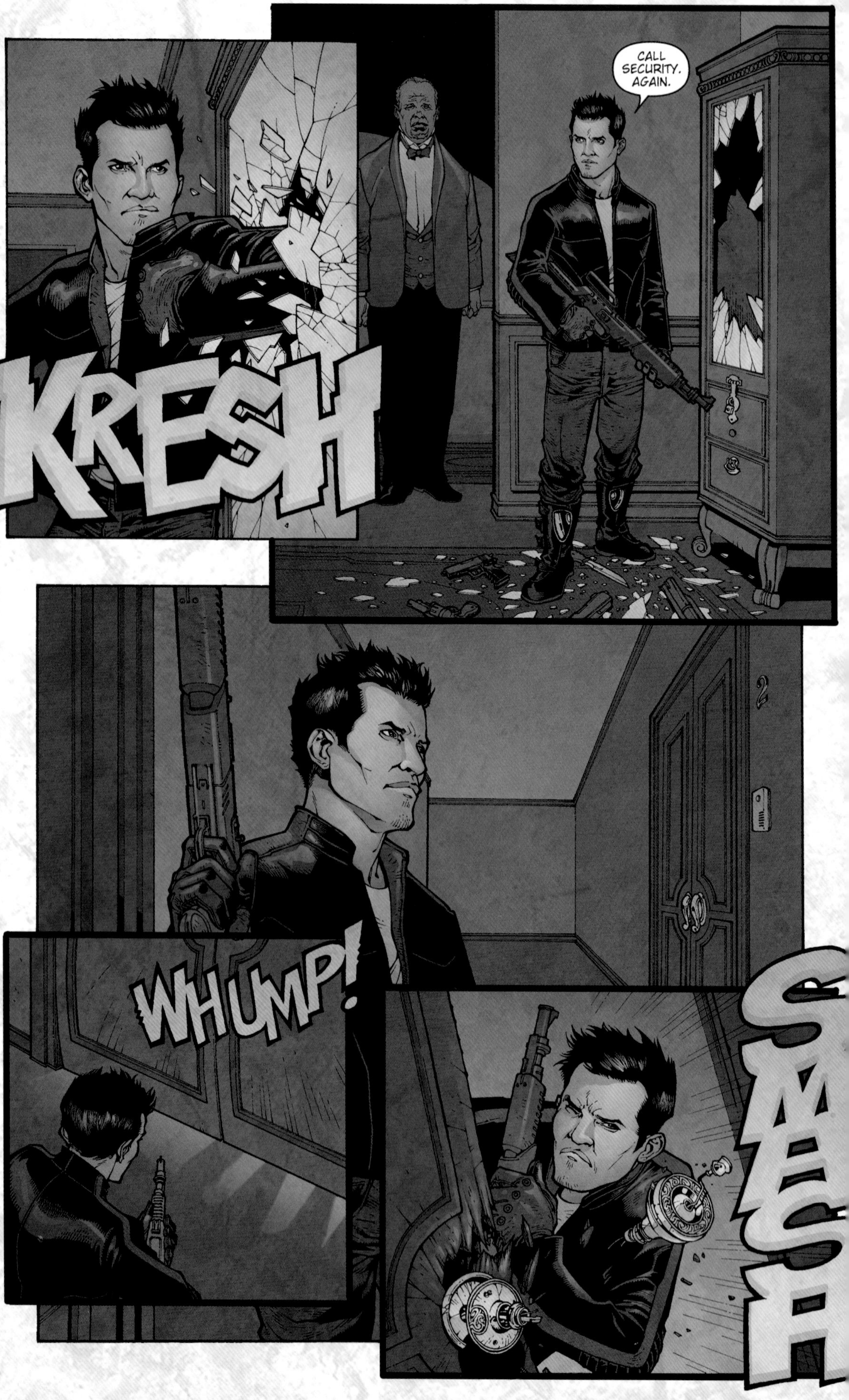
KRESH
CALL SECURITY. AGAIN.
WHUMP!
SMASH

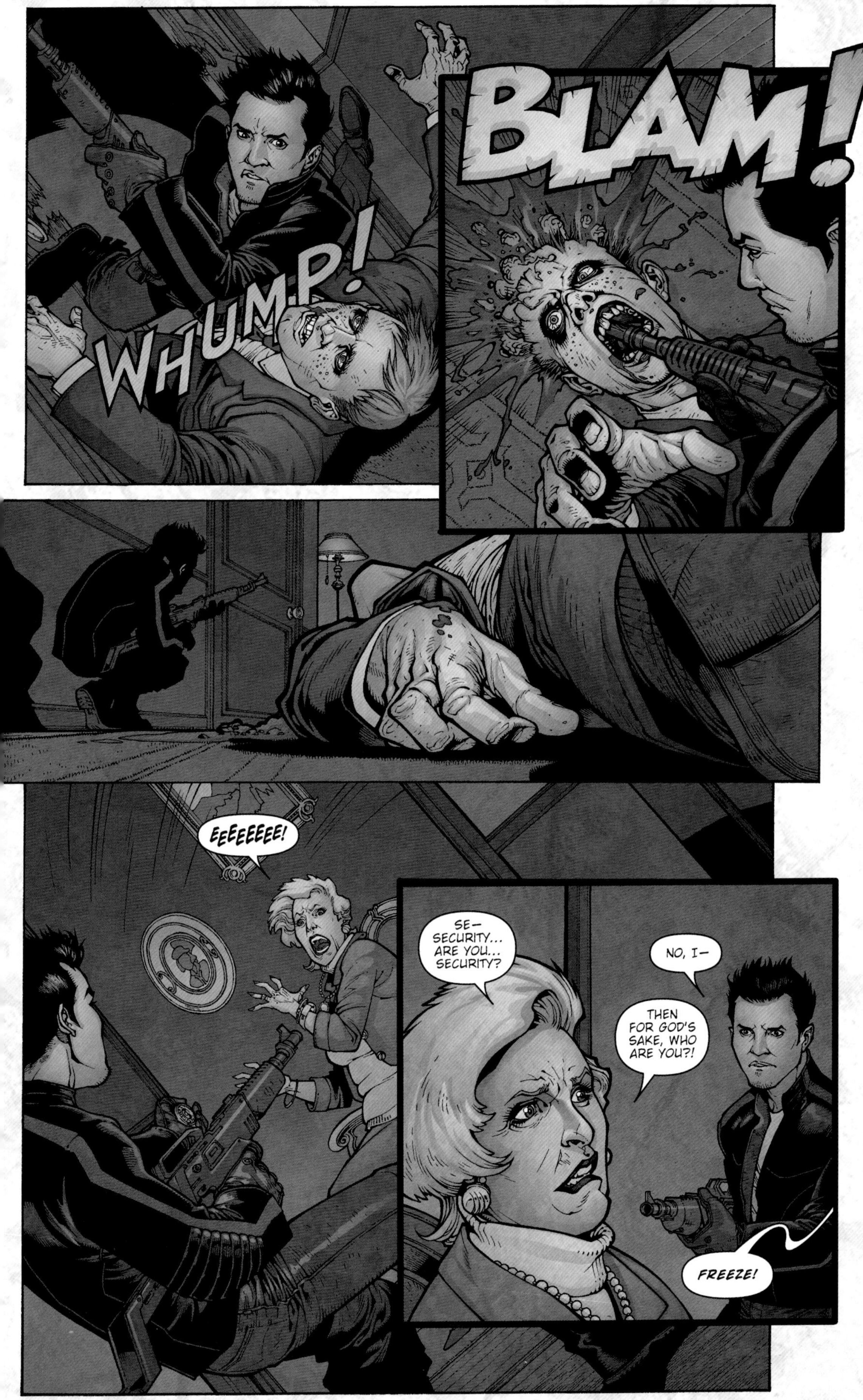
WHUMP!
BLAM!
EEEEEEEE!
SE— SECURITY... ARE YOU... SECURITY?
NO, I—
THEN FOR GOD'S SAKE, WHO ARE YOU?!
FREEZE!

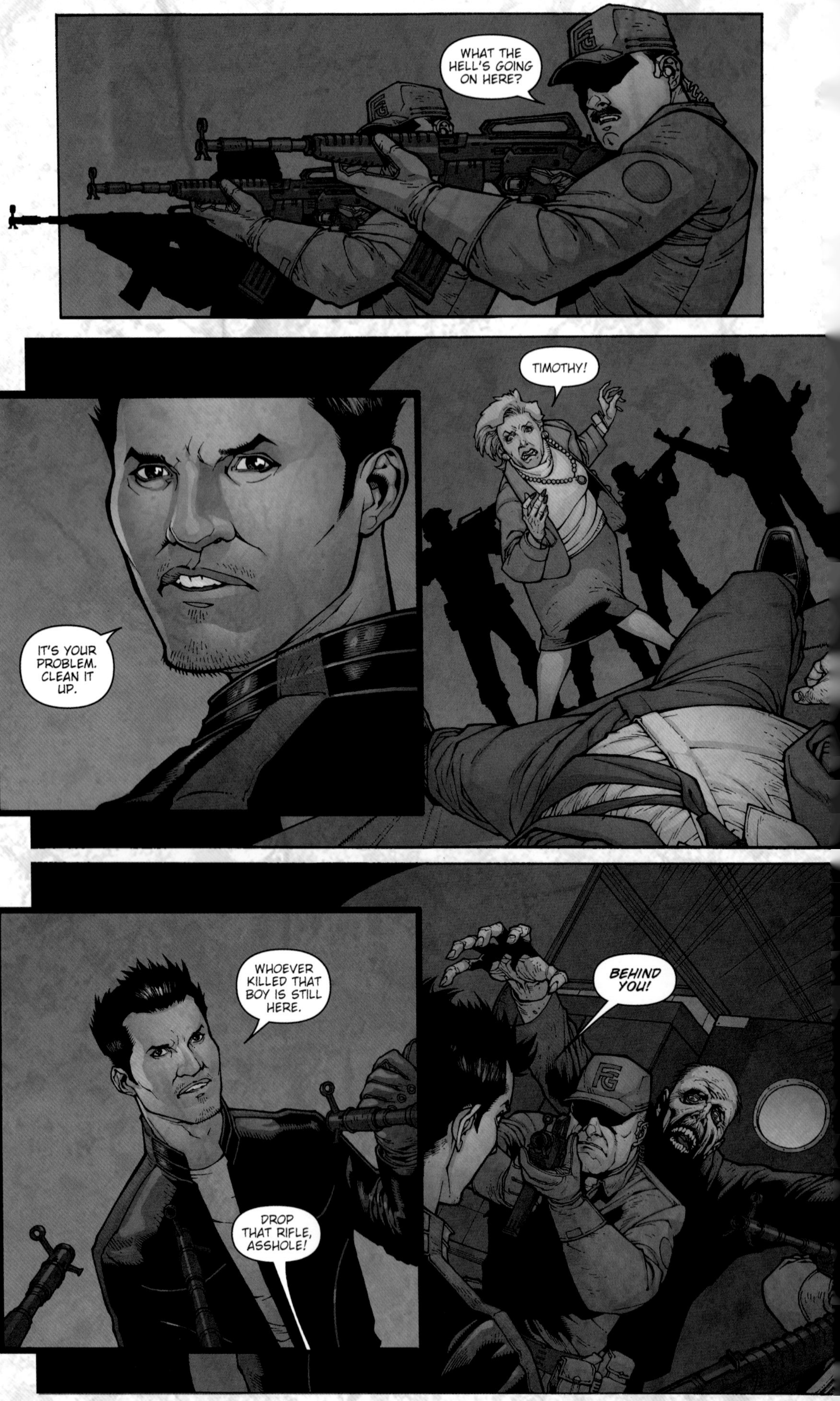
WHAT THE HELL'S GOING ON HERE?
IT'S YOUR PROBLEM. CLEAN IT UP.
TIMOTHY!
WHOEVER KILLED THAT BOY IS STILL HERE.
DROP THAT RIFLE, ASSHOLE!
BEHIND YOU!

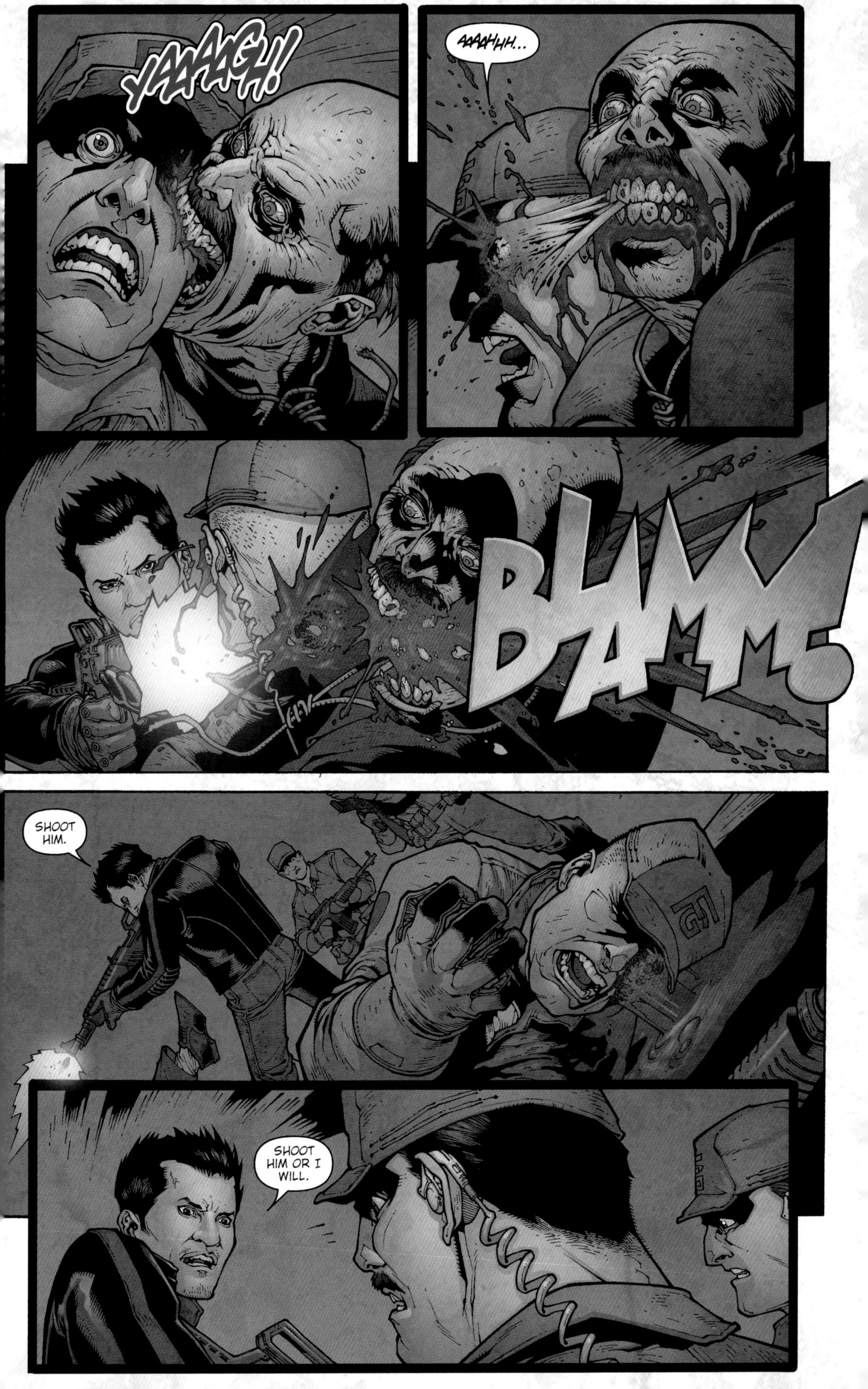
YAAAGH!
AAAHHH...
BLAMM!
SHOOT HIM.
SHOOT HIM OR I WILL.

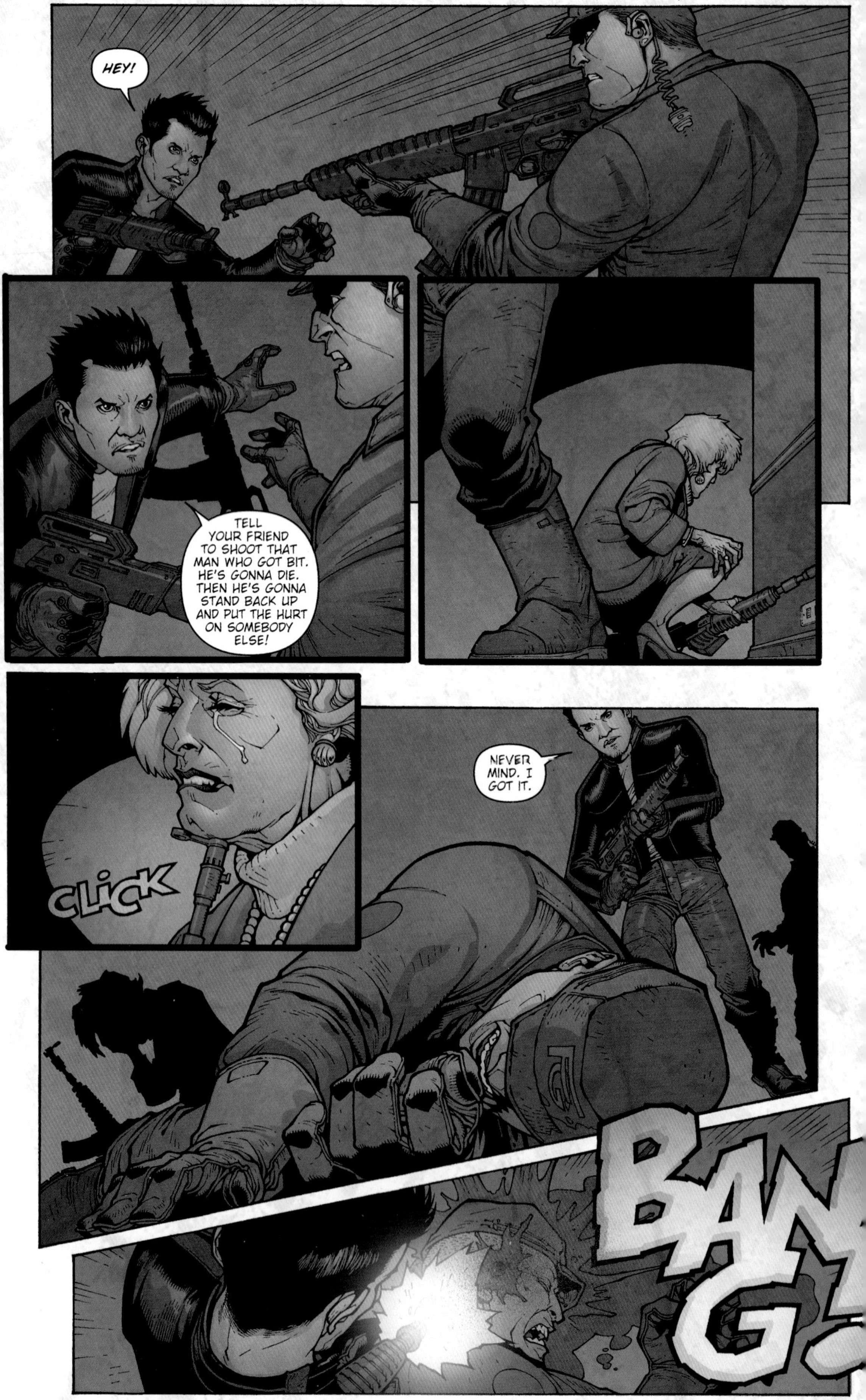
HEY!
TELL YOUR FRIEND TO SHOOT THAT MAN WHO GOT BIT. HE'S GONNA DIE. THEN HE'S GONNA STAND BACK UP AND PUT THE HURT ON SOMEBODY ELSE!
CLICK
NEVER MIND. I GOT IT.

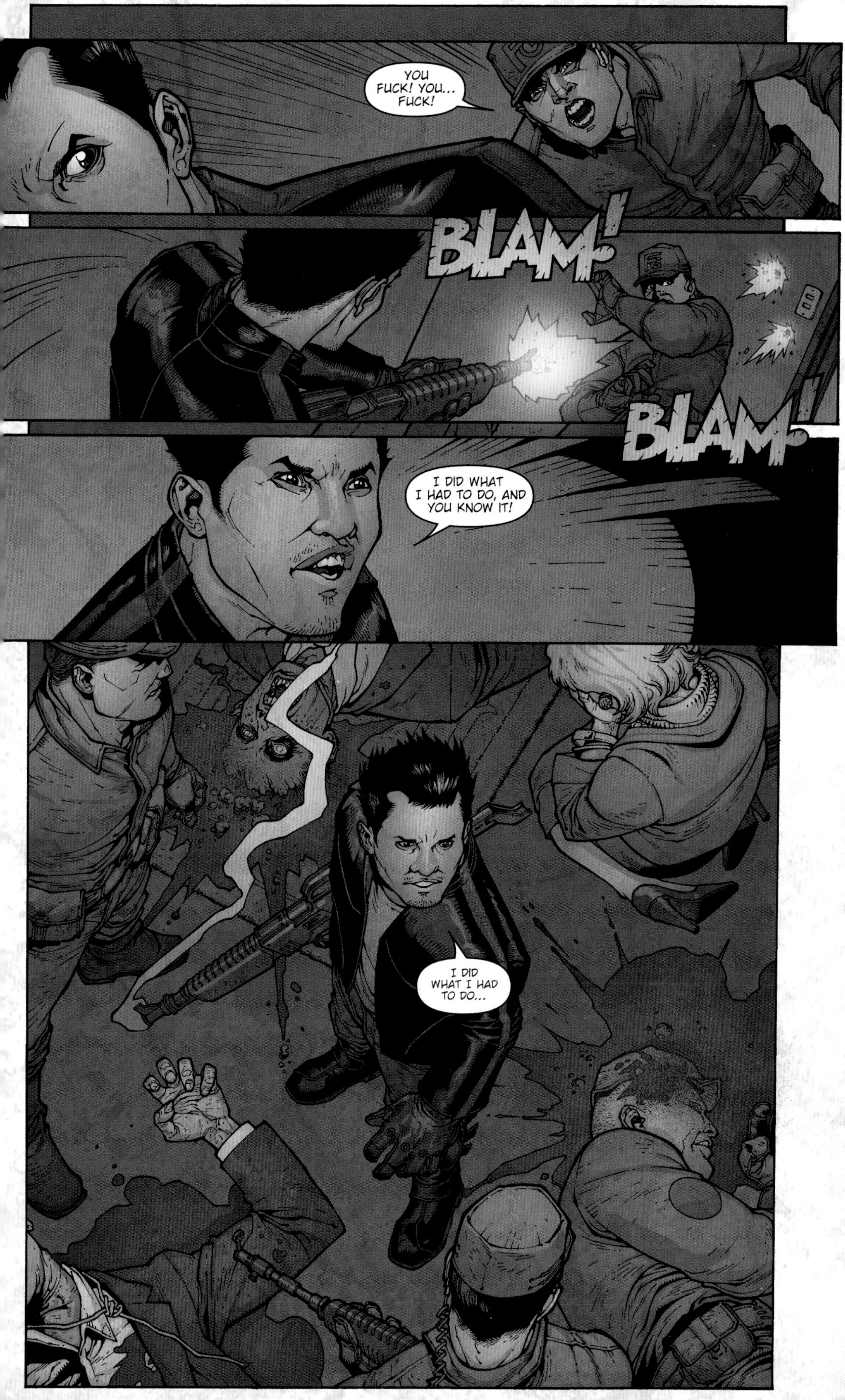
YOU FUCK! YOU... FUCK!
BLAM!
BLAM!
I DID WHAT I HAD TO DO, AND YOU KNOW IT!
I DID WHAT I HAD TO DO...

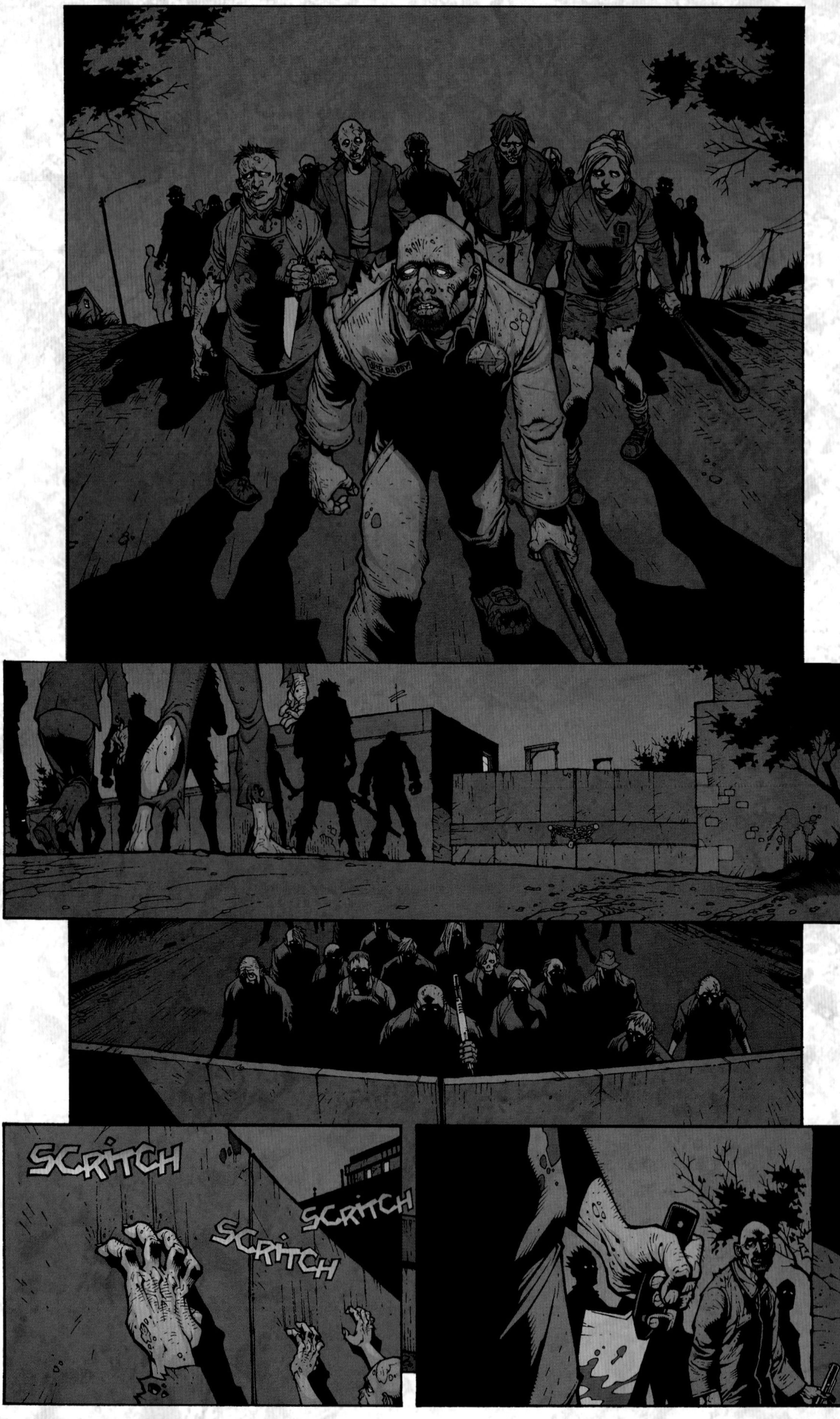
SCRITCH
SCRITCH
SCRITCH

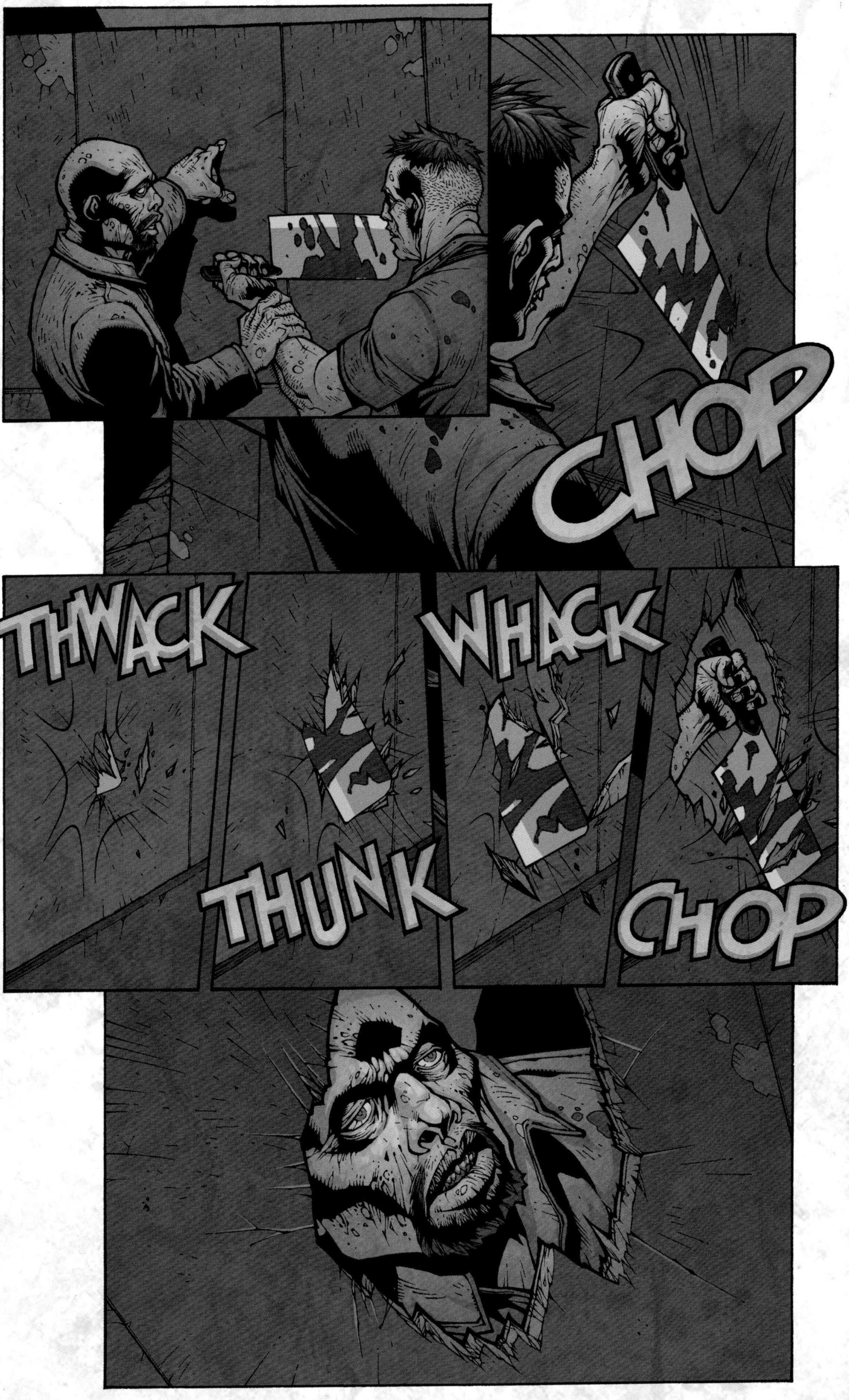
CHOP
THWACK
THUNK
WHACK
CHOP

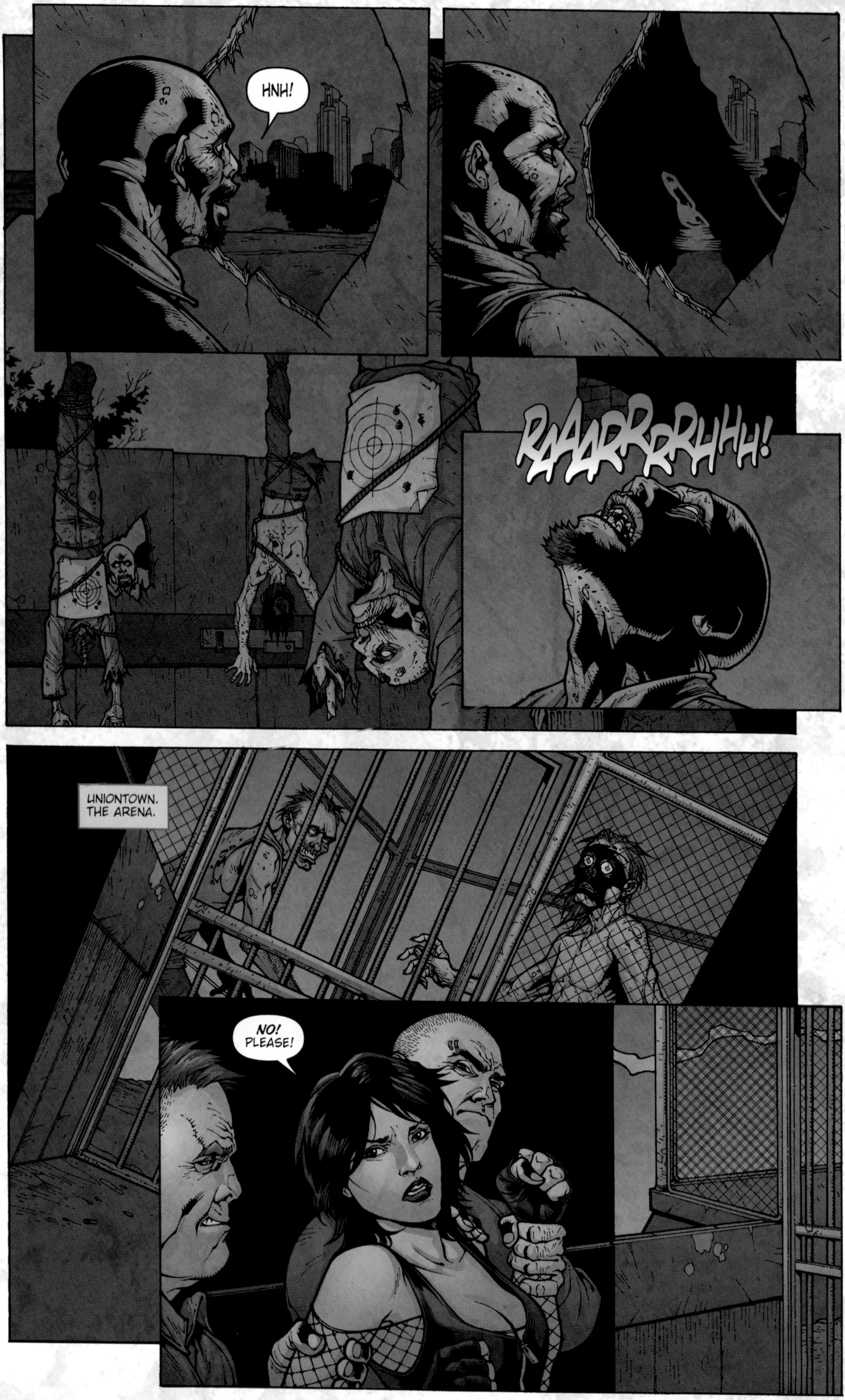
HNH!
RAAARRRRHHH!
UNIONTOWN.
THE ARENA.
NO!
PLEASE!

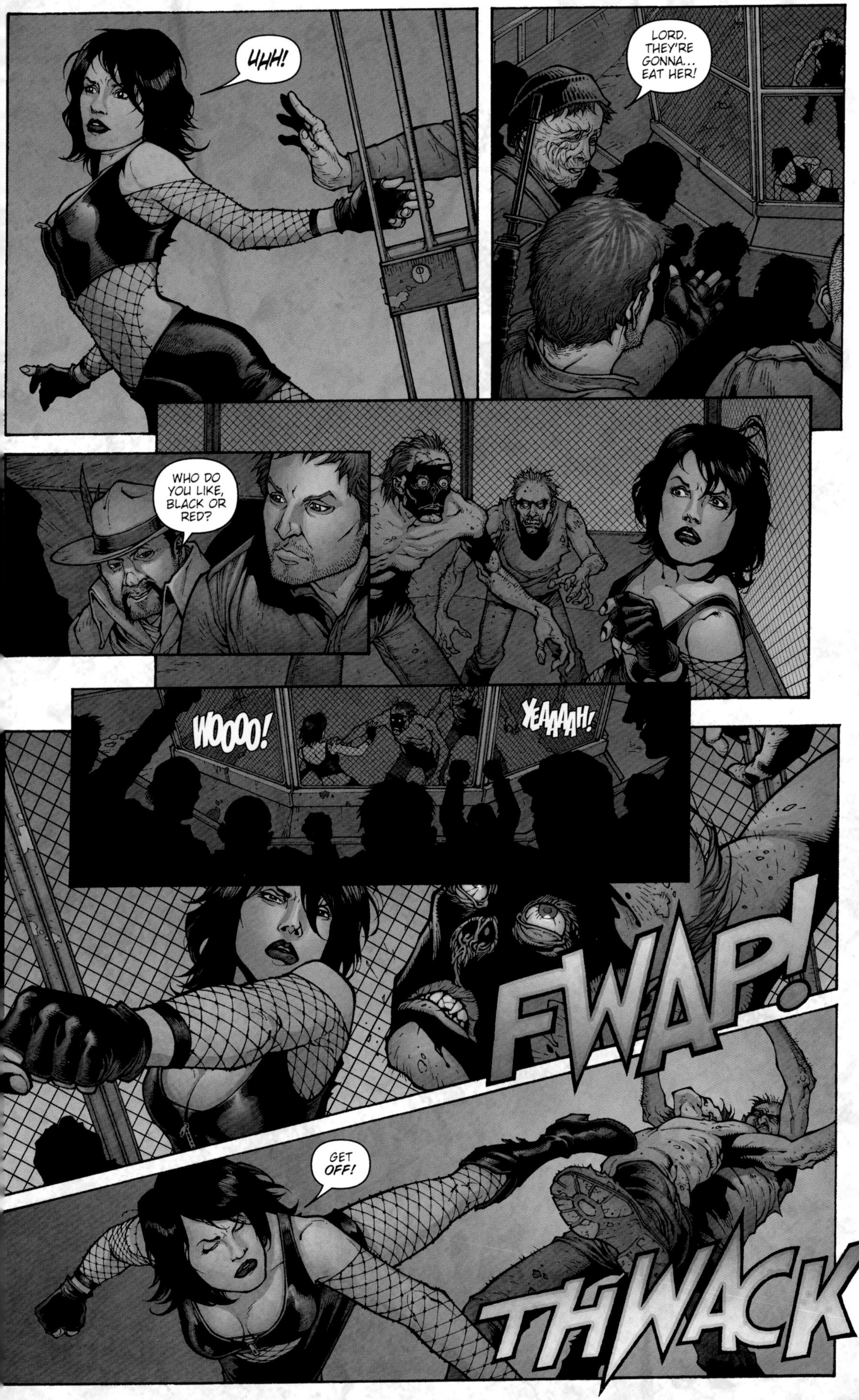
UHH!
LORD. THEY'RE GONNA... EAT HER!
WHO DO YOU LIKE, BLACK OR RED?
WOOOO!
YEAAAAH!
FWAP!
GET OFF!
THWACK

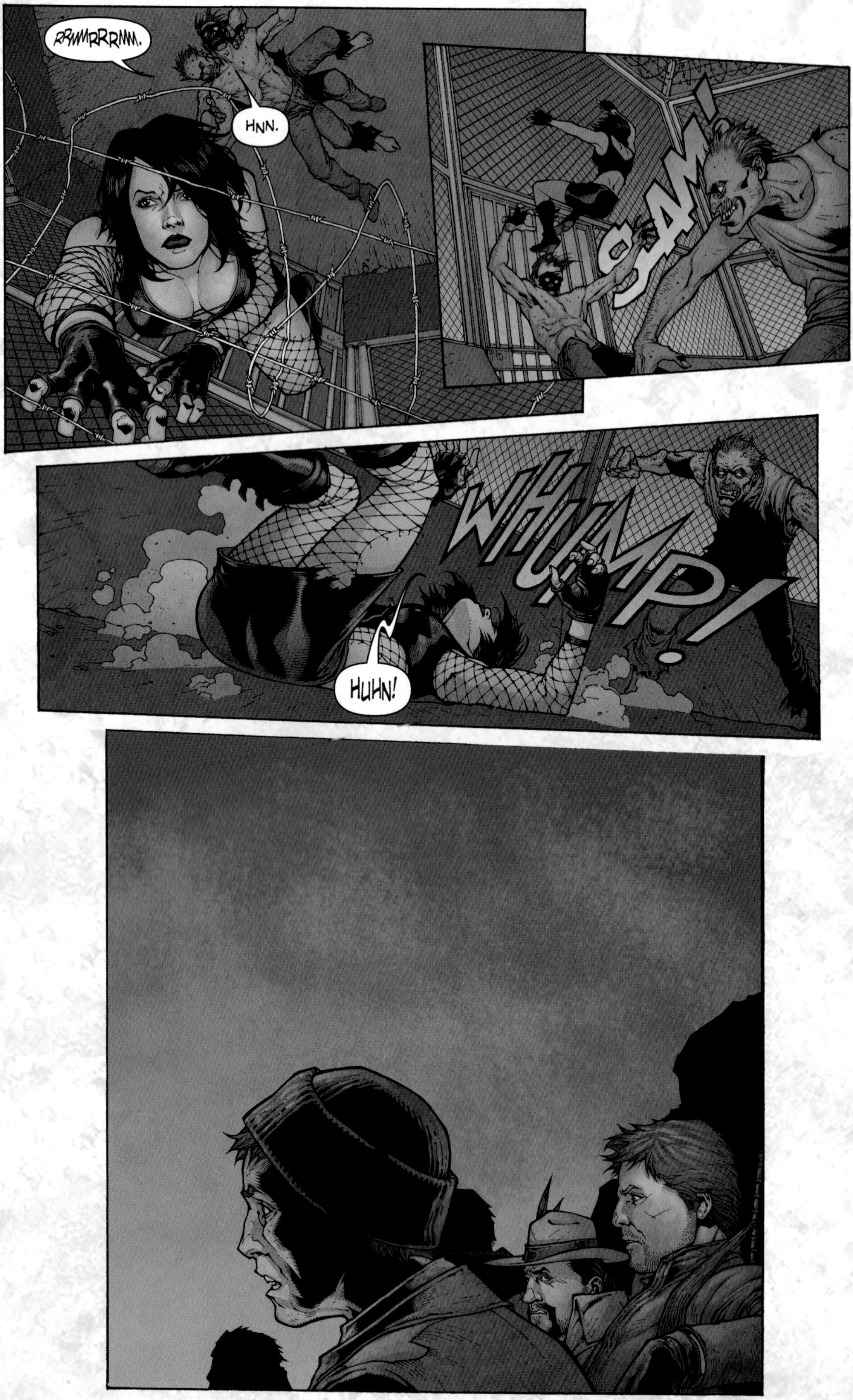
RRWMRRRMM.
HNN.
SAM!
WHUMP!
HUHN!

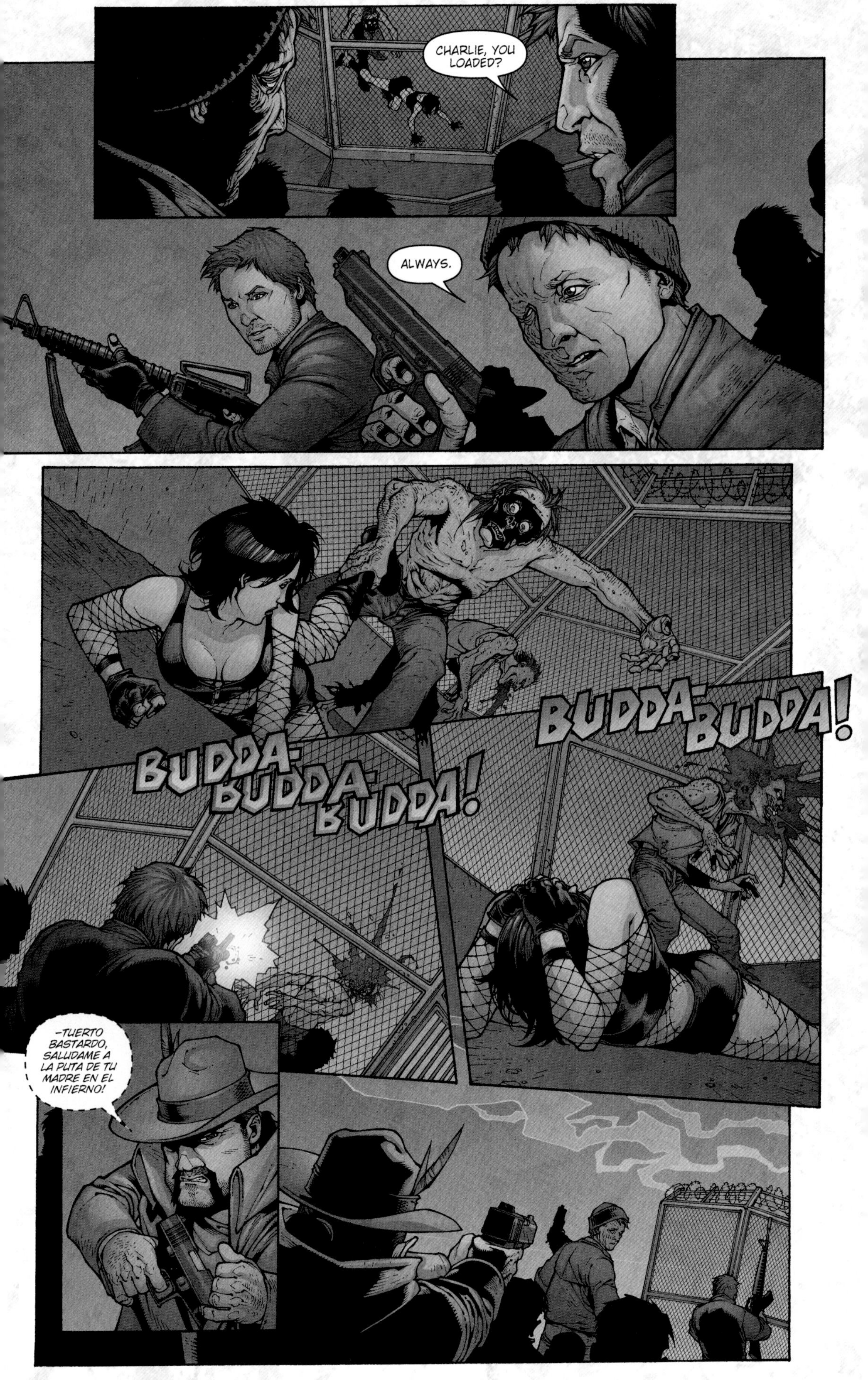

CHARLIE, YOU LOADED?
ALWAYS.
BUDDA-BUDDA!
BUDDA-BUDDA-BUDDA!
–TUERTO BASTARDO, SALUDAME A LA PUTA DE TU MADRE EN EL INFIERNO!

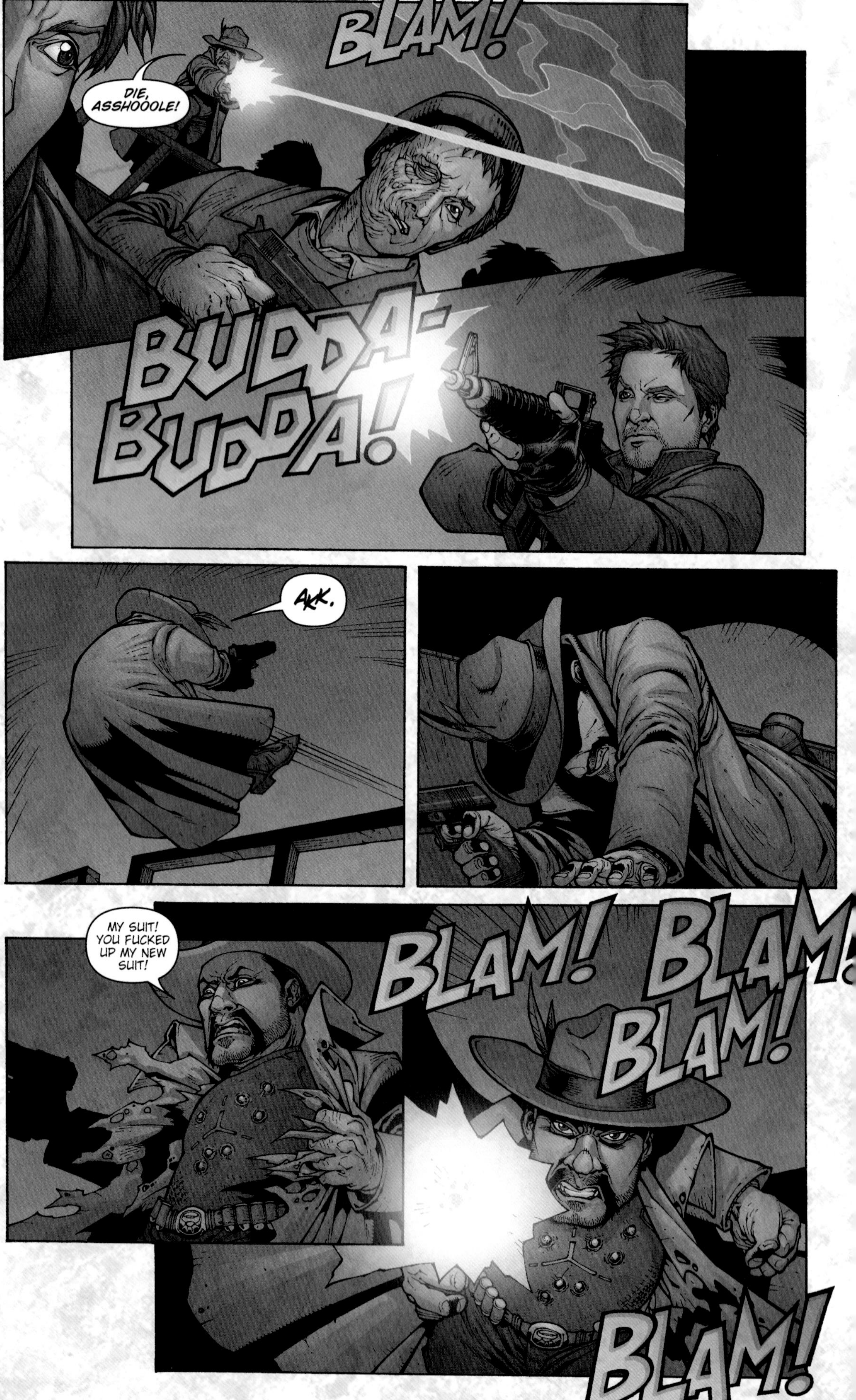
BLAM!
DIE, ASSHOOOLE!
BUDDA-BUDDA!
AKK.
MY SUIT! YOU FUCKED UP MY NEW SUIT!
BLAM! BLAM!
BLAM!
BLAM!

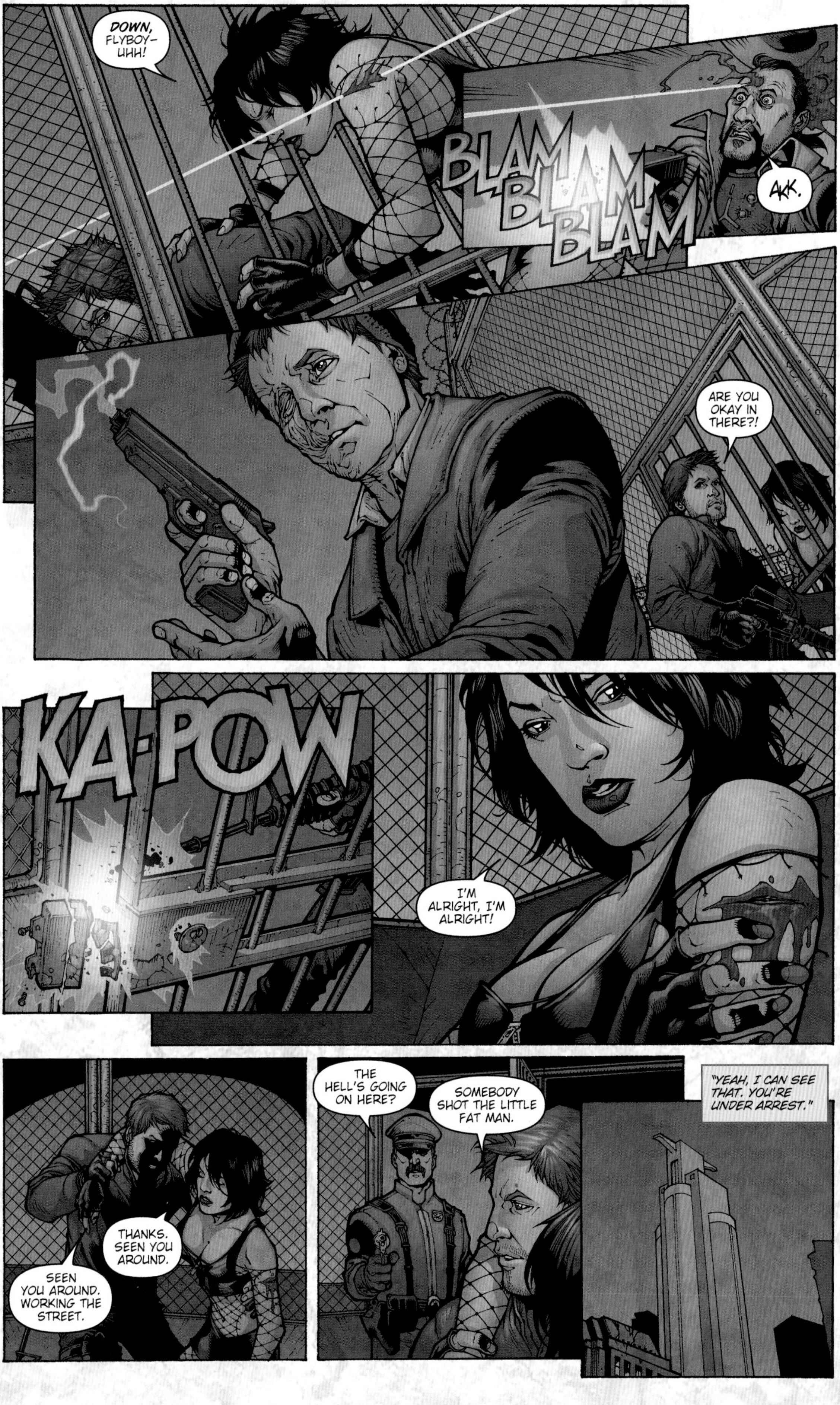
DOWN, FLYBOY- UHH!
BLAM BLAM BLAM
AKK.
ARE YOU OKAY IN THERE?!
KA-POW
I'M ALRIGHT, I'M ALRIGHT!
THANKS. SEEN YOU AROUND.
SEEN YOU AROUND. WORKING THE STREET.
THE HELL'S GOING ON HERE?
SOMEBODY SHOT THE LITTLE FAT MAN.
"YEAH, I CAN SEE THAT. YOU'RE UNDER ARREST."

WHY YOU? IN THAT ARENA? WHY'D THE LITTLE FAT MAN THROW YOU IN WITH THOSE THINGS?

IT WASN'T THE LITTLE MAN. IT WAS THE BIG MAN. THE MAN UPSTAIRS. MR. K.

HE'S GOT HIS FINGERS IN EVERYTHING. IF YOU CAN DRINK IT, SHOOT IT, FUCK IT, OR GAMBLE IT, IT BELONGS TO HIM. HE'S JUST SEEING THAT WE GET A FEW CHEAP KICKS.

YOU DIDN'T ANSWER HIS QUESTION. HE ASKED YOU WHY...

I KNOW WHAT HE ASKED. THEY FOUND OUT I WAS HELPING MULLIGAN AND HIS PEOPLE.

I'M TIRED OF KAUFMAN EATING STEAK WHILE WE GET THE BONES.

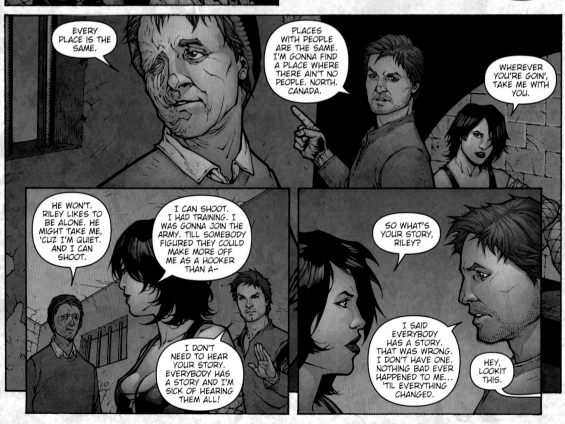

EVERY PLACE IS THE SAME.

PLACES WITH PEOPLE ARE THE SAME. I'M GONNA FIND A PLACE WHERE THERE AIN'T NO PEOPLE. NORTH CANADA.

WHEREVER YOU'RE GOIN', TAKE ME WITH YOU.

HE WON'T. RILEY LIKES TO BE ALONE. HE MIGHT TAKE ME, 'CUZ I'M QUIET. AND I CAN SHOOT.

I CAN SHOOT. I HAD TRAINING. I WAS GONNA JOIN THE ARMY. TILL SOMEBODY FIGURED THEY COULD MAKE MORE OFF ME AS A HOOKER THAN A—

I DON'T NEED TO HEAR YOUR STORY. EVERYBODY HAS A STORY AND I'M SICK OF HEARING THEM ALL!

SO WHAT'S YOUR STORY, RILEY?

I SAID EVERYBODY HAS A STORY. THAT WAS WRONG. I DON'T HAVE ONE. NOTHING BAD EVER HAPPENED TO ME... 'TIL EVERYTHING CHANGED.

HEY, LOOKIT THIS.

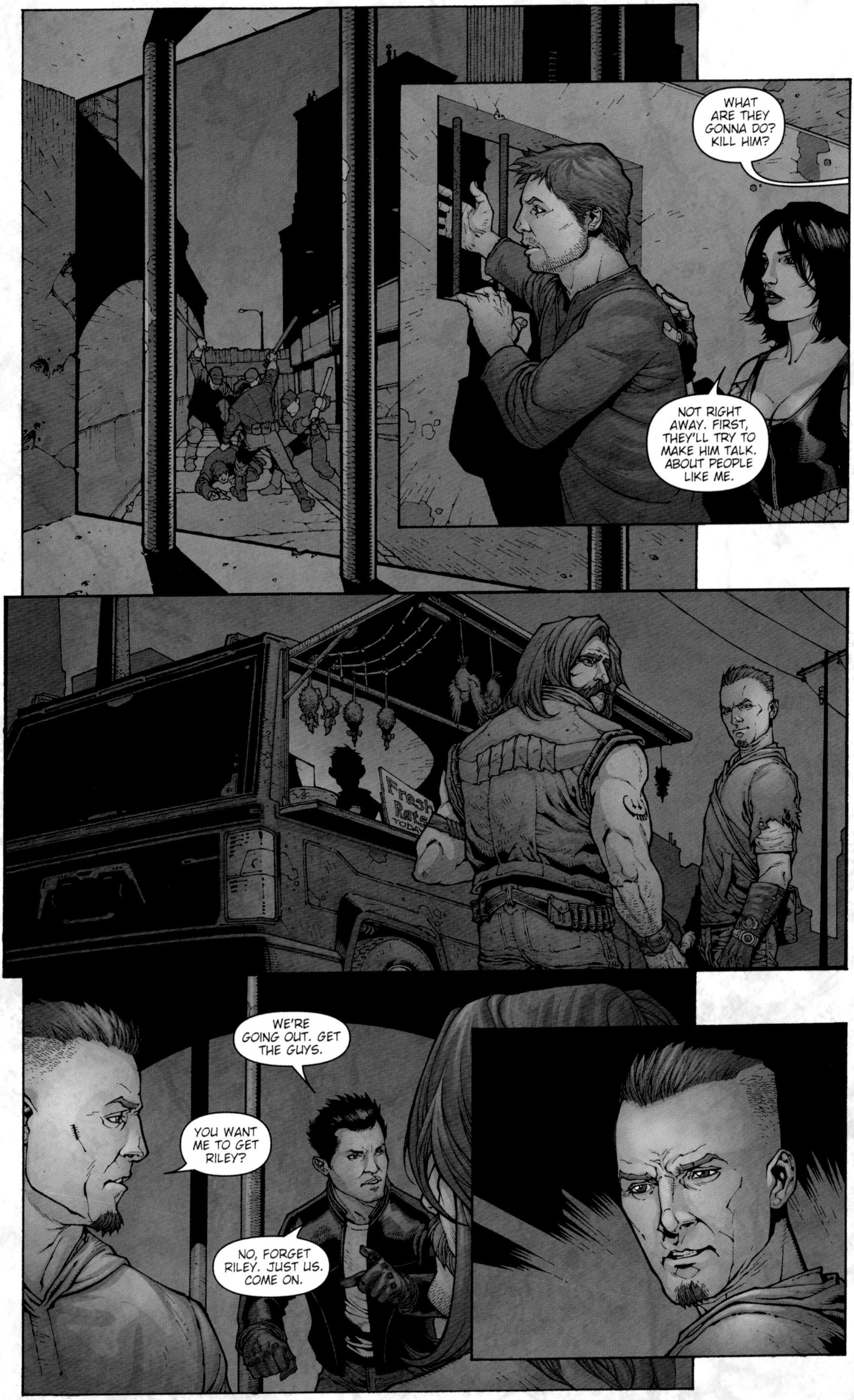
WHAT ARE THEY GONNA DO? KILL HIM?
NOT RIGHT AWAY. FIRST, THEY'LL TRY TO MAKE HIM TALK. ABOUT PEOPLE LIKE ME.
Fresh Rats
WE'RE GOING OUT. GET THE GUYS.
YOU WANT ME TO GET RILEY?
NO, FORGET RILEY. JUST US. COME ON.

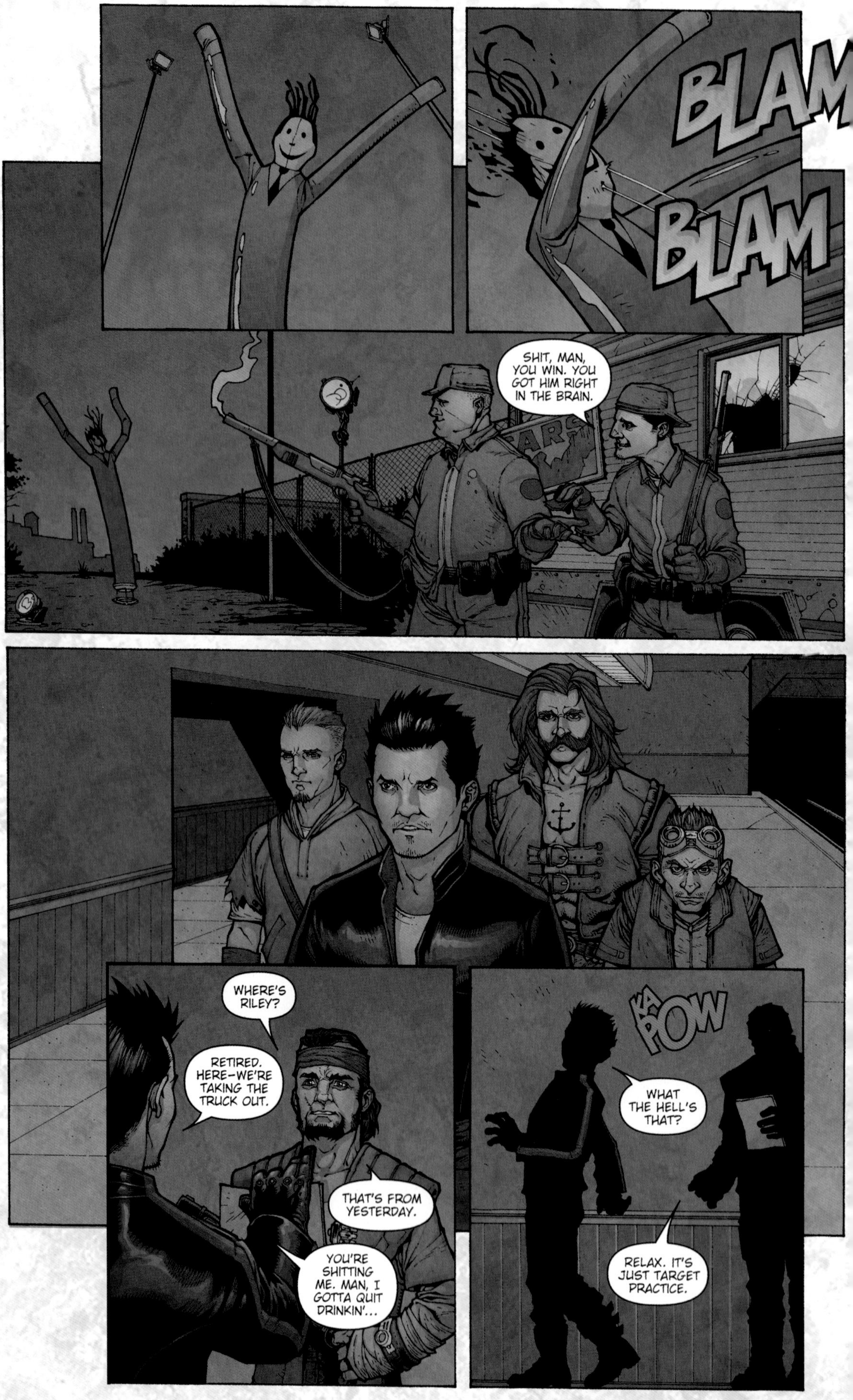
BLAM
BLAM
SHIT, MAN, YOU WIN. YOU GOT HIM RIGHT IN THE BRAIN.
WHERE'S RILEY?
RETIRED. HERE—WE'RE TAKING THE TRUCK OUT.
THAT'S FROM YESTERDAY.
YOU'RE SHITTING ME. MAN, I GOTTA QUIT DRINKIN'...
KA POW
WHAT THE HELL'S THAT?
RELAX. IT'S JUST TARGET PRACTICE.

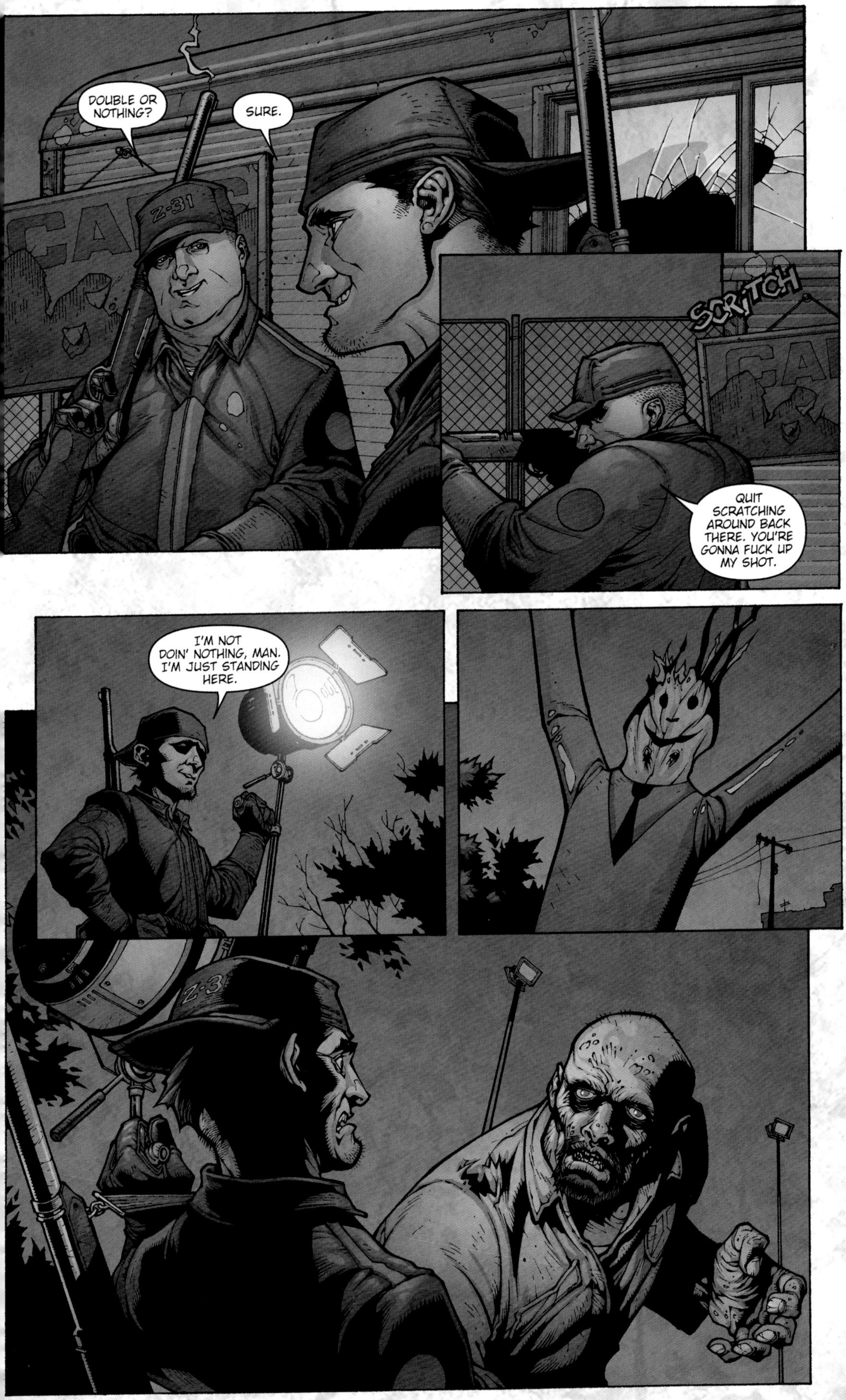
DOUBLE OR NOTHING?
SURE.
SCRITCH
QUIT SCRATCHING AROUND BACK THERE. YOU'RE GONNA FUCK UP MY SHOT.
I'M NOT DOIN' NOTHING, MAN. I'M JUST STANDING HERE.

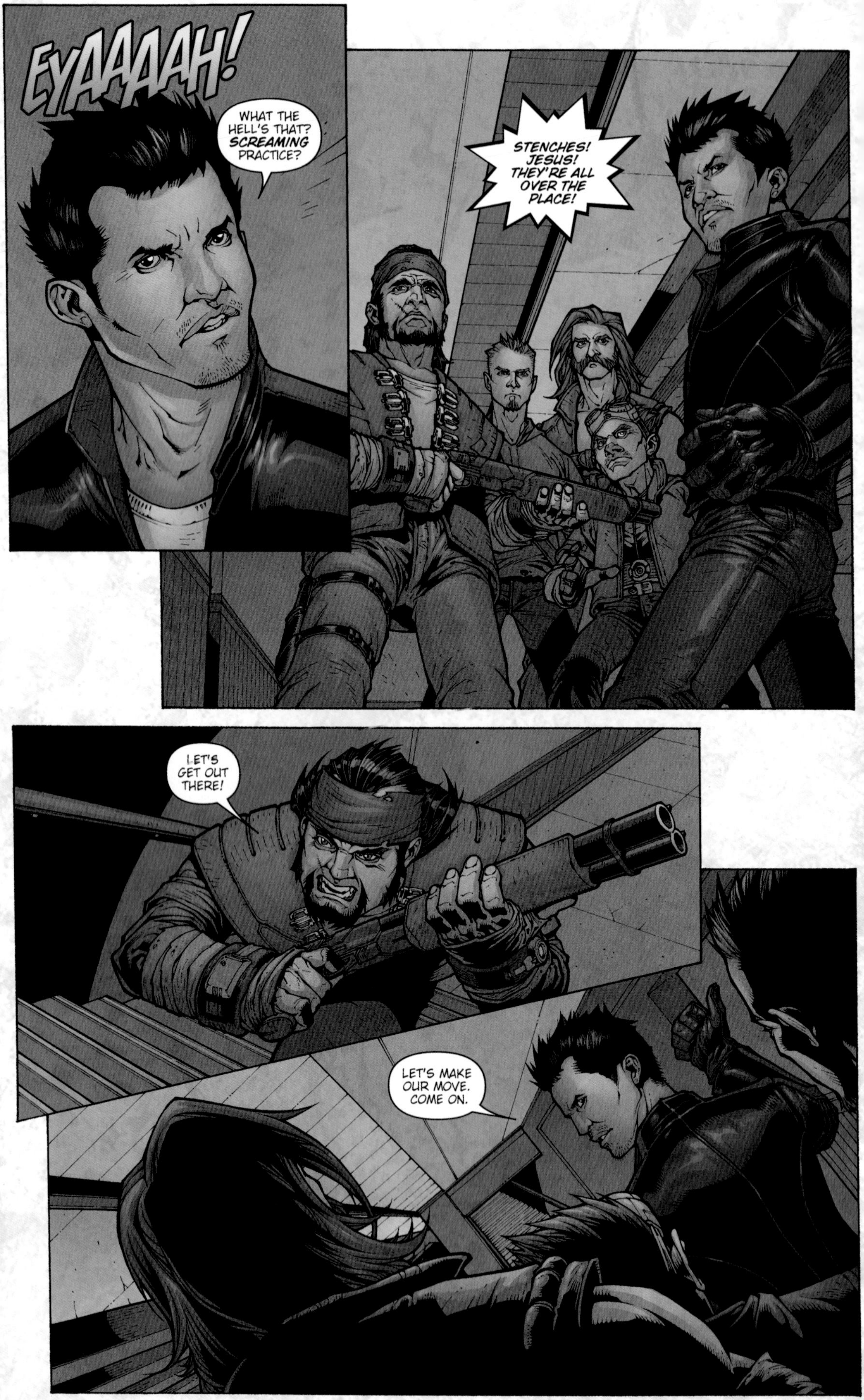
EYAAAAH!
WHAT THE HELL'S THAT? SCREAMING PRACTICE?
STENCHES! JESUS! THEY'RE ALL OVER THE PLACE!
LET'S GET OUT THERE!
LET'S MAKE OUR MOVE. COME ON.

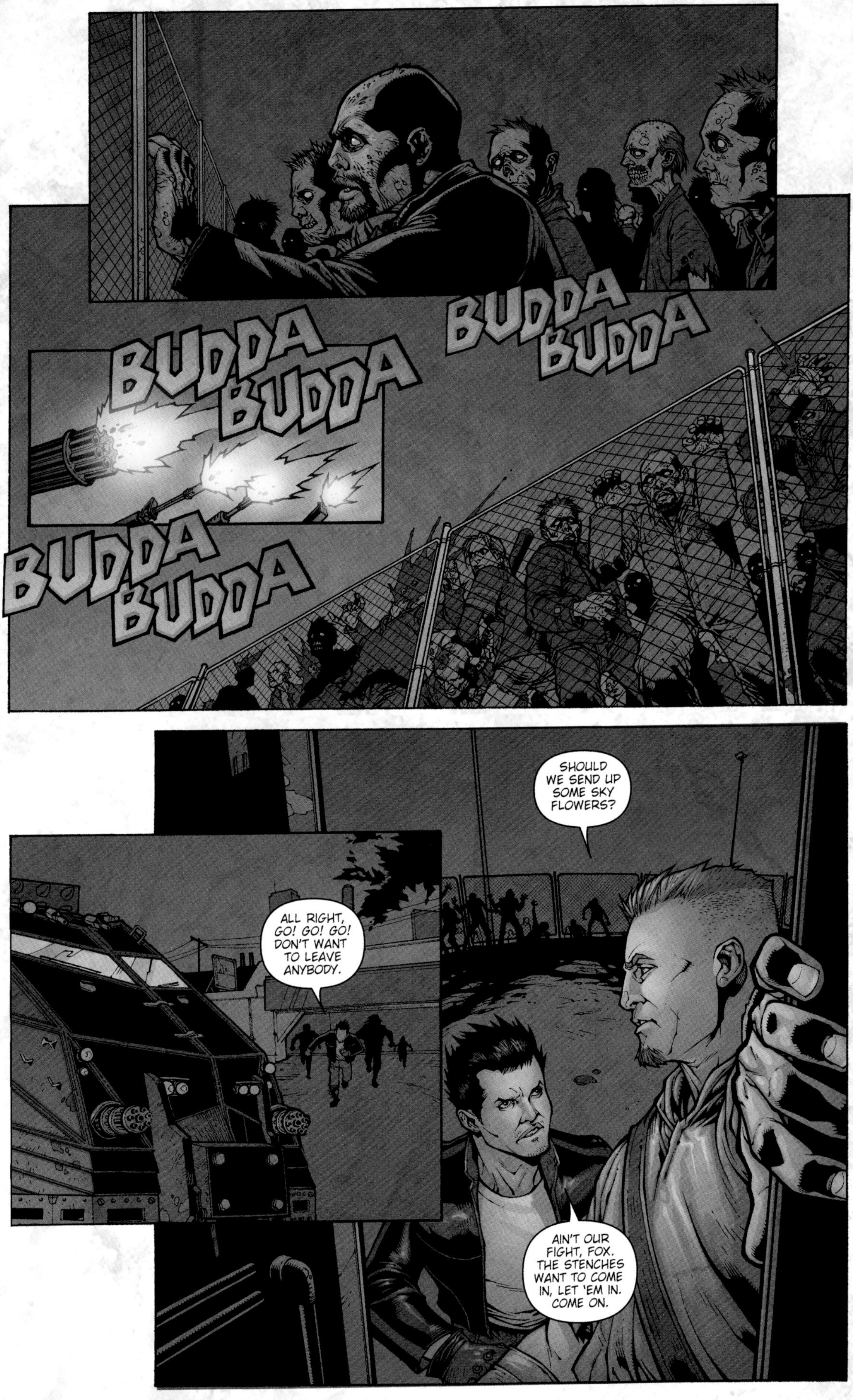
BUDDA BUDDA
BUDDA BUDDA
BUDDA BUDDA
SHOULD WE SEND UP SOME SKY FLOWERS?
ALL RIGHT, GO! GO! GO! DON'T WANT TO LEAVE ANYBODY.
AIN'T OUR FIGHT, FOX. THE STENCHES WANT TO COME IN, LET 'EM IN. COME ON.

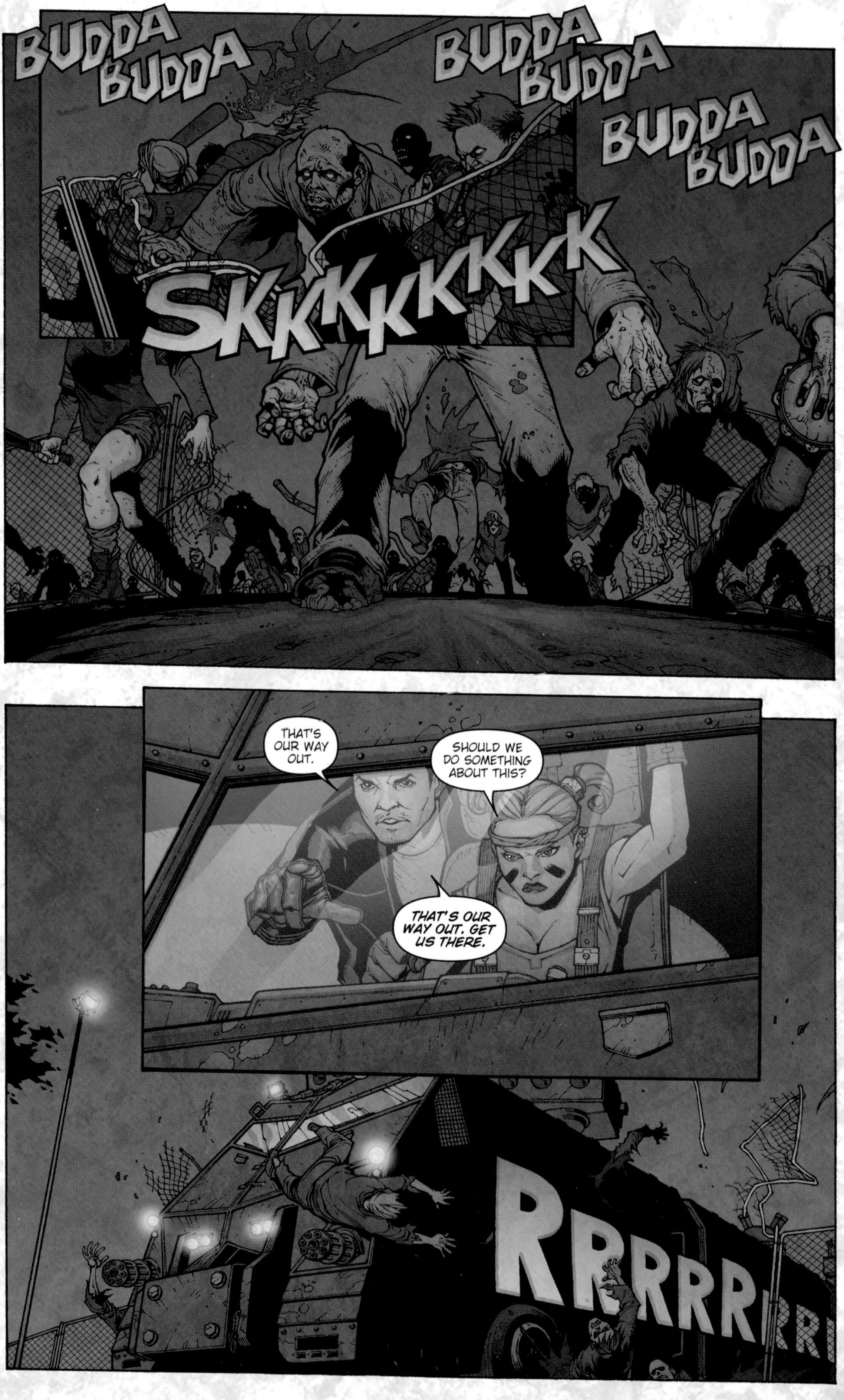
BUDDA BUDDA
BUDDA BUDDA
BUDDA BUDDA
SKKKKKKK
THAT'S OUR WAY OUT.
SHOULD WE DO SOMETHING ABOUT THIS?
THAT'S OUR WAY OUT. GET US THERE.
RRRRRRR

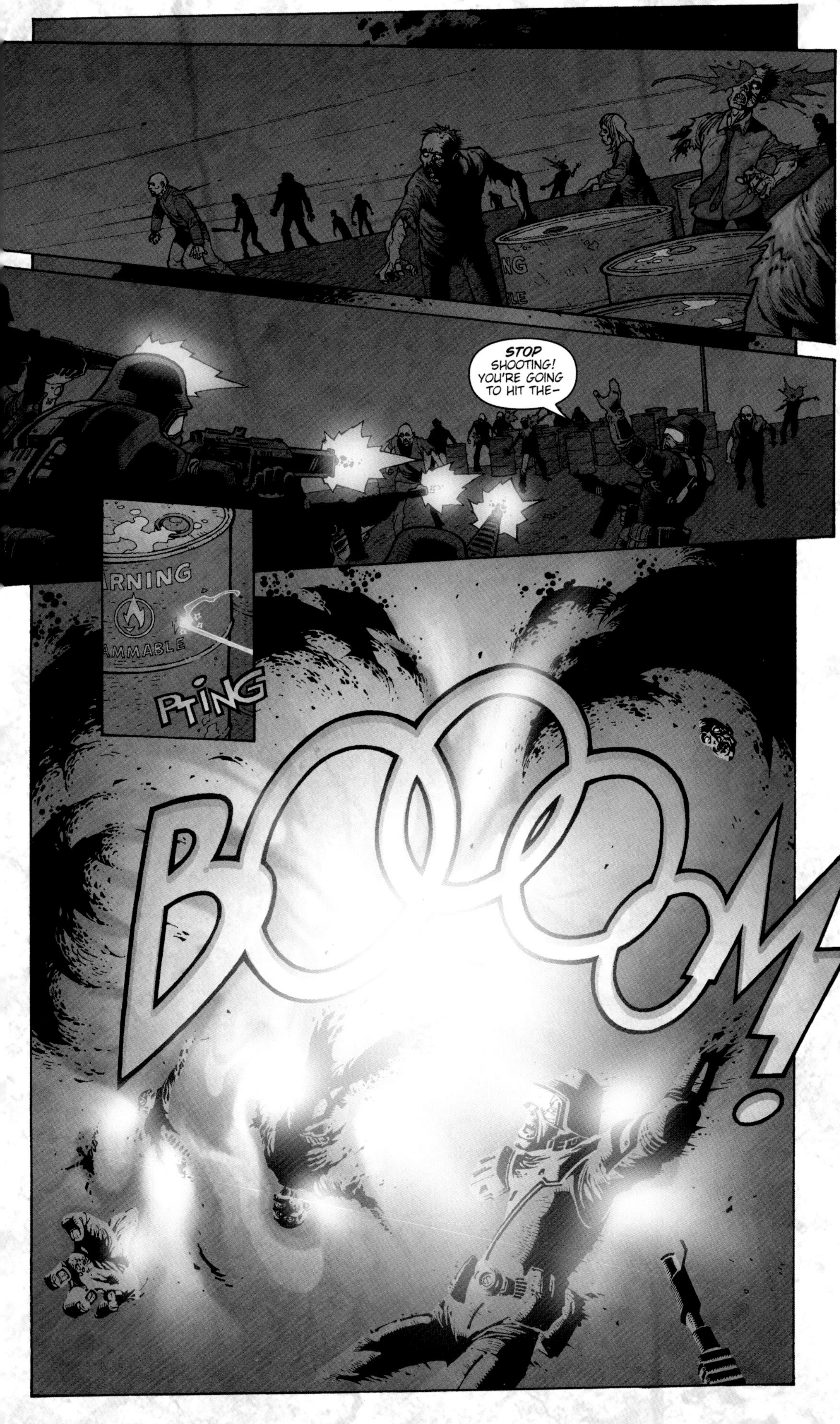

STOP SHOOTING! YOU'RE GOING TO HIT THE-
RNING
AMMABLE
PTING
BOOOOM!

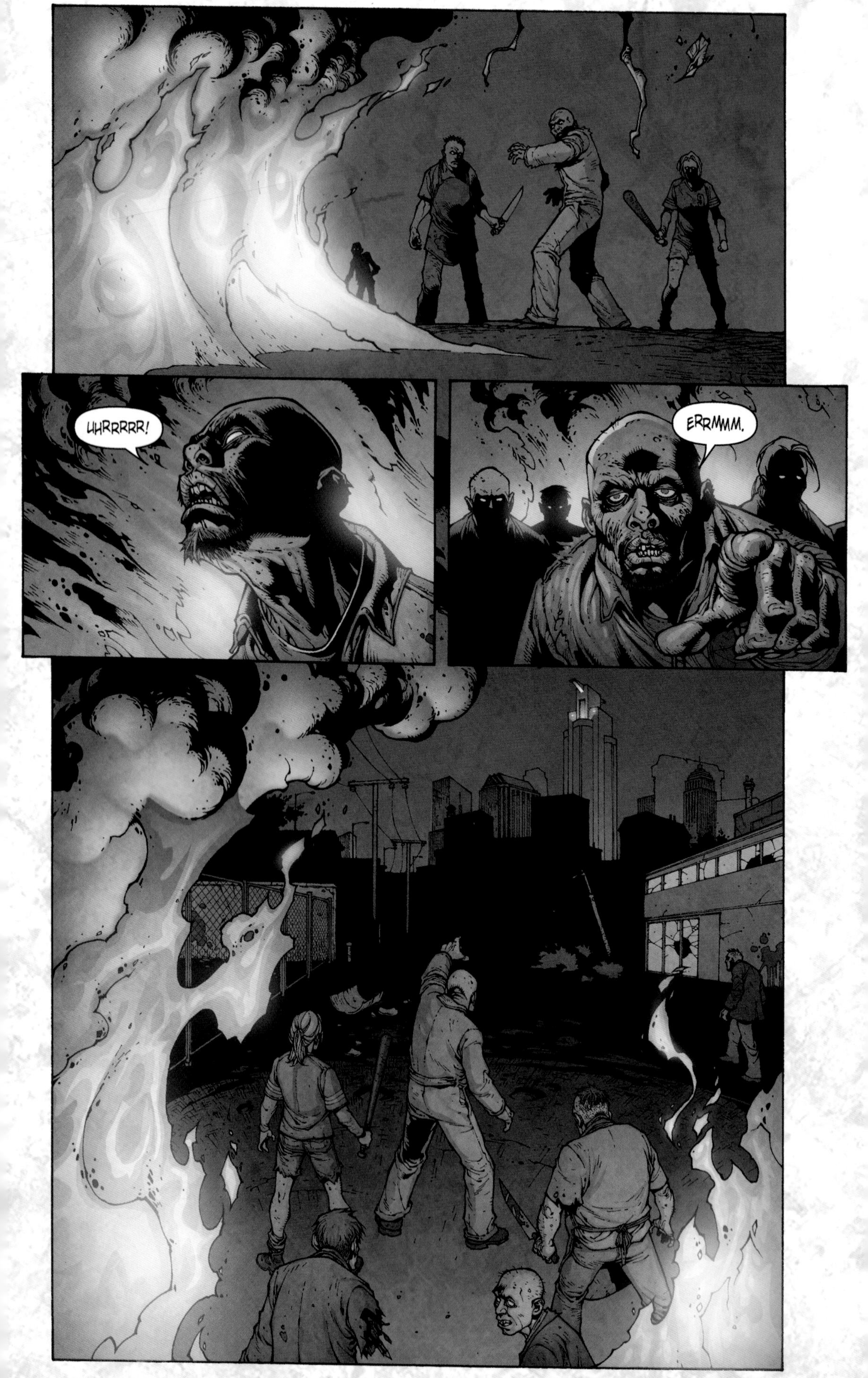
UHRRRRR!
ERRMMM.

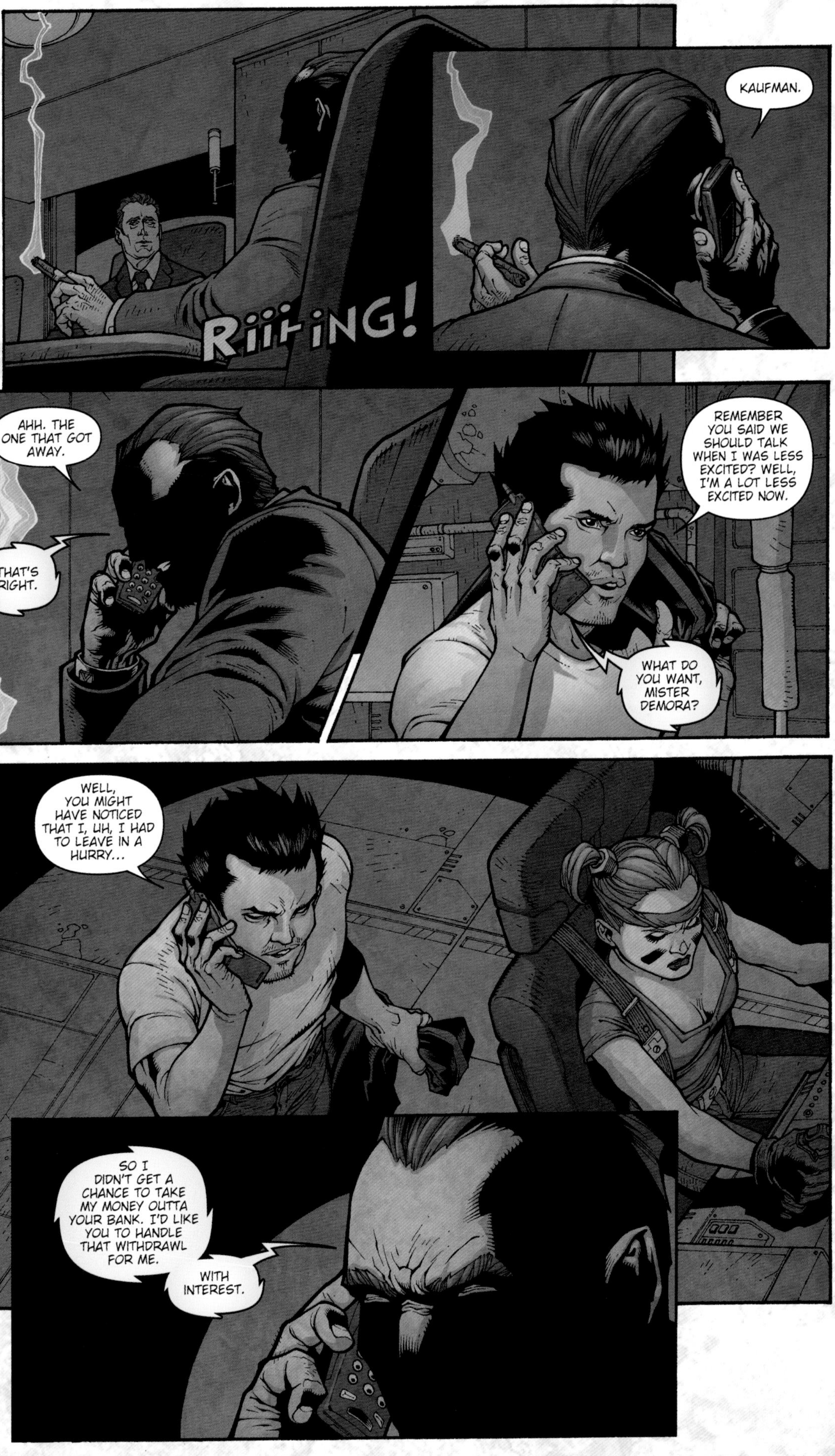
RIIING!
KAUFMAN.
AHH. THE ONE THAT GOT AWAY.
THAT'S RIGHT.
REMEMBER YOU SAID WE SHOULD TALK WHEN I WAS LESS EXCITED? WELL, I'M A LOT LESS EXCITED NOW.
WHAT DO YOU WANT, MISTER DEMORA?
WELL, YOU MIGHT HAVE NOTICED THAT I, UH, I HAD TO LEAVE IN A HURRY...
SO I DIDN'T GET A CHANCE TO TAKE MY MONEY OUTTA YOUR BANK. I'D LIKE YOU TO HANDLE THAT WITHDRAWL FOR ME.
WITH INTEREST.

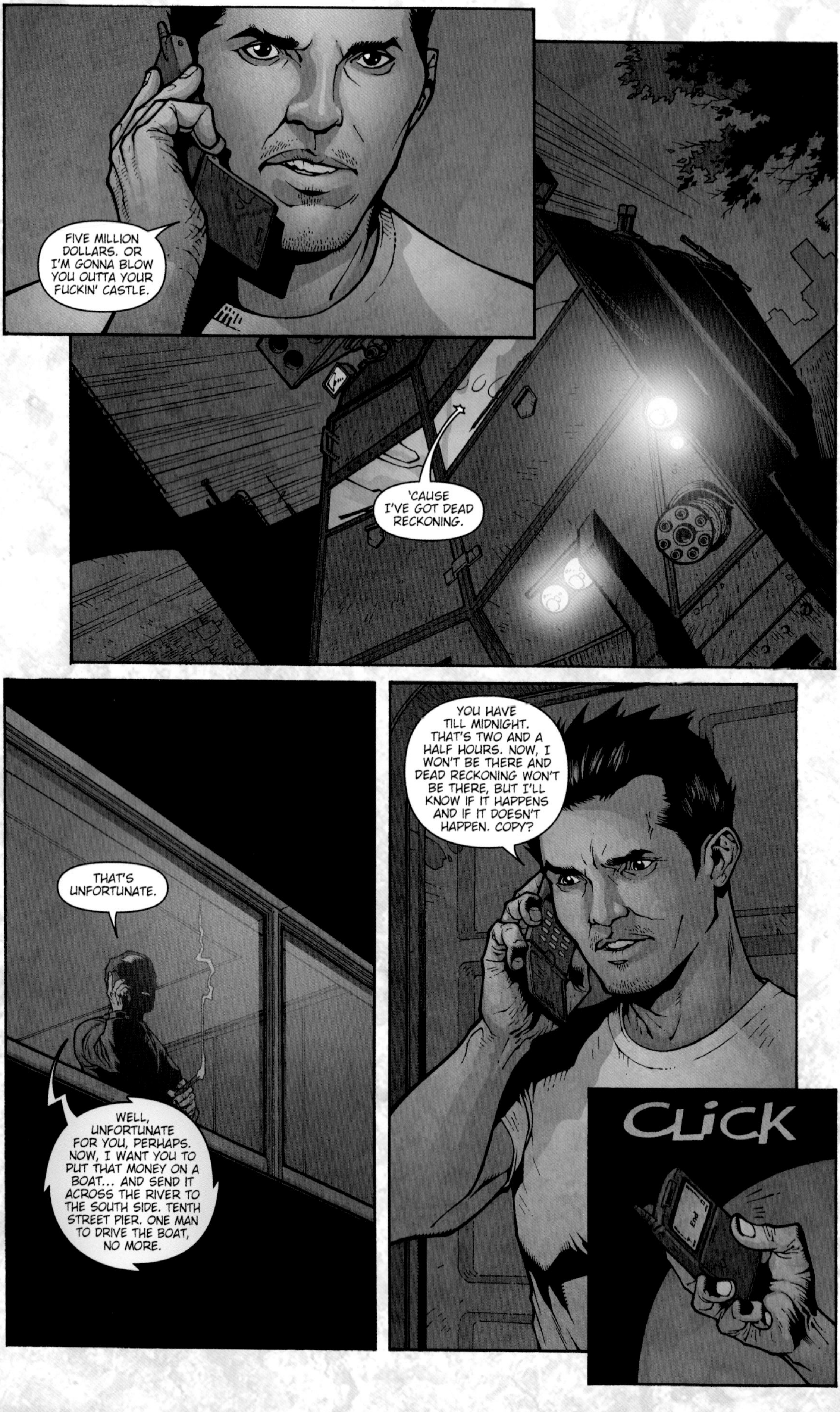

FIVE MILLION DOLLARS. OR I'M GONNA BLOW YOU OUTTA YOUR FUCKIN' CASTLE.
'CAUSE I'VE GOT DEAD RECKONING.
THAT'S UNFORTUNATE.
WELL, UNFORTUNATE FOR YOU, PERHAPS. NOW, I WANT YOU TO PUT THAT MONEY ON A BOAT... AND SEND IT ACROSS THE RIVER TO THE SOUTH SIDE. TENTH STREET PIER. ONE MAN TO DRIVE THE BOAT, NO MORE.
YOU HAVE TILL MIDNIGHT. THAT'S TWO AND A HALF HOURS. NOW, I WON'T BE THERE AND DEAD RECKONING WON'T BE THERE, BUT I'LL KNOW IF IT HAPPENS AND IF IT DOESN'T HAPPEN. COPY?
CLICK

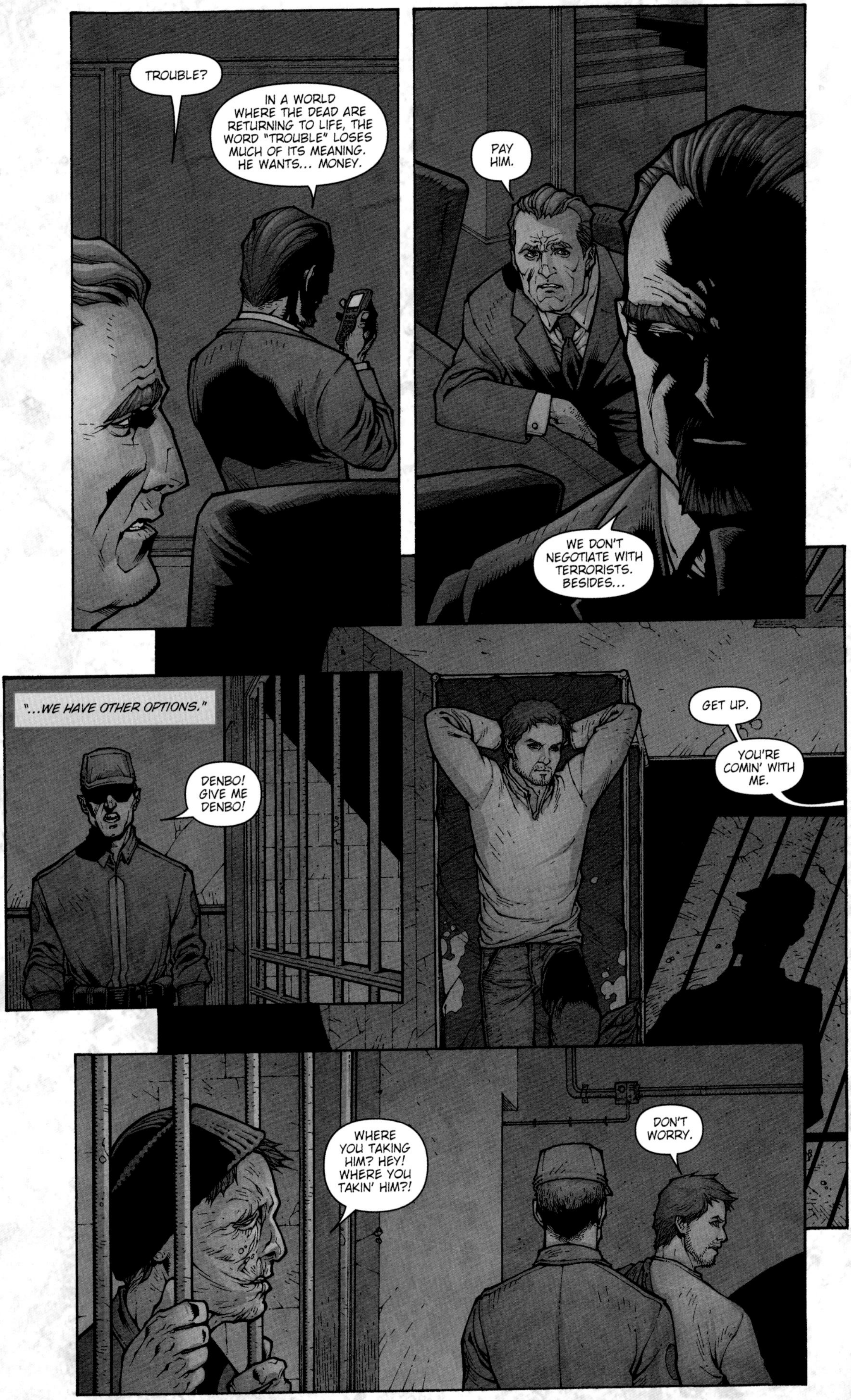
TROUBLE?
IN A WORLD WHERE THE DEAD ARE RETURNING TO LIFE, THE WORD "TROUBLE" LOSES MUCH OF ITS MEANING. HE WANTS... MONEY.
PAY HIM.
WE DON'T NEGOTIATE WITH TERRORISTS. BESIDES...
"...WE HAVE OTHER OPTIONS."
DENBO! GIVE ME DENBO!
GET UP.
YOU'RE COMIN' WITH ME.
WHERE YOU TAKING HIM? HEY! WHERE YOU TAKIN' HIM?!
DON'T WORRY.

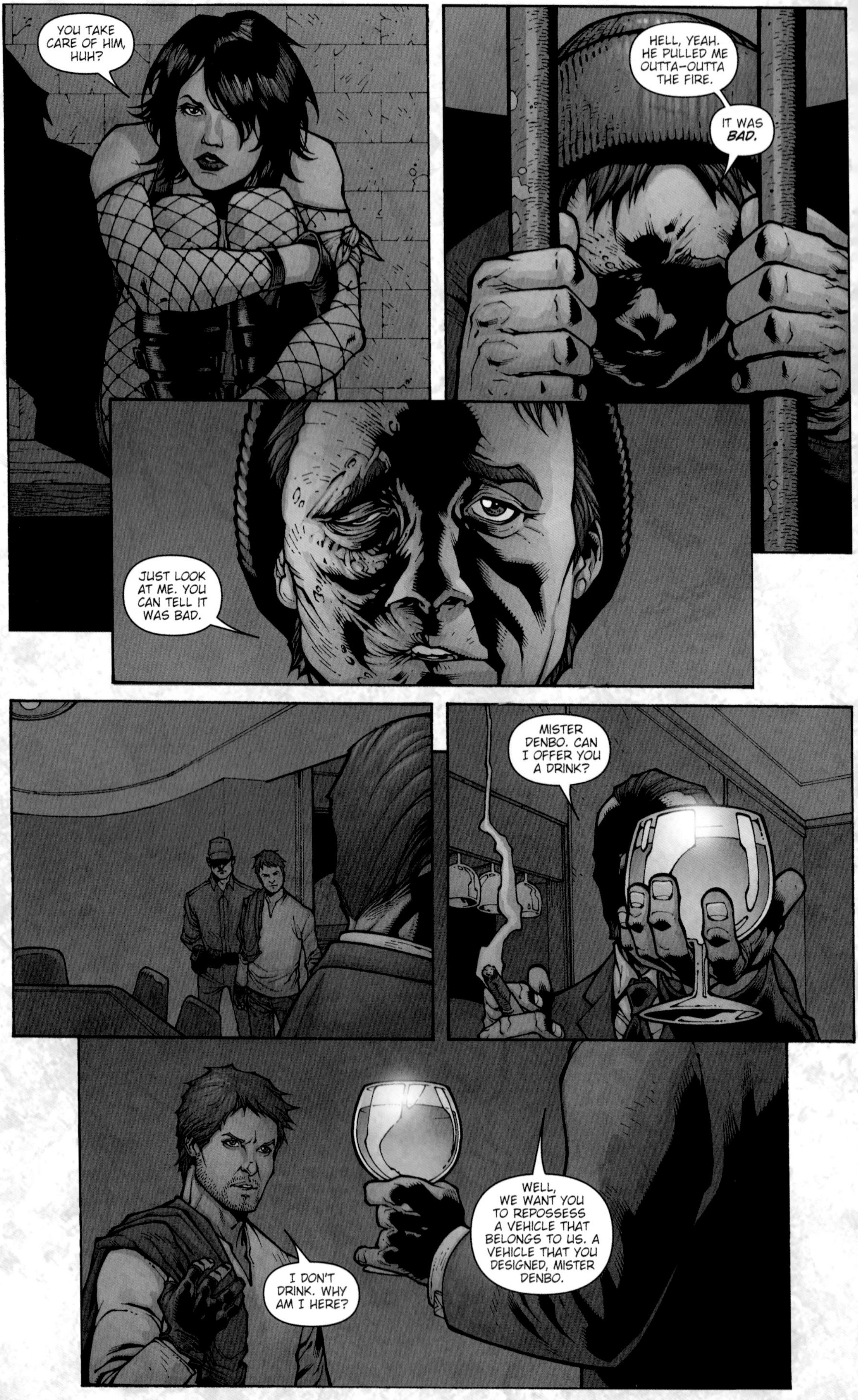
YOU TAKE CARE OF HIM, HUH?
HELL, YEAH. HE PULLED ME OUTTA–OUTTA THE FIRE.
IT WAS BAD.
JUST LOOK AT ME. YOU CAN TELL IT WAS BAD.
MISTER DENBO. CAN I OFFER YOU A DRINK?
I DON'T DRINK. WHY AM I HERE?
WELL, WE WANT YOU TO REPOSSESS A VEHICLE THAT BELONGS TO US. A VEHICLE THAT YOU DESIGNED, MISTER DENBO.

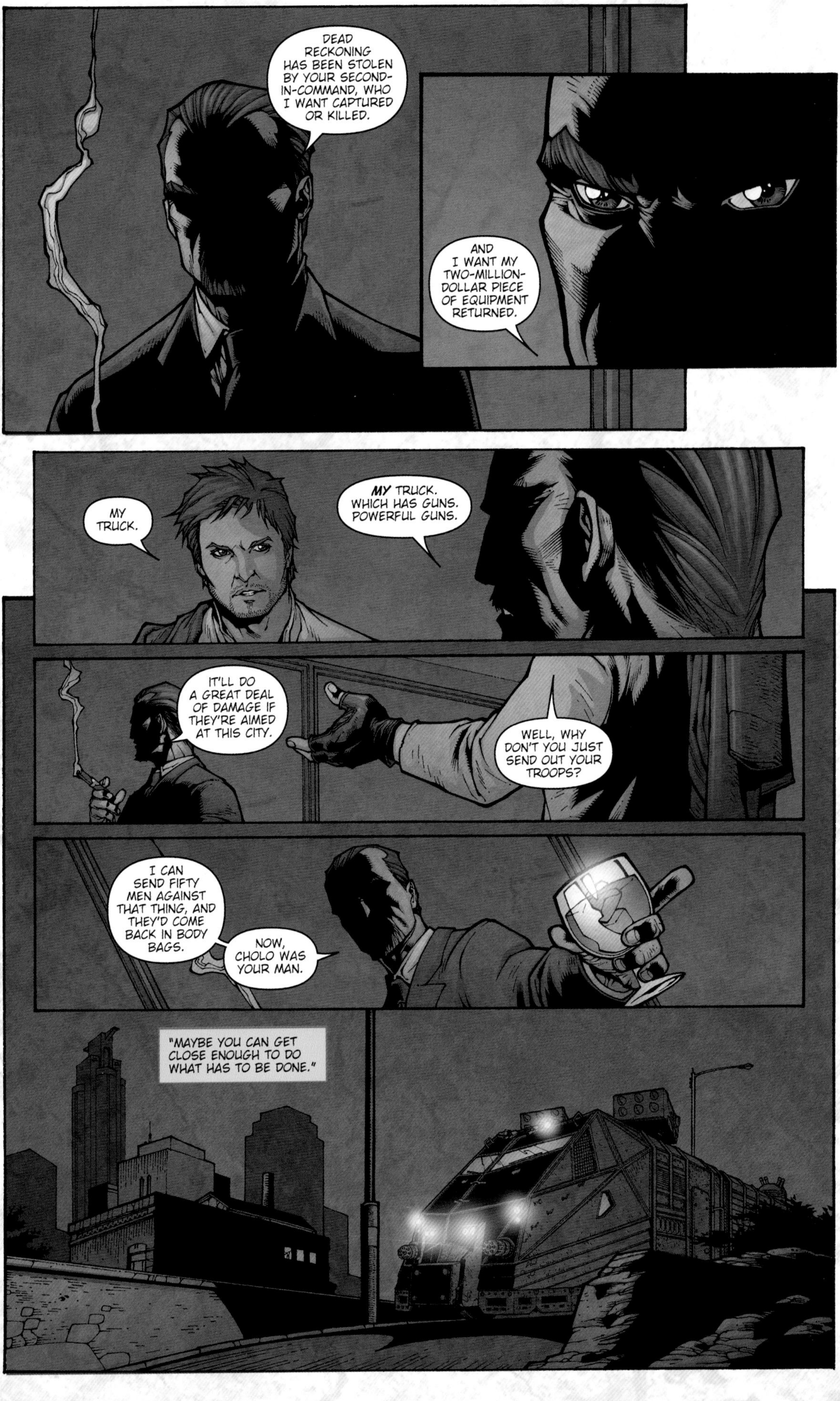
DEAD RECKONING HAS BEEN STOLEN BY YOUR SECOND-IN-COMMAND, WHO I WANT CAPTURED OR KILLED.
AND I WANT MY TWO-MILLION-DOLLAR PIECE OF EQUIPMENT RETURNED.
MY TRUCK.
MY TRUCK. WHICH HAS GUNS. POWERFUL GUNS.
IT'LL DO A GREAT DEAL OF DAMAGE IF THEY'RE AIMED AT THIS CITY.
WELL, WHY DON'T YOU JUST SEND OUT YOUR TROOPS?
I CAN SEND FIFTY MEN AGAINST THAT THING, AND THEY'D COME BACK IN BODY BAGS.
NOW, CHOLO WAS YOUR MAN.
"MAYBE YOU CAN GET CLOSE ENOUGH TO DO WHAT HAS TO BE DONE."

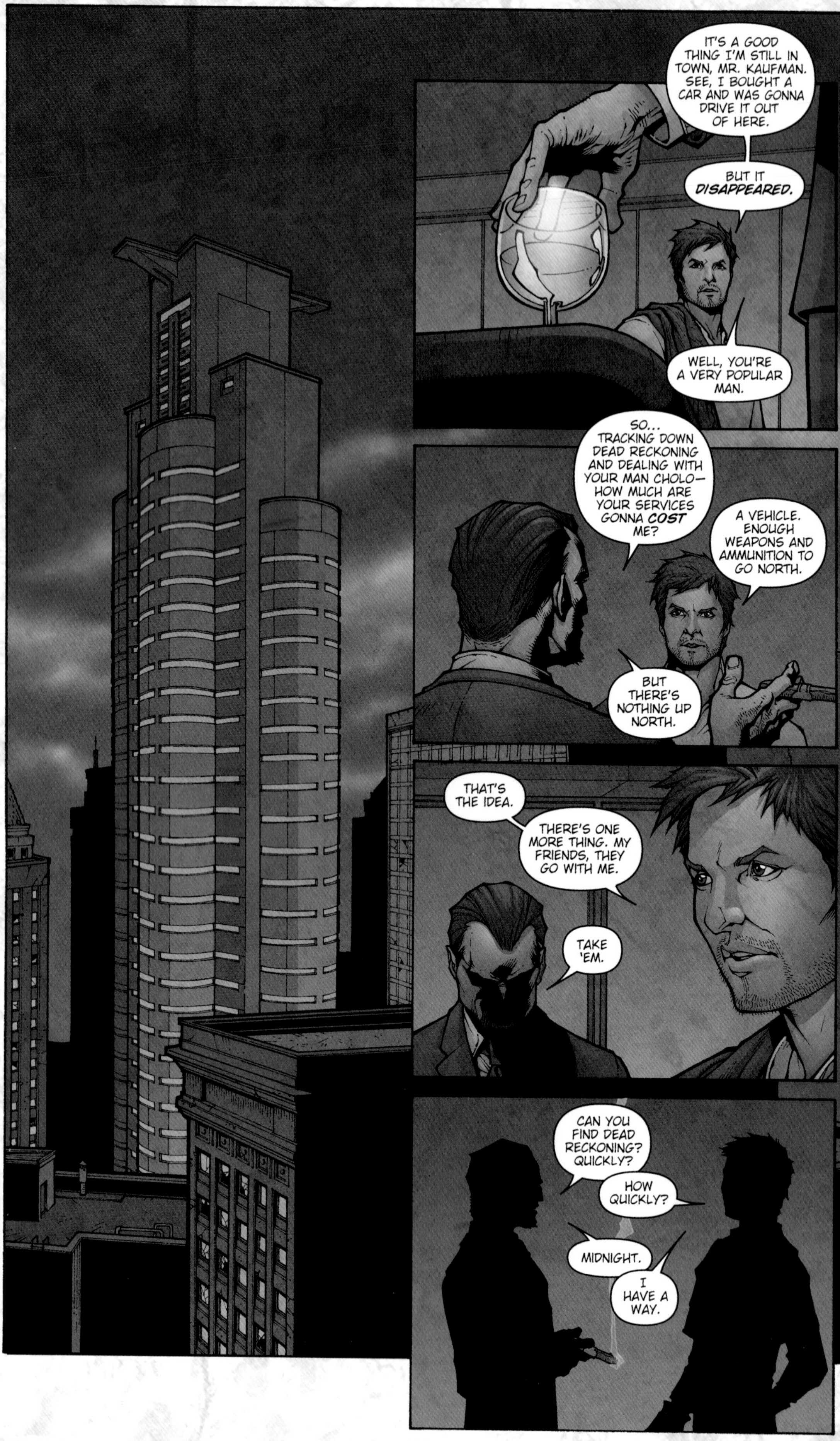
IT'S A GOOD THING I'M STILL IN TOWN, MR. KAUFMAN. SEE, I BOUGHT A CAR AND WAS GONNA DRIVE IT OUT OF HERE.
BUT IT *DISAPPEARED.*
WELL, YOU'RE A VERY POPULAR MAN.
SO... TRACKING DOWN DEAD RECKONING AND DEALING WITH YOUR MAN CHOLO— HOW MUCH ARE YOUR SERVICES GONNA **COST** ME?
A VEHICLE. ENOUGH WEAPONS AND AMMUNITION TO GO NORTH.
BUT THERE'S NOTHING UP NORTH.
THAT'S THE IDEA.
THERE'S ONE MORE THING. MY FRIENDS, THEY GO WITH ME.
TAKE 'EM.
CAN YOU FIND DEAD RECKONING? QUICKLY?
HOW QUICKLY?
MIDNIGHT.
I HAVE A WAY.

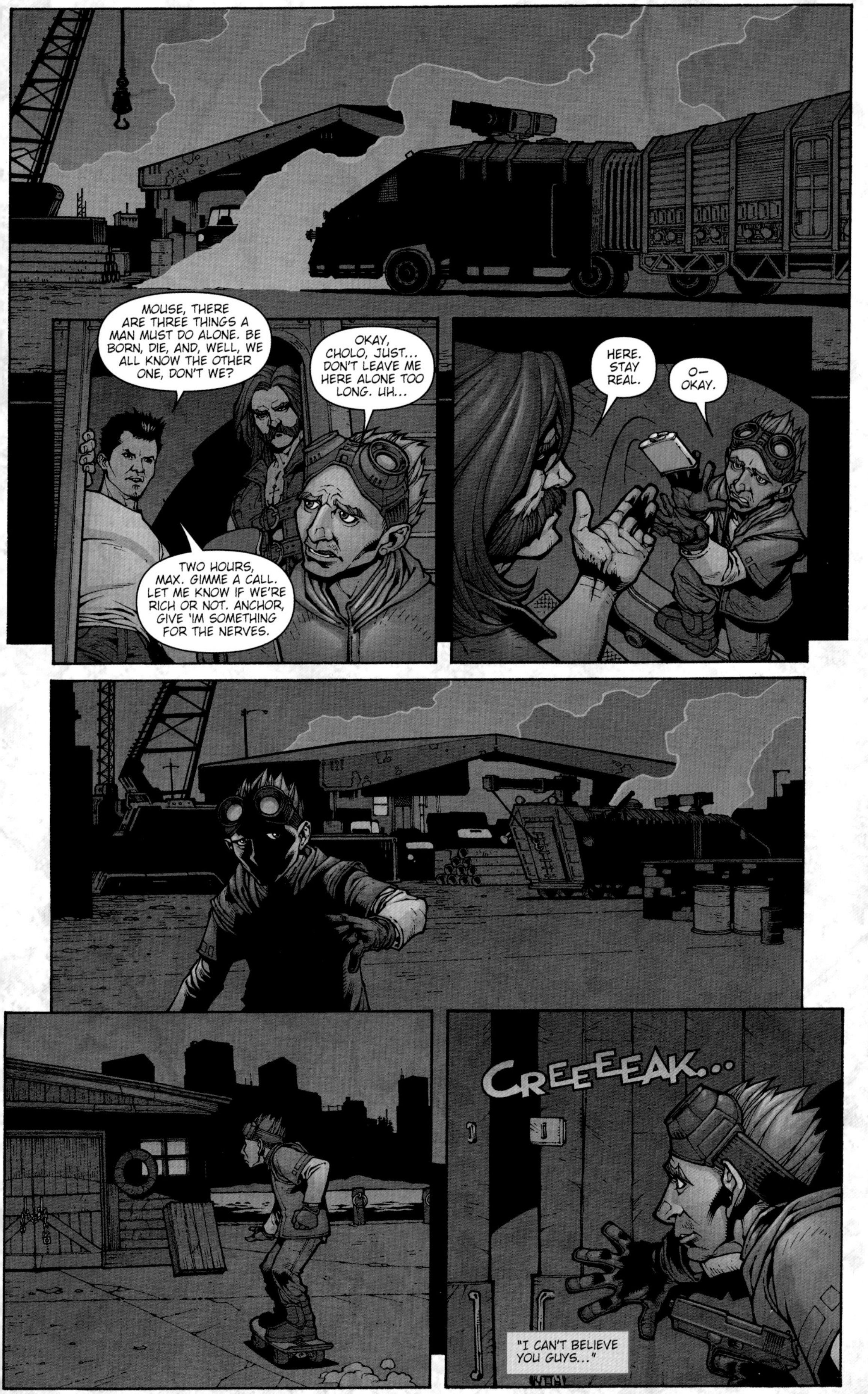
MOUSE, THERE ARE THREE THINGS A MAN MUST DO ALONE. BE BORN, DIE, AND, WELL, WE ALL KNOW THE OTHER ONE, DON'T WE?
OKAY, CHOLO, JUST... DON'T LEAVE ME HERE ALONE TOO LONG. UH...
TWO HOURS, MAX. GIMME A CALL. LET ME KNOW IF WE'RE RICH OR NOT. ANCHOR, GIVE 'IM SOMETHING FOR THE NERVES.
HERE. STAY REAL.
O— OKAY.
CREEEEAK...
"I CAN'T BELIEVE YOU GUYS..."

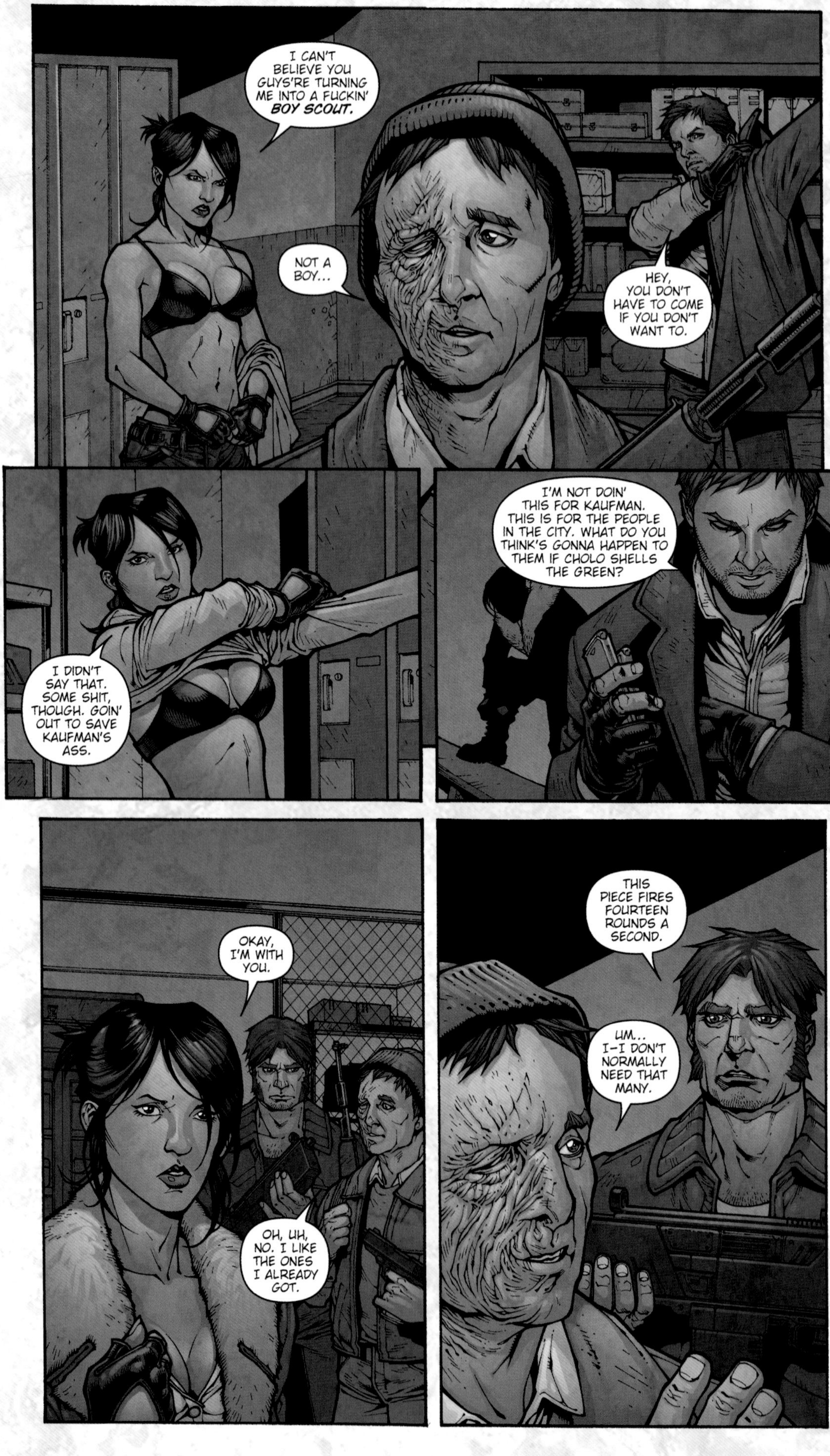
I CAN'T BELIEVE YOU GUYS'RE TURNING ME INTO A FUCKIN' **BOY SCOUT.**
NOT A BOY...
HEY, YOU DON'T HAVE TO COME IF YOU DON'T WANT TO.
I DIDN'T SAY THAT. SOME SHIT, THOUGH. GOIN' OUT TO SAVE KAUFMAN'S ASS.
I'M NOT DOIN' THIS FOR KAUFMAN. THIS IS FOR THE PEOPLE IN THE CITY. WHAT DO YOU THINK'S GONNA HAPPEN TO THEM IF CHOLO SHELLS THE GREEN?
OKAY, I'M WITH YOU.
OH, UH, NO. I LIKE THE ONES I ALREADY GOT.
THIS PIECE FIRES FOURTEEN ROUNDS A SECOND.
UM... I-I DON'T NORMALLY NEED THAT MANY.

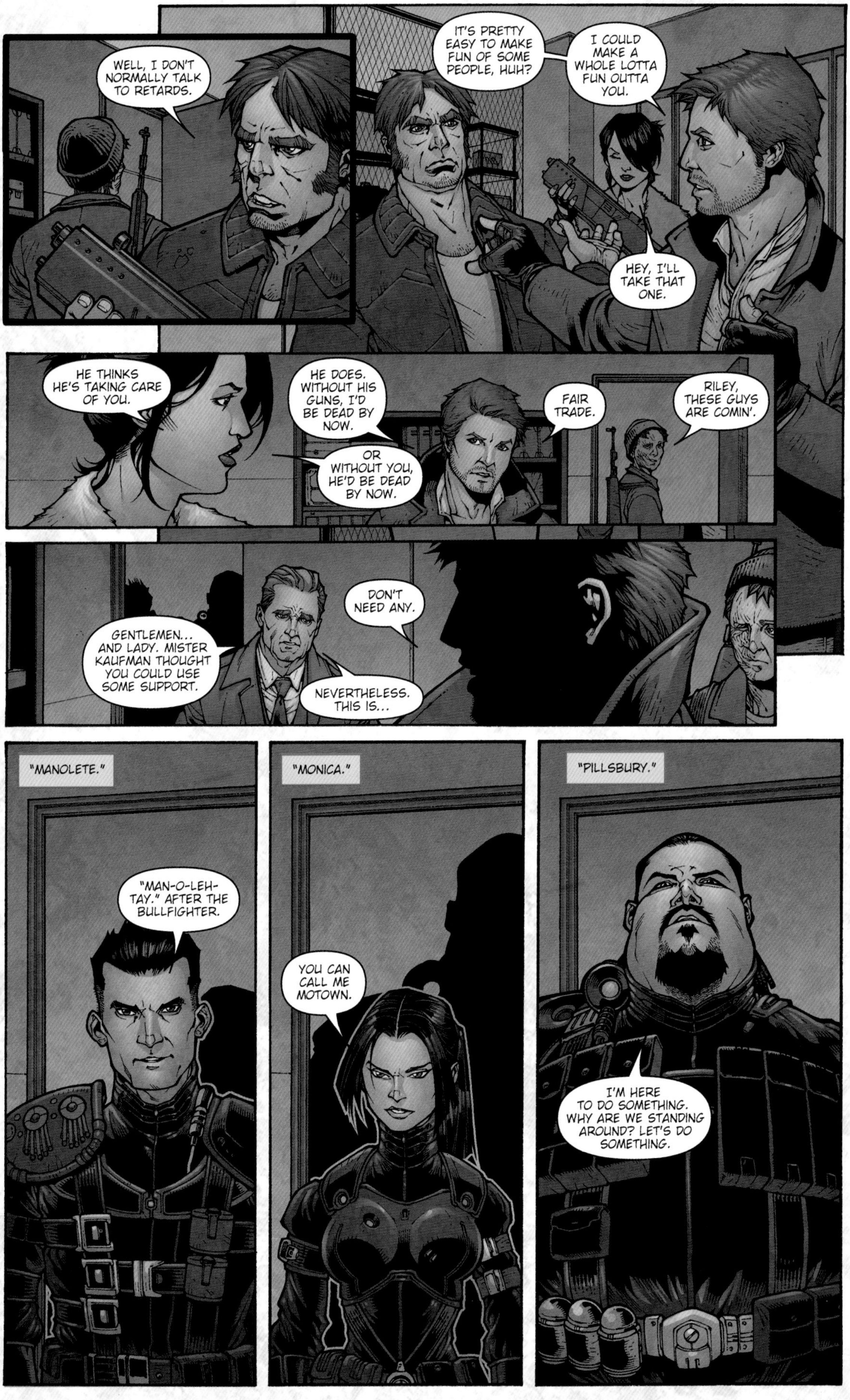
WELL, I DON'T NORMALLY TALK TO RETARDS.
IT'S PRETTY EASY TO MAKE FUN OF SOME PEOPLE, HUH?
I COULD MAKE A WHOLE LOTTA FUN OUTTA YOU.
HEY, I'LL TAKE THAT ONE.
HE THINKS HE'S TAKING CARE OF YOU.
HE DOES. WITHOUT HIS GUNS, I'D BE DEAD BY NOW.
OR WITHOUT YOU, HE'D BE DEAD BY NOW.
FAIR TRADE.
RILEY, THESE GUYS ARE COMIN'.
GENTLEMEN... AND LADY. MISTER KAUFMAN THOUGHT YOU COULD USE SOME SUPPORT.
DON'T NEED ANY.
NEVERTHELESS. THIS IS...
"MANOLETE."
"MAN-O-LEH-TAY." AFTER THE BULLFIGHTER.
"MONICA."
YOU CAN CALL ME MOTOWN.
"PILLSBURY."
I'M HERE TO DO SOMETHING. WHY ARE WE STANDING AROUND? LET'S DO SOMETHING.

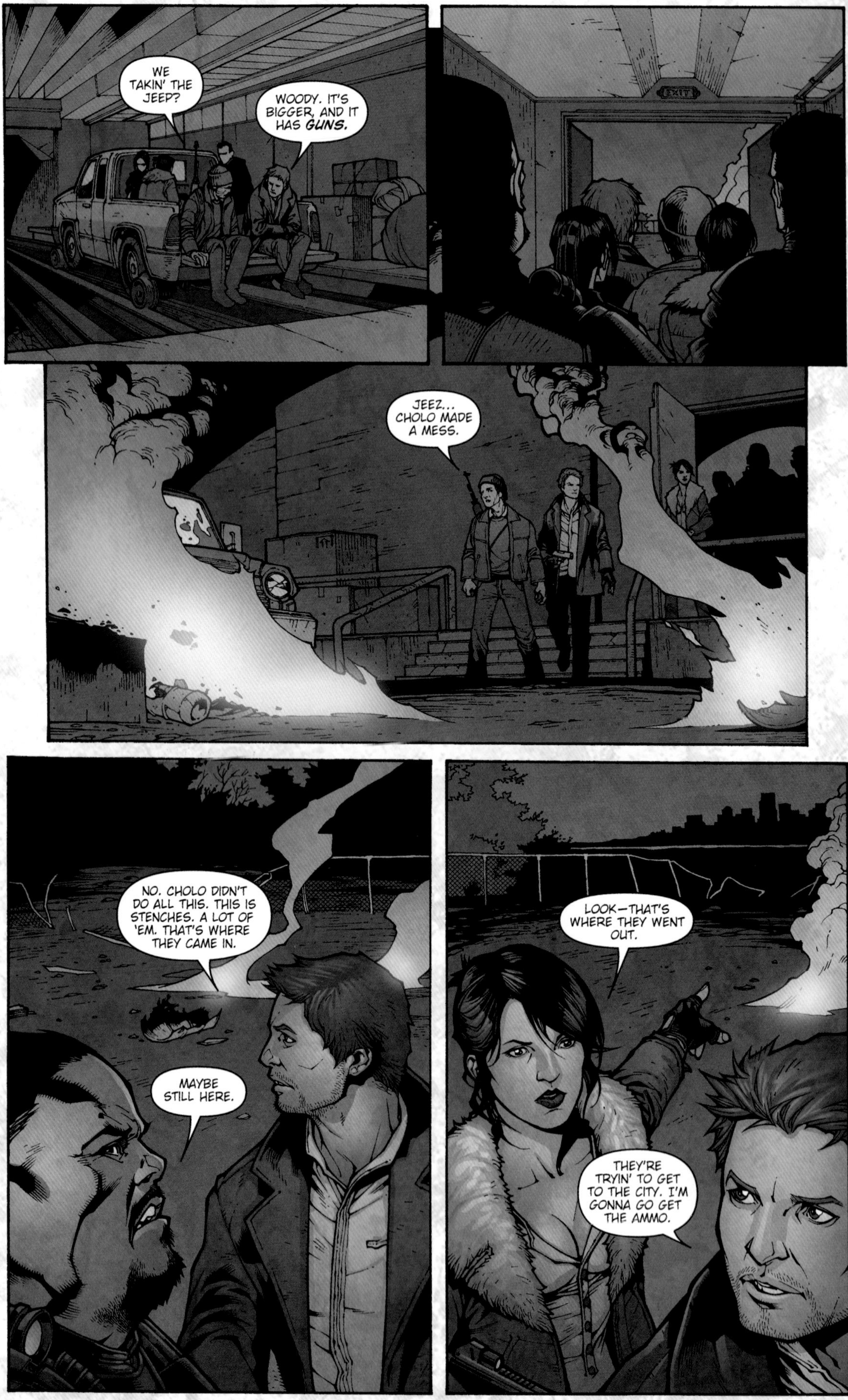
WE TAKIN' THE JEEP?
WOODY. IT'S BIGGER, AND IT HAS **GUNS.**
JEEZ... CHOLO MADE A MESS.
NO. CHOLO DIDN'T DO ALL THIS. THIS IS STENCHES. A LOT OF 'EM. THAT'S WHERE THEY CAME IN.
MAYBE STILL HERE.
LOOK—THAT'S WHERE THEY WENT OUT.
THEY'RE TRYIN' TO GET TO THE CITY. I'M GONNA GO GET THE AMMO.

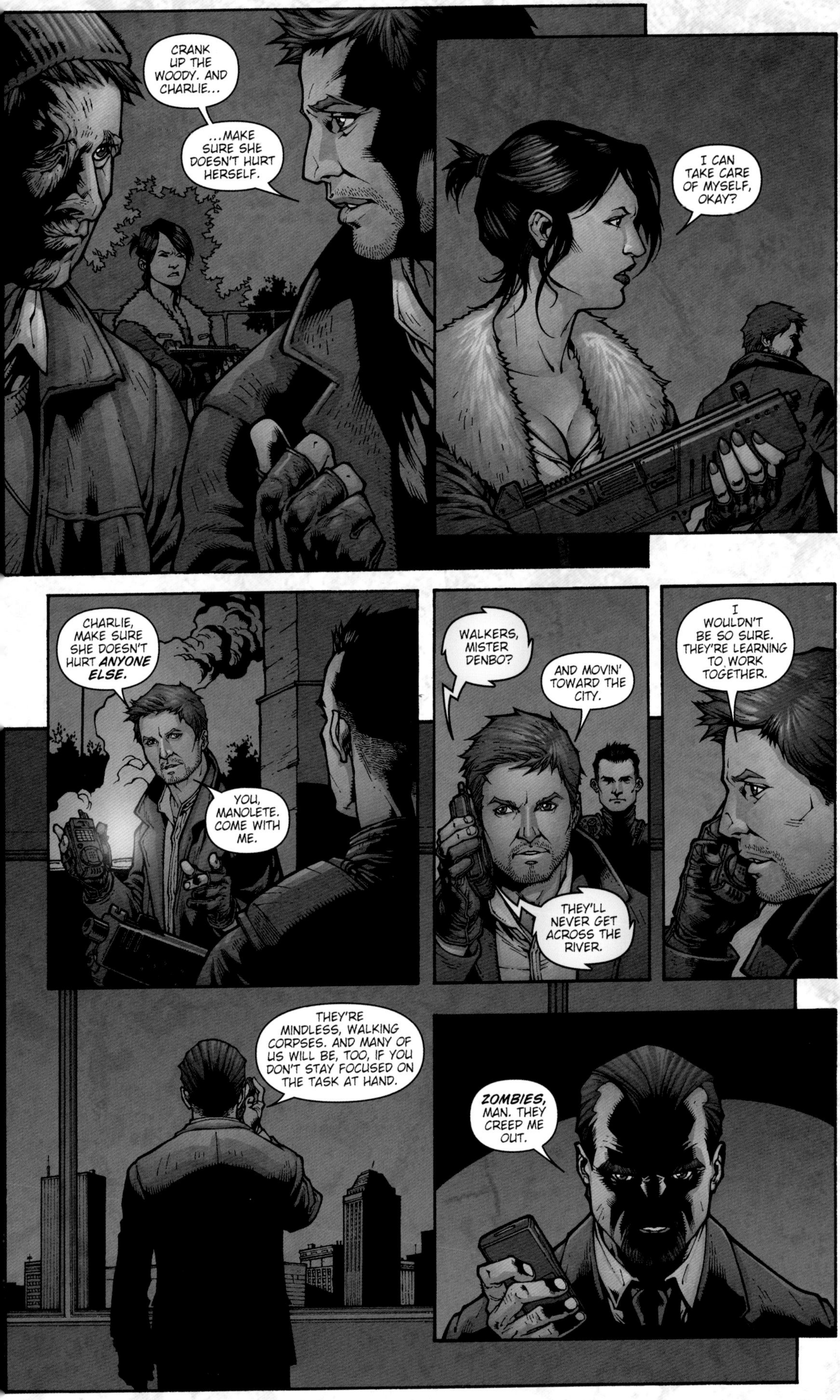
CRANK UP THE WOODY. AND CHARLIE...
...MAKE SURE SHE DOESN'T HURT HERSELF.
I CAN TAKE CARE OF MYSELF, OKAY?
CHARLIE, MAKE SURE SHE DOESN'T HURT **ANYONE ELSE.**
YOU, MANOLETE. COME WITH ME.
WALKERS, MISTER DENBO?
AND MOVIN' TOWARD THE CITY.
THEY'LL NEVER GET ACROSS THE RIVER.
I WOULDN'T BE SO SURE. THEY'RE LEARNING TO WORK TOGETHER.
THEY'RE MINDLESS, WALKING CORPSES. AND MANY OF US WILL BE, TOO, IF YOU DON'T STAY FOCUSED ON THE TASK AT HAND.
ZOMBIES, MAN. THEY CREEP ME OUT.

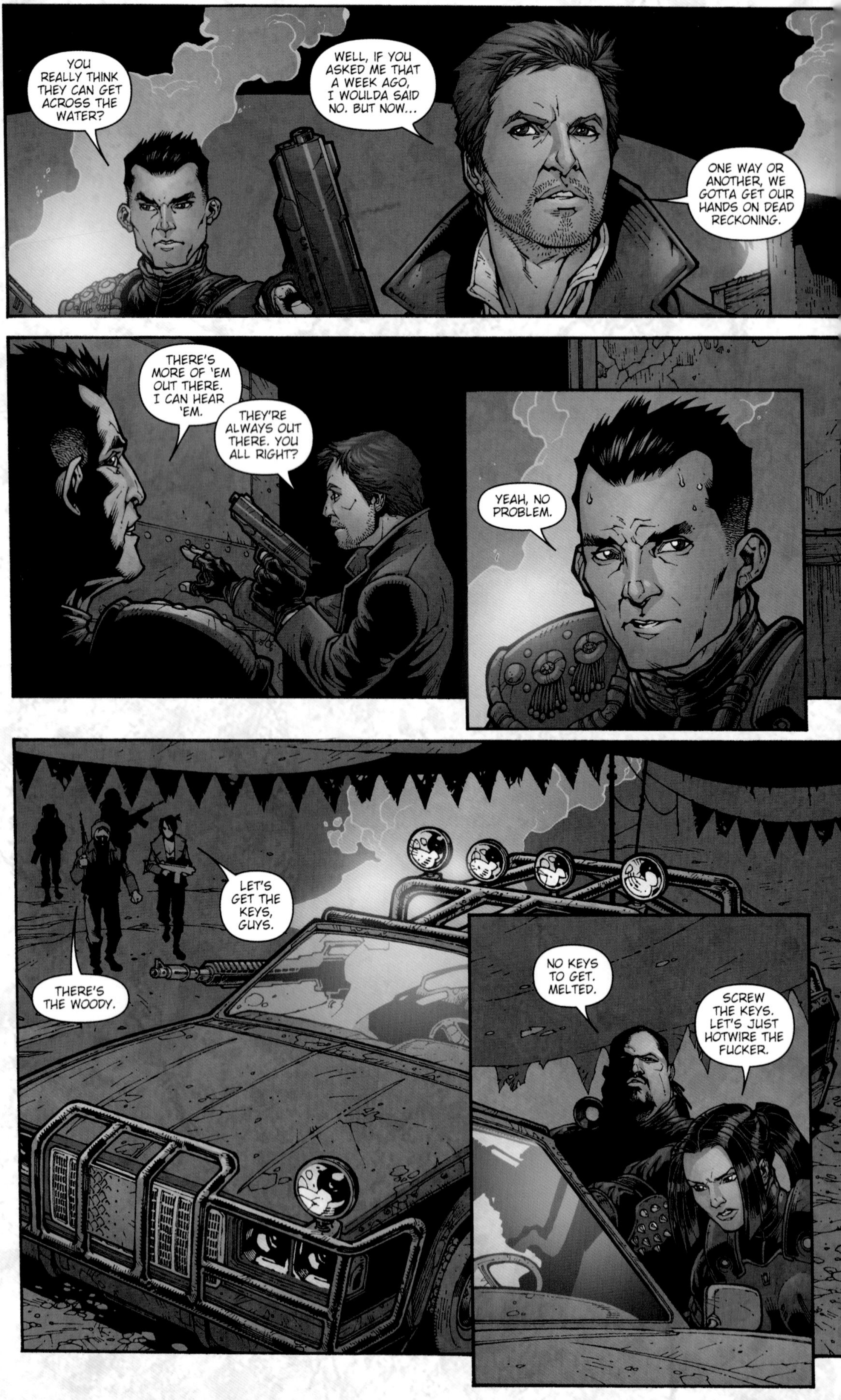
YOU REALLY THINK THEY CAN GET ACROSS THE WATER?
WELL, IF YOU ASKED ME THAT A WEEK AGO, I WOULDA SAID NO. BUT NOW...
ONE WAY OR ANOTHER, WE GOTTA GET OUR HANDS ON DEAD RECKONING.
THERE'S MORE OF 'EM OUT THERE. I CAN HEAR 'EM.
THEY'RE ALWAYS OUT THERE. YOU ALL RIGHT?
YEAH, NO PROBLEM.
LET'S GET THE KEYS, GUYS.
THERE'S THE WOODY.
NO KEYS TO GET. MELTED.
SCREW THE KEYS. LET'S JUST HOTWIRE THE FUCKER.

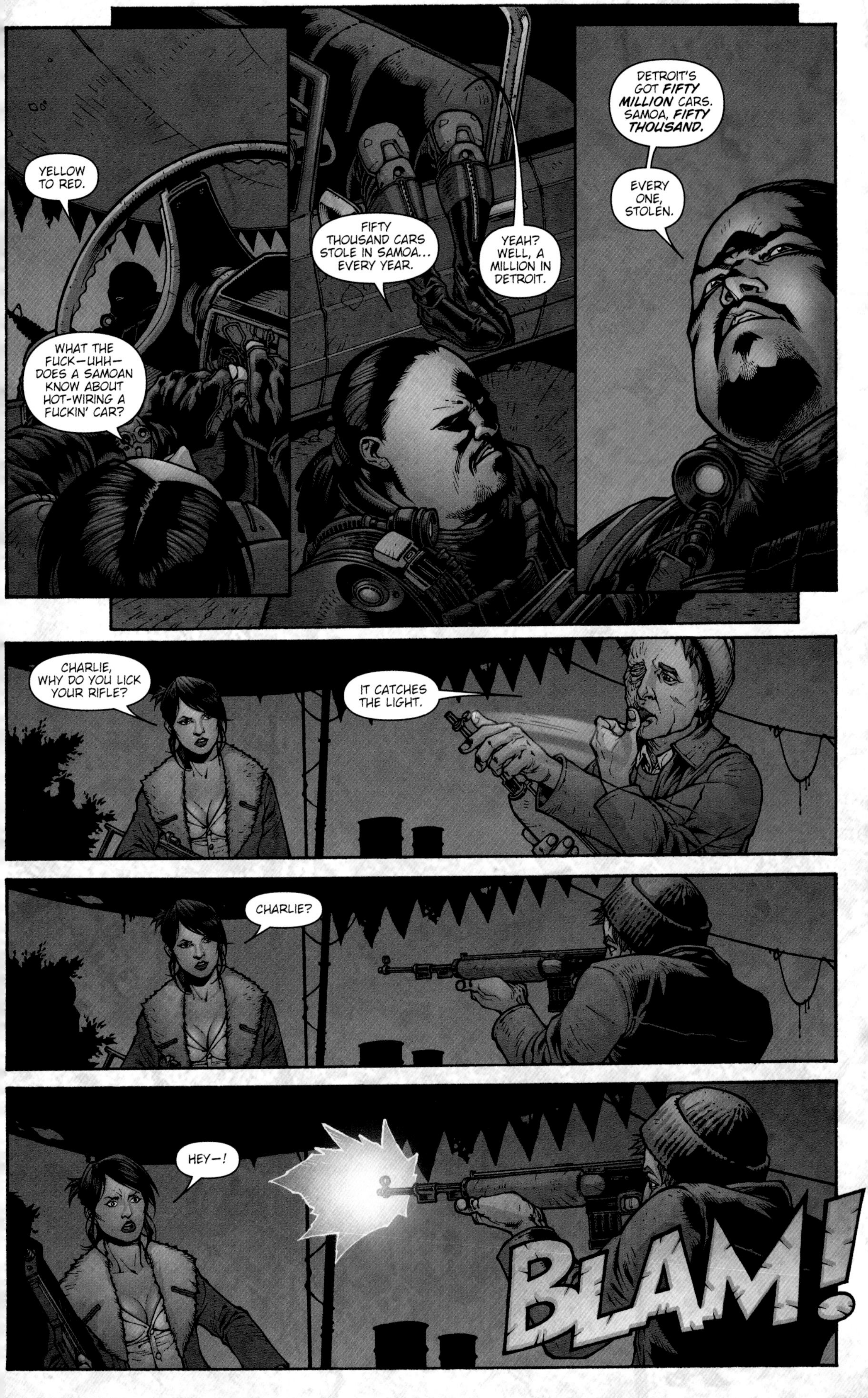

YELLOW TO RED.
WHAT THE FUCK—UHH—DOES A SAMOAN KNOW ABOUT HOT-WIRING A FUCKIN' CAR?
FIFTY THOUSAND CARS STOLE IN SAMOA... EVERY YEAR.
YEAH? WELL, A MILLION IN DETROIT.
DETROIT'S GOT FIFTY MILLION CARS. SAMOA, FIFTY THOUSAND.
EVERY ONE, STOLEN.
CHARLIE, WHY DO YOU LICK YOUR RIFLE?
IT CATCHES THE LIGHT.
CHARLIE?
HEY—!
BLAM!

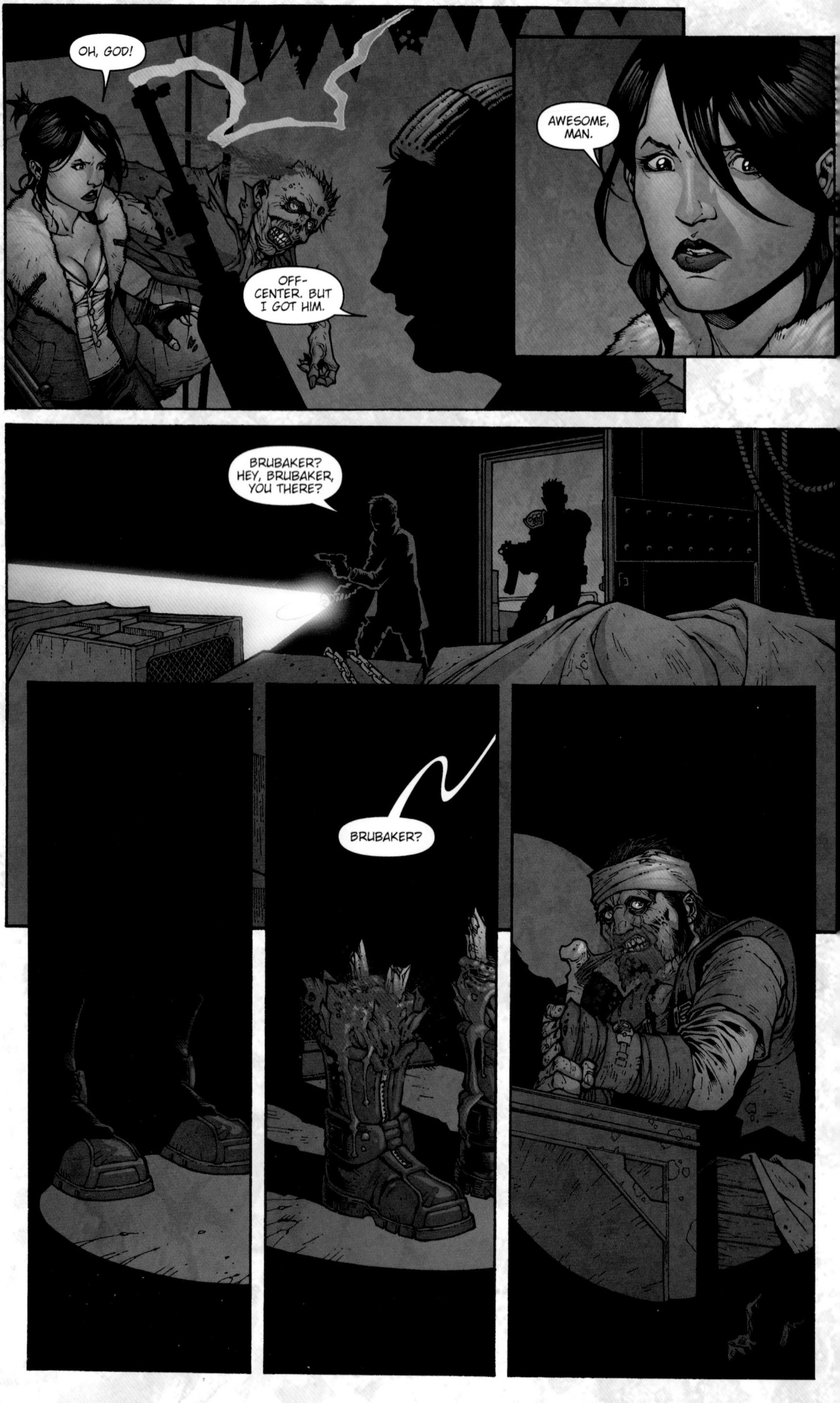
OH, GOD!
OFF-CENTER. BUT I GOT HIM.
AWESOME, MAN.
BRUBAKER? HEY, BRUBAKER, YOU THERE?
BRUBAKER?

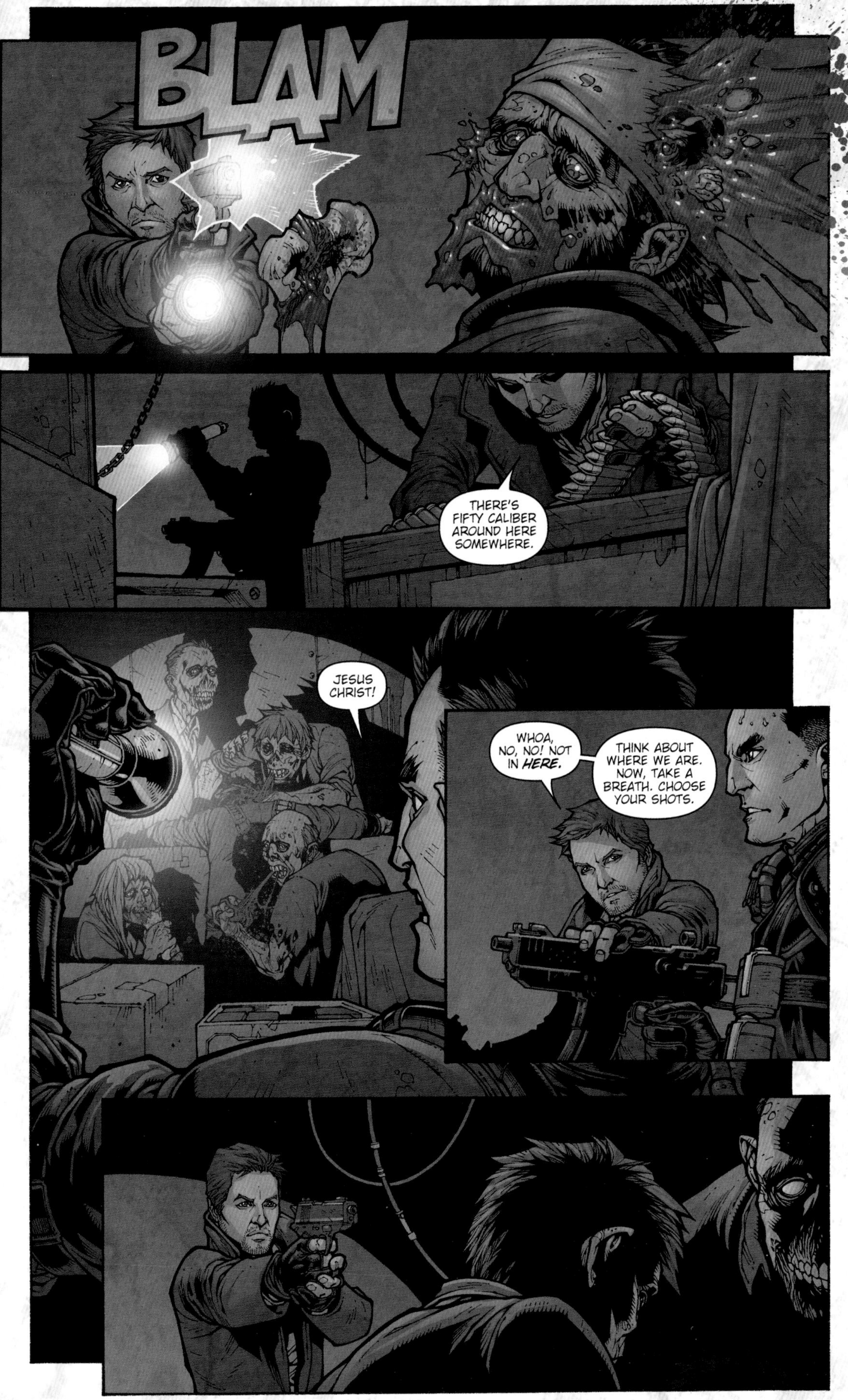
BLAM
THERE'S FIFTY CALIBER AROUND HERE SOMEWHERE.
JESUS CHRIST!
WHOA, NO, NO! NOT IN *HERE.*
THINK ABOUT WHERE WE ARE. NOW, TAKE A BREATH. CHOOSE YOUR SHOTS.

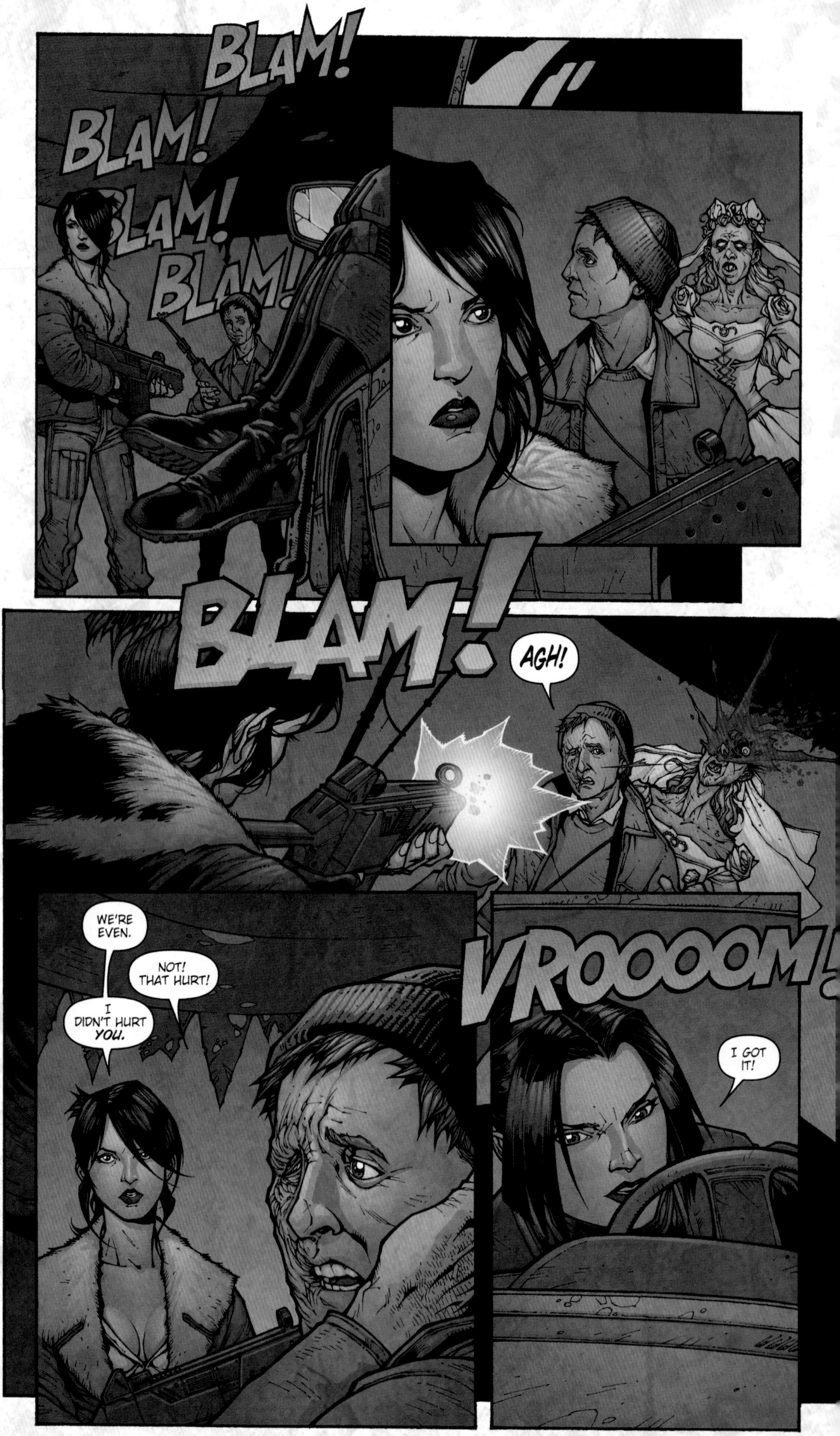
BLAM!
BLAM!
BLAM!
BLAM!
BLAM!
AGH!
WE'RE EVEN.
NOT! THAT HURT!
I DIDN'T HURT YOU.
VROOOOM!
I GOT IT!

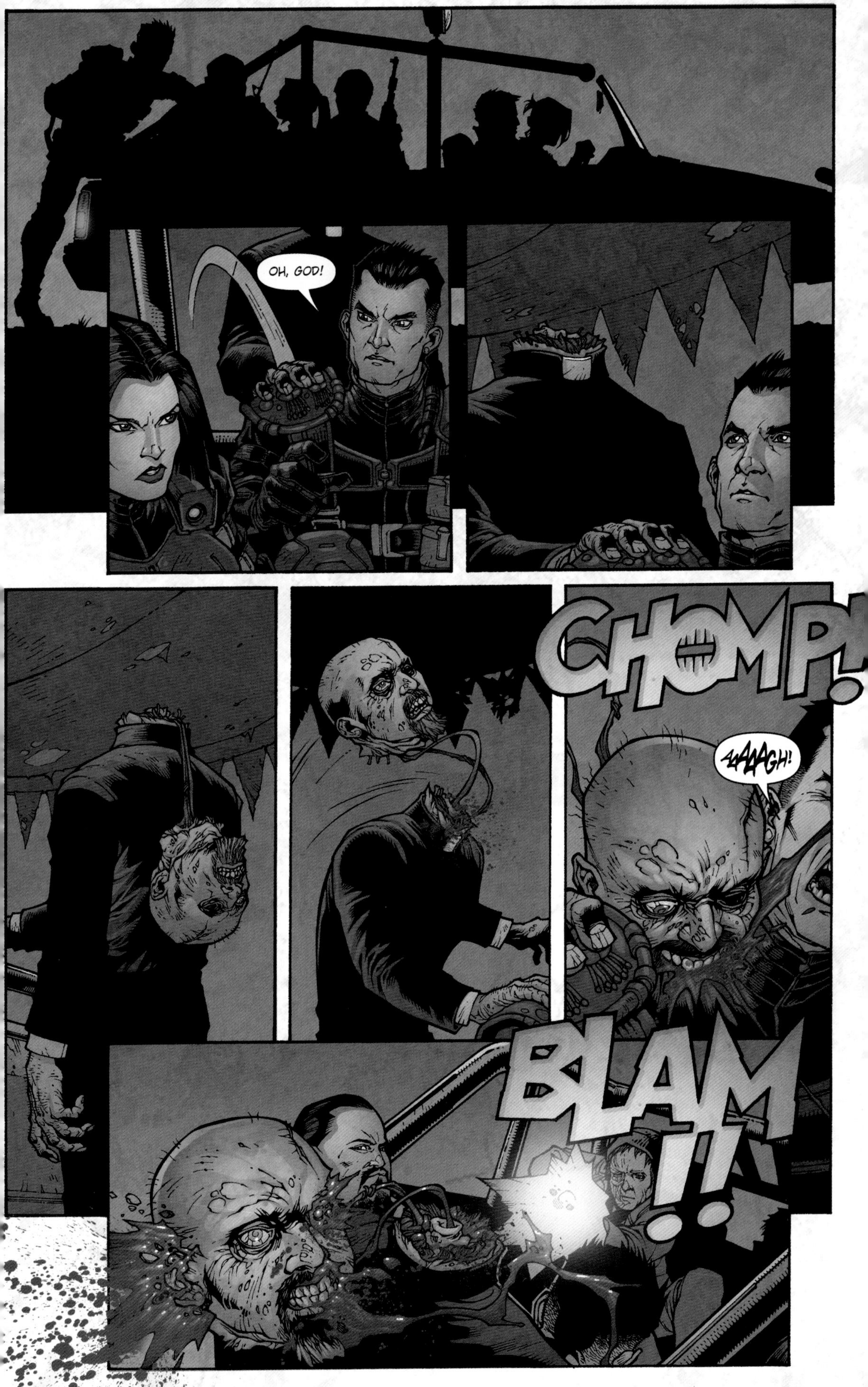
OH, GOD!
CHOMP!
AAAAAGH!
BLAM!!

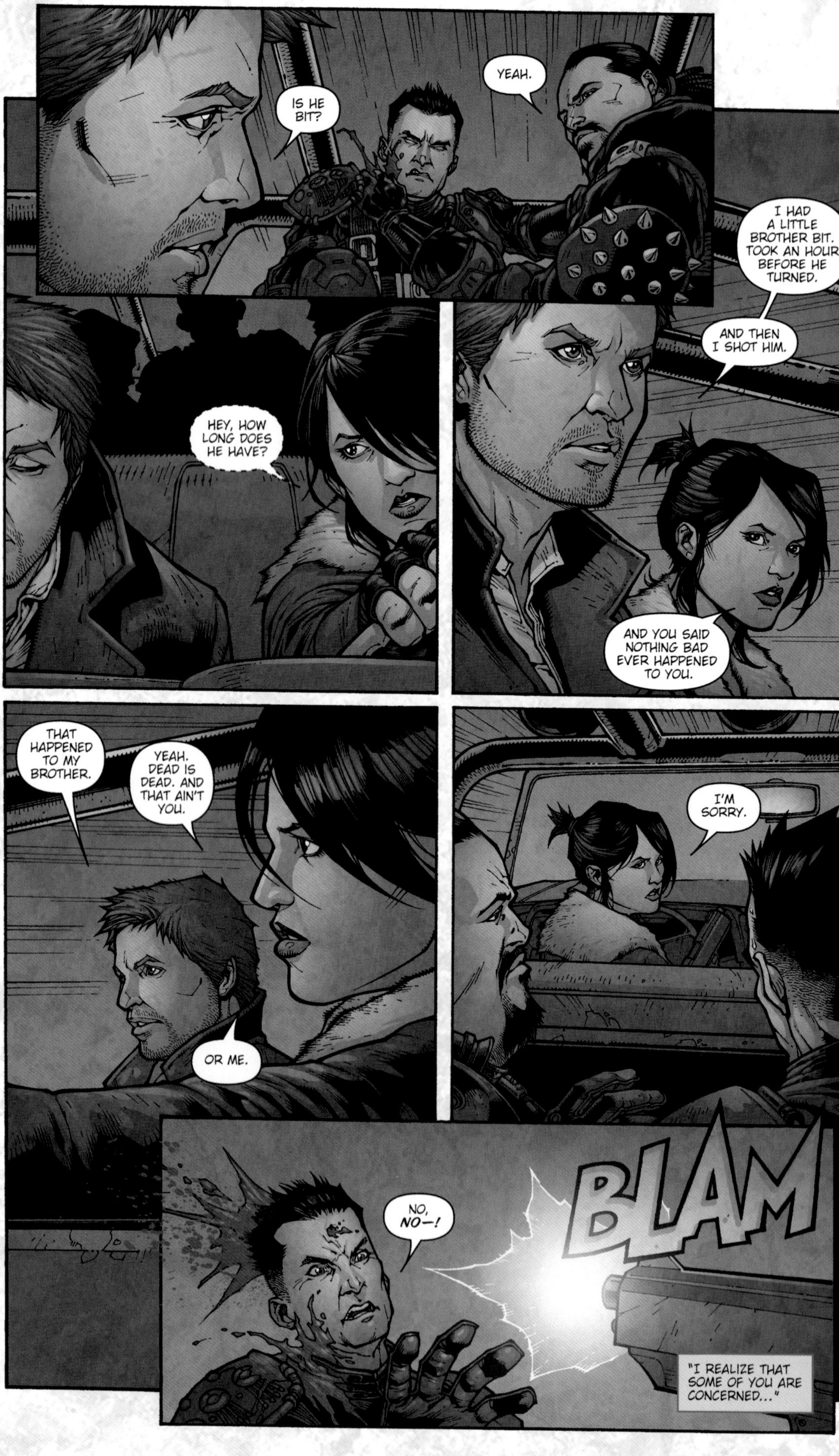

IS HE BIT?
YEAH.
I HAD A LITTLE BROTHER BIT. TOOK AN HOUR BEFORE HE TURNED.
AND THEN I SHOT HIM.
HEY, HOW LONG DOES HE HAVE?
AND YOU SAID NOTHING BAD EVER HAPPENED TO YOU.
THAT HAPPENED TO MY BROTHER.
YEAH. DEAD IS DEAD. AND THAT AIN'T YOU.
OR ME.
I'M SORRY.
BLAM
NO, NO—!
"I REALIZE THAT SOME OF YOU ARE CONCERNED..."

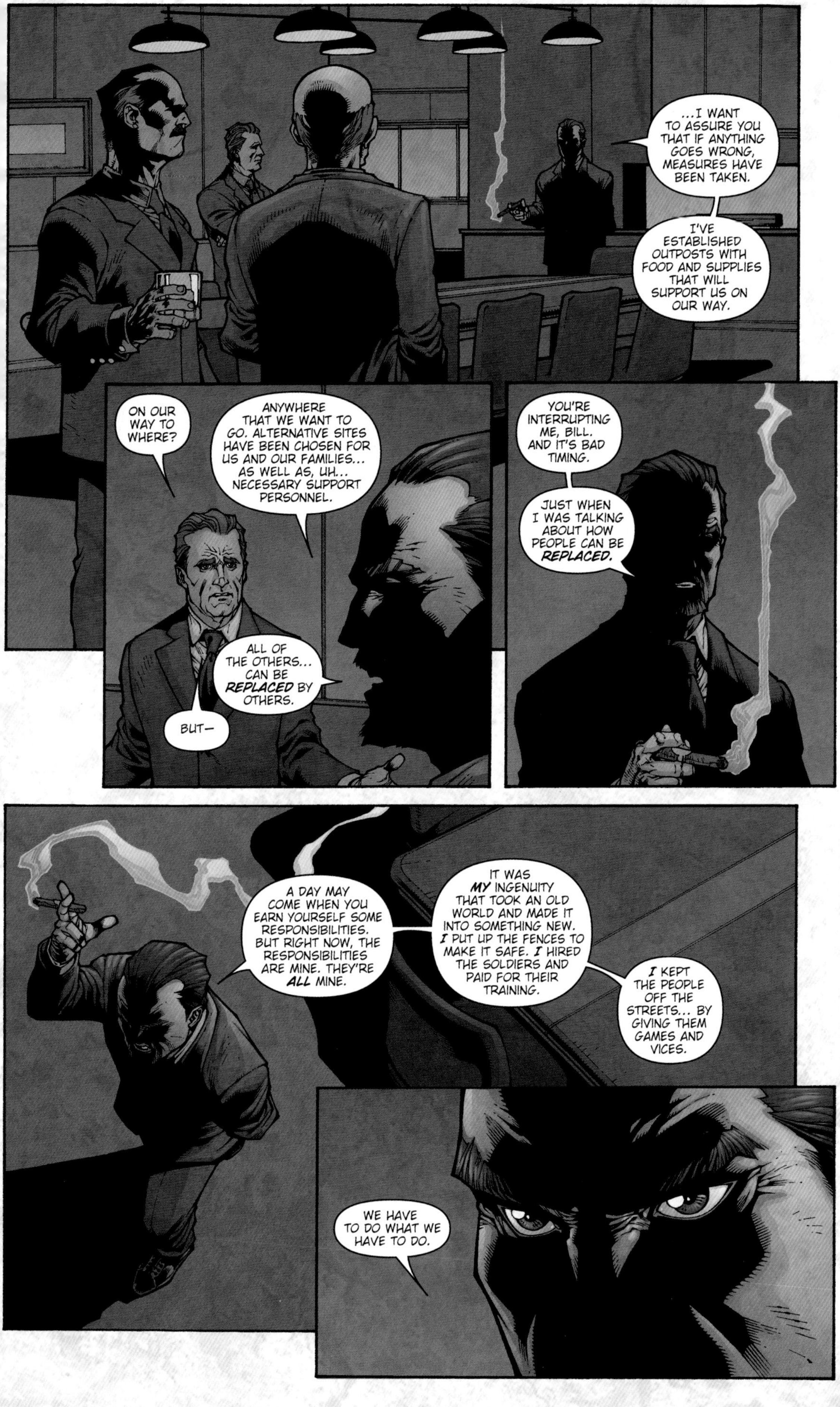

...I WANT TO ASSURE YOU THAT IF ANYTHING GOES WRONG, MEASURES HAVE BEEN TAKEN.
I'VE ESTABLISHED OUTPOSTS WITH FOOD AND SUPPLIES THAT WILL SUPPORT US ON OUR WAY.
ON OUR WAY TO WHERE?
ANYWHERE THAT WE WANT TO GO. ALTERNATIVE SITES HAVE BEEN CHOSEN FOR US AND OUR FAMILIES... AS WELL AS, UH... NECESSARY SUPPORT PERSONNEL.
ALL OF THE OTHERS... CAN BE *REPLACED* BY OTHERS.
BUT—
YOU'RE INTERRUPTING ME, BILL. AND IT'S BAD TIMING.
JUST WHEN I WAS TALKING ABOUT HOW PEOPLE CAN BE *REPLACED.*
A DAY MAY COME WHEN YOU EARN YOURSELF SOME RESPONSIBILITIES. BUT RIGHT NOW, THE RESPONSIBILITIES ARE MINE. THEY'RE *ALL* MINE.
IT WAS *MY* INGENUITY THAT TOOK AN OLD WORLD AND MADE IT INTO SOMETHING NEW. *I* PUT UP THE FENCES TO MAKE IT SAFE. *I* HIRED THE SOLDIERS AND PAID FOR THEIR TRAINING.
I KEPT THE PEOPLE OFF THE STREETS... BY GIVING THEM GAMES AND VICES.
WE HAVE TO DO WHAT WE HAVE TO DO.

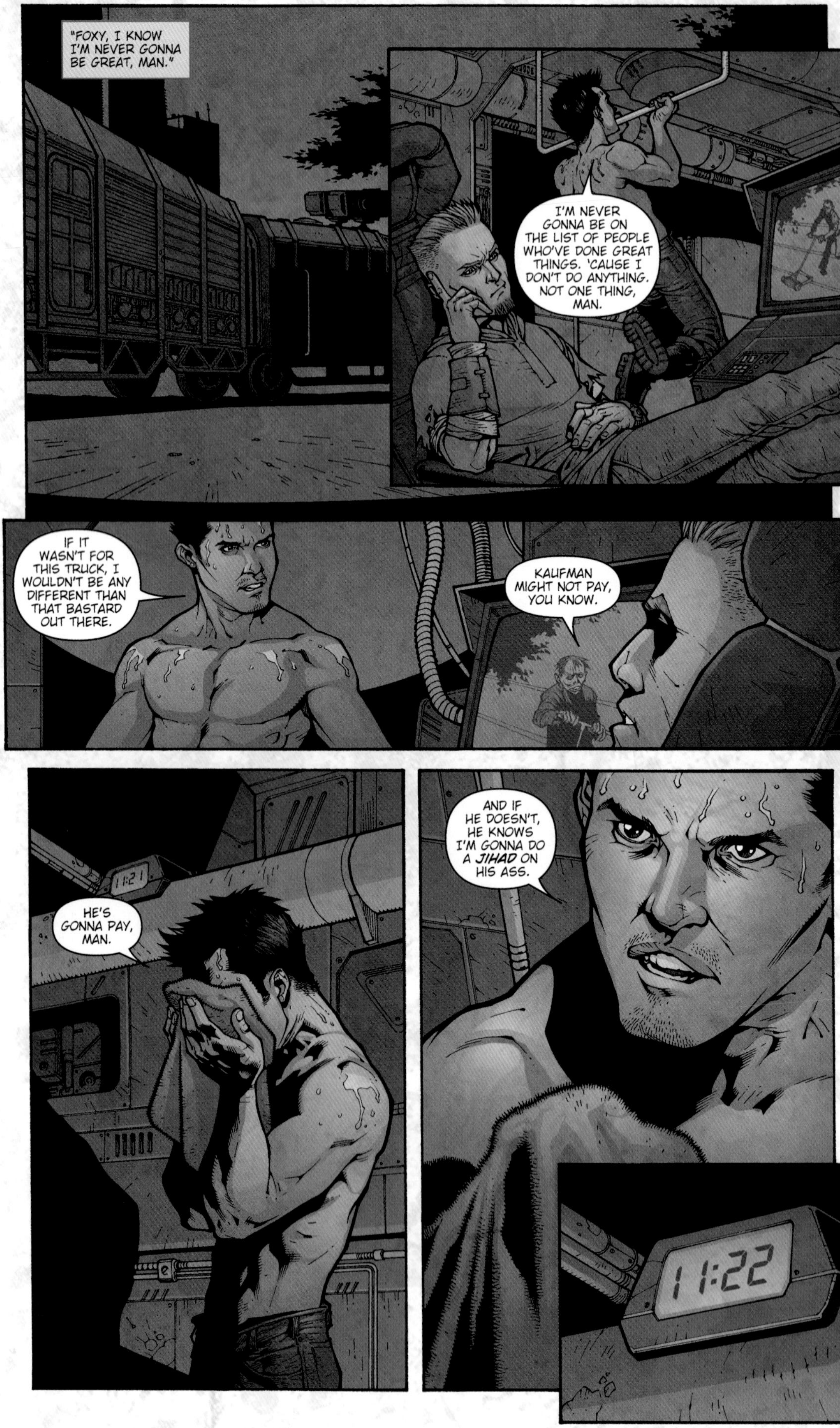
"FOXY, I KNOW I'M NEVER GONNA BE GREAT, MAN."
I'M NEVER GONNA BE ON THE LIST OF PEOPLE WHO'VE DONE GREAT THINGS. 'CAUSE I DON'T DO ANYTHING. NOT ONE THING, MAN.
IF IT WASN'T FOR THIS TRUCK, I WOULDN'T BE ANY DIFFERENT THAN THAT BASTARD OUT THERE.
KAUFMAN MIGHT NOT PAY, YOU KNOW.
11:21
HE'S GONNA PAY, MAN.
AND IF HE DOESN'T, HE KNOWS I'M GONNA DO A *JIHAD* ON HIS ASS.
11:22

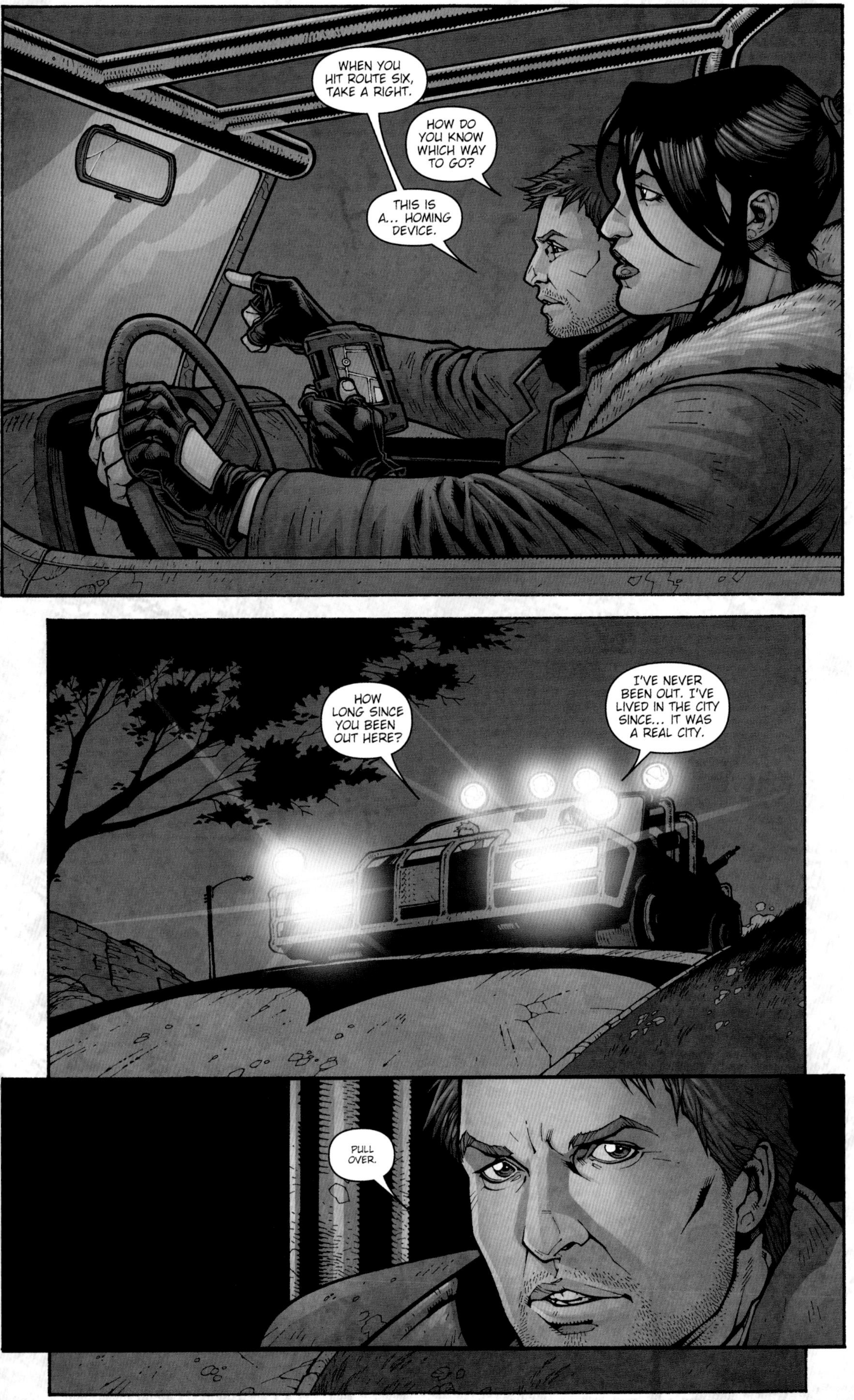
WHEN YOU HIT ROUTE SIX, TAKE A RIGHT.
HOW DO YOU KNOW WHICH WAY TO GO?
THIS IS A... HOMING DEVICE.
HOW LONG SINCE YOU BEEN OUT HERE?
I'VE NEVER BEEN OUT. I'VE LIVED IN THE CITY SINCE... IT WAS A REAL CITY.
PULL OVER.

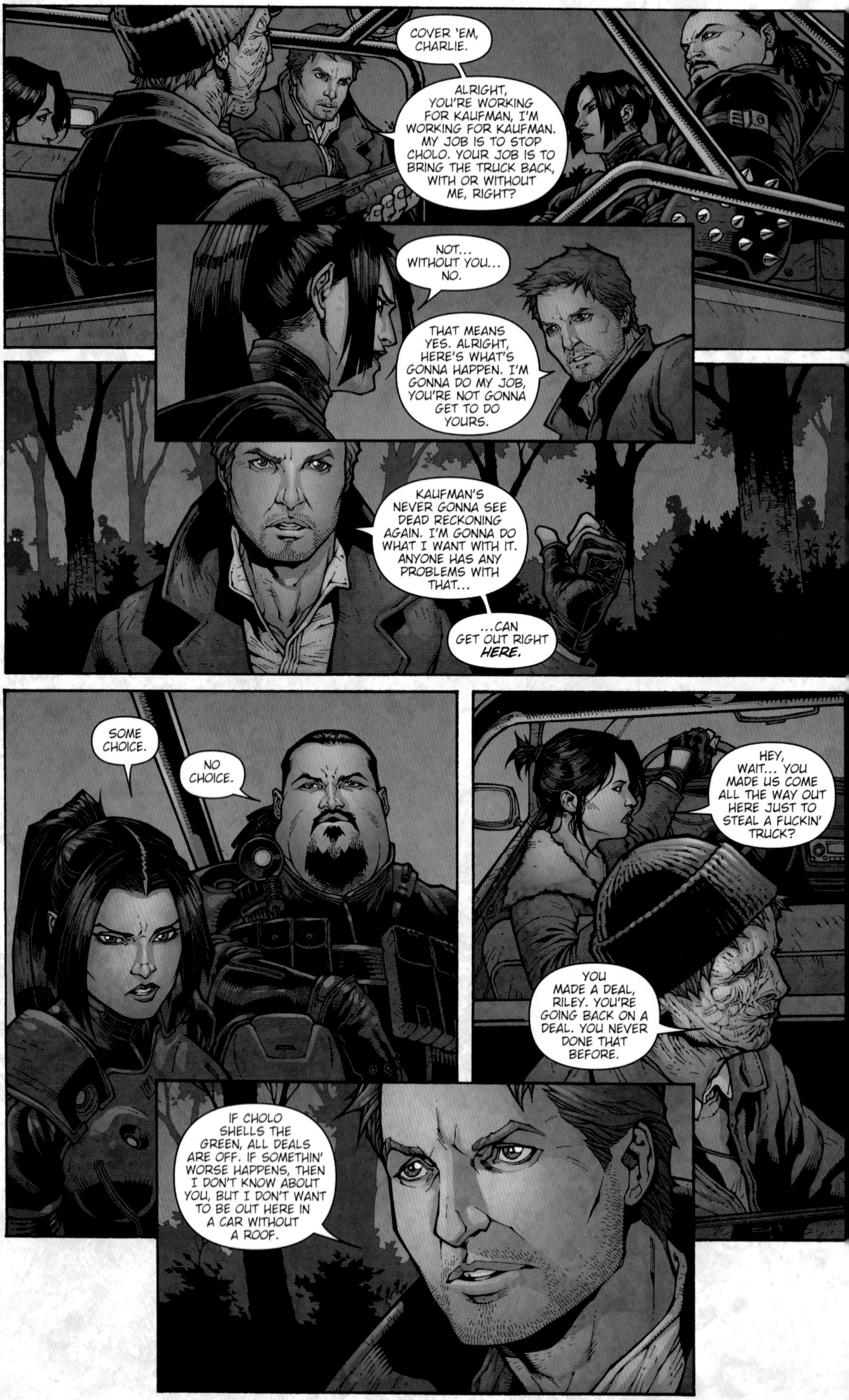
COVER 'EM, CHARLIE.
ALRIGHT, YOU'RE WORKING FOR KAUFMAN, I'M WORKING FOR KAUFMAN. MY JOB IS TO STOP CHOLO. YOUR JOB IS TO BRING THE TRUCK BACK, WITH OR WITHOUT ME, RIGHT?
NOT... WITHOUT YOU... NO.
THAT MEANS YES. ALRIGHT, HERE'S WHAT'S GONNA HAPPEN. I'M GONNA DO MY JOB, YOU'RE NOT GONNA GET TO DO YOURS.
KAUFMAN'S NEVER GONNA SEE DEAD RECKONING AGAIN. I'M GONNA DO WHAT I WANT WITH IT. ANYONE HAS ANY PROBLEMS WITH THAT...
...CAN GET OUT RIGHT *HERE.*
SOME CHOICE.
NO CHOICE.
HEY, WAIT... YOU MADE US COME ALL THE WAY OUT HERE JUST TO STEAL A FUCKIN' TRUCK?
YOU MADE A DEAL, RILEY. YOU'RE GOING BACK ON A DEAL. YOU NEVER DONE THAT BEFORE.
IF CHOLO SHELLS THE GREEN, ALL DEALS ARE OFF. IF SOMETHIN' WORSE HAPPENS, THEN I DON'T KNOW ABOUT YOU, BUT I DON'T WANT TO BE OUT HERE IN A CAR WITHOUT A ROOF.

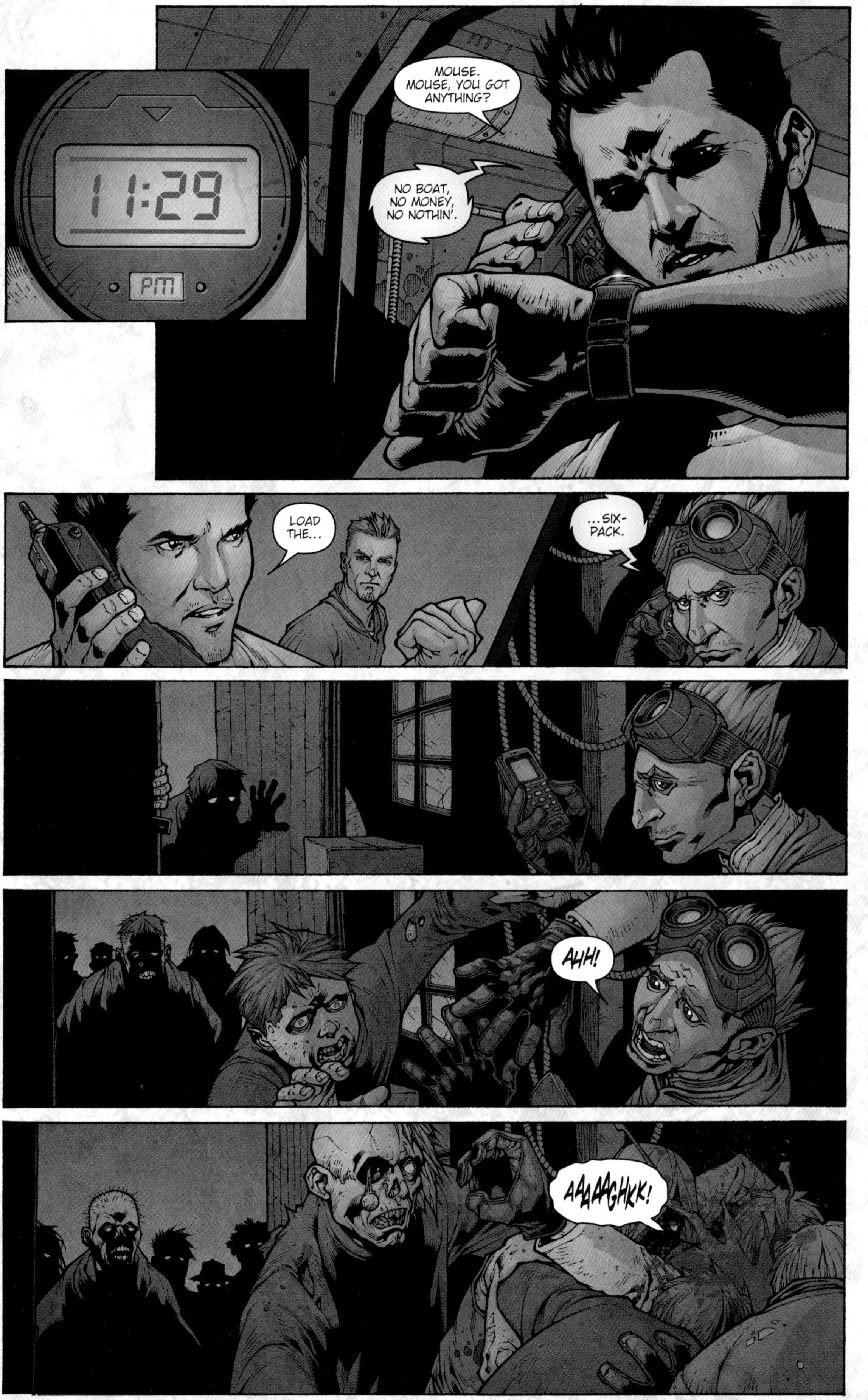
11:29
PM
MOUSE. MOUSE, YOU GOT ANYTHING?
NO BOAT, NO MONEY, NO NOTHIN'.
LOAD THE...
...SIX-PACK.
AHH!
AAAAAGHKK!

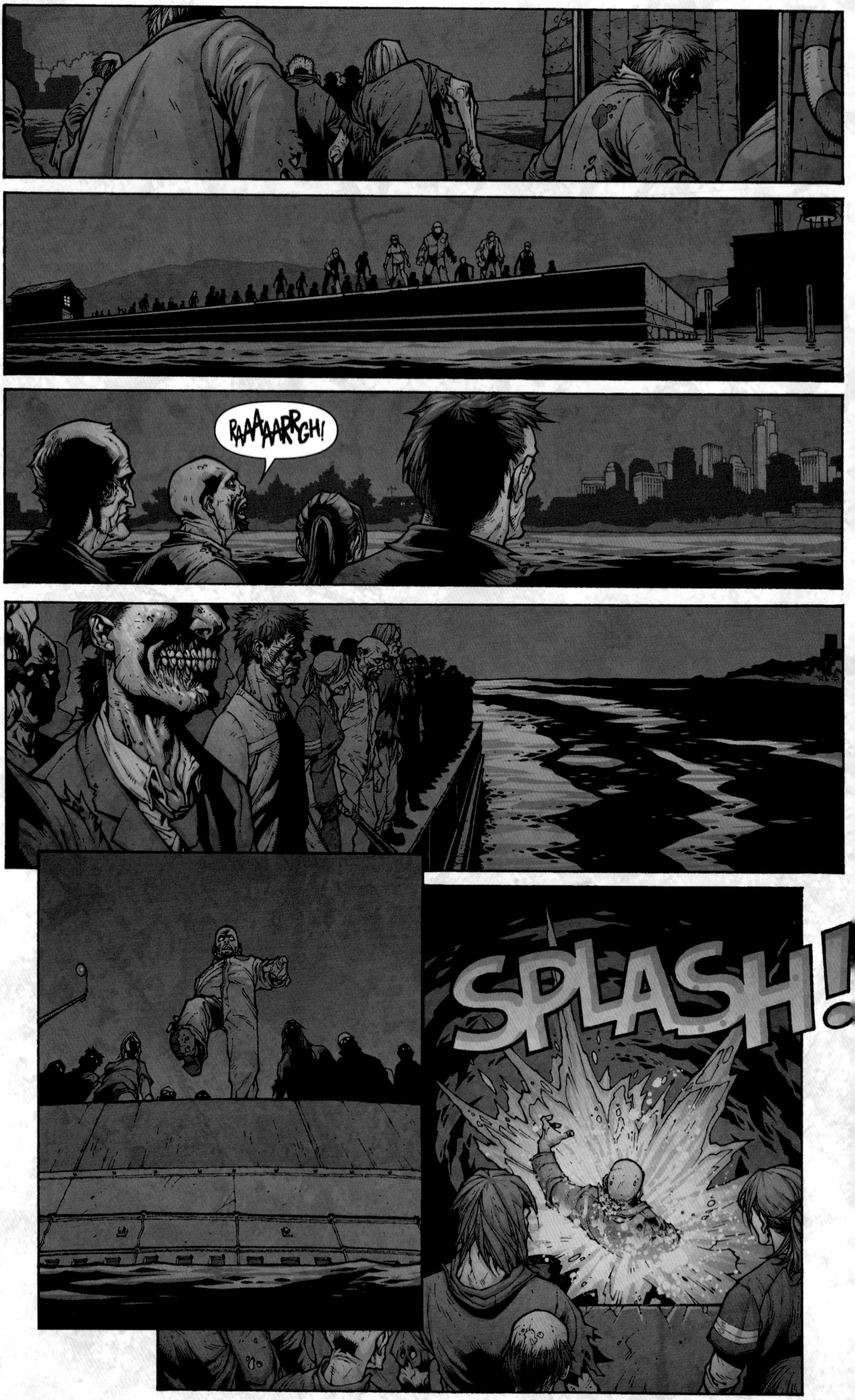
RAAAAARRGH!
SPLASH!

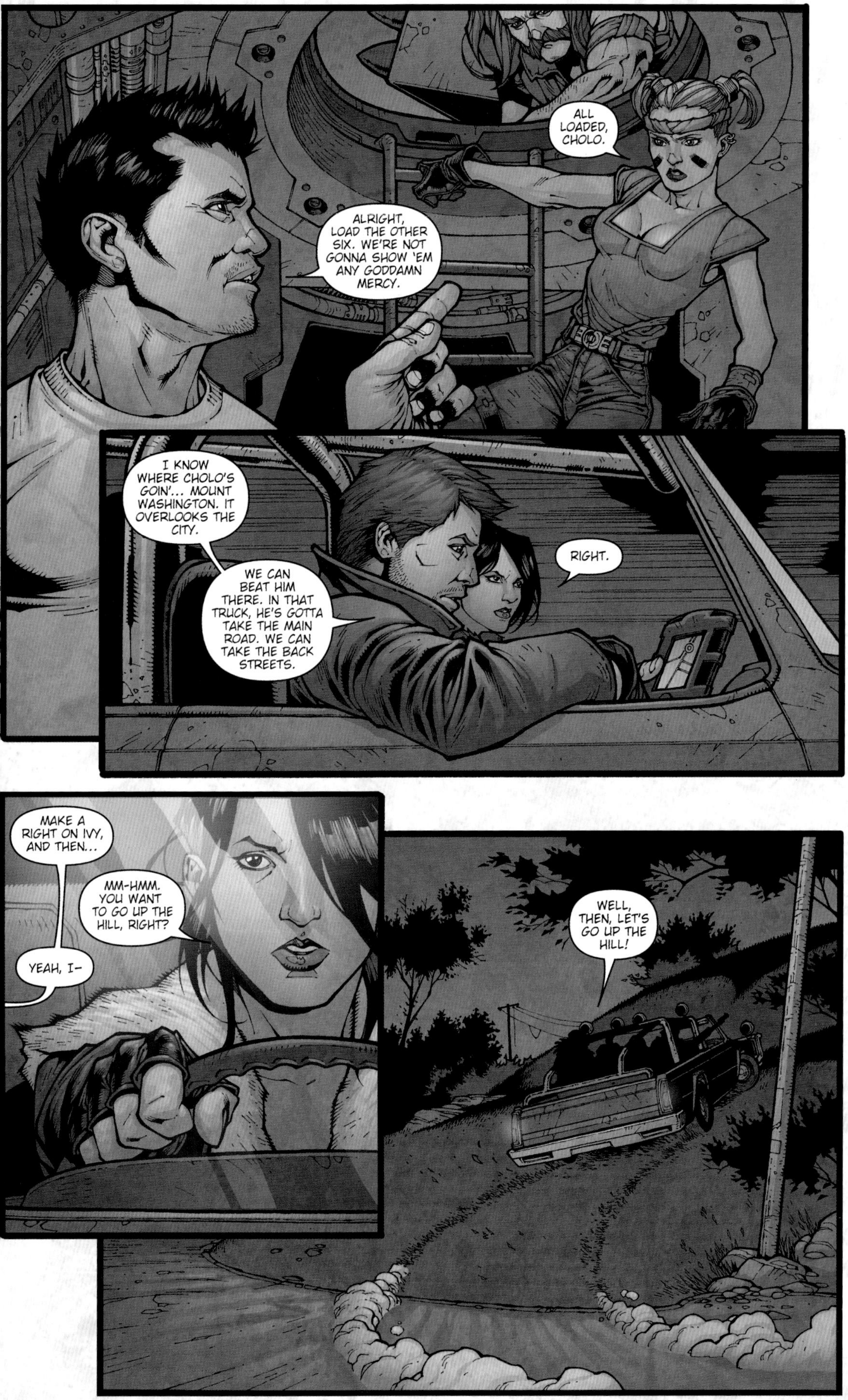
ALL LOADED, CHOLO.
ALRIGHT, LOAD THE OTHER SIX. WE'RE NOT GONNA SHOW 'EM ANY GODDAMN MERCY.
I KNOW WHERE CHOLO'S GOIN'... MOUNT WASHINGTON. IT OVERLOOKS THE CITY.
WE CAN BEAT HIM THERE. IN THAT TRUCK, HE'S GOTTA TAKE THE MAIN ROAD. WE CAN TAKE THE BACK STREETS.
RIGHT.
MAKE A RIGHT ON IVY, AND THEN...
MM-HMM. YOU WANT TO GO UP THE HILL, RIGHT?
YEAH, I-
WELL, THEN, LET'S GO UP THE HILL!

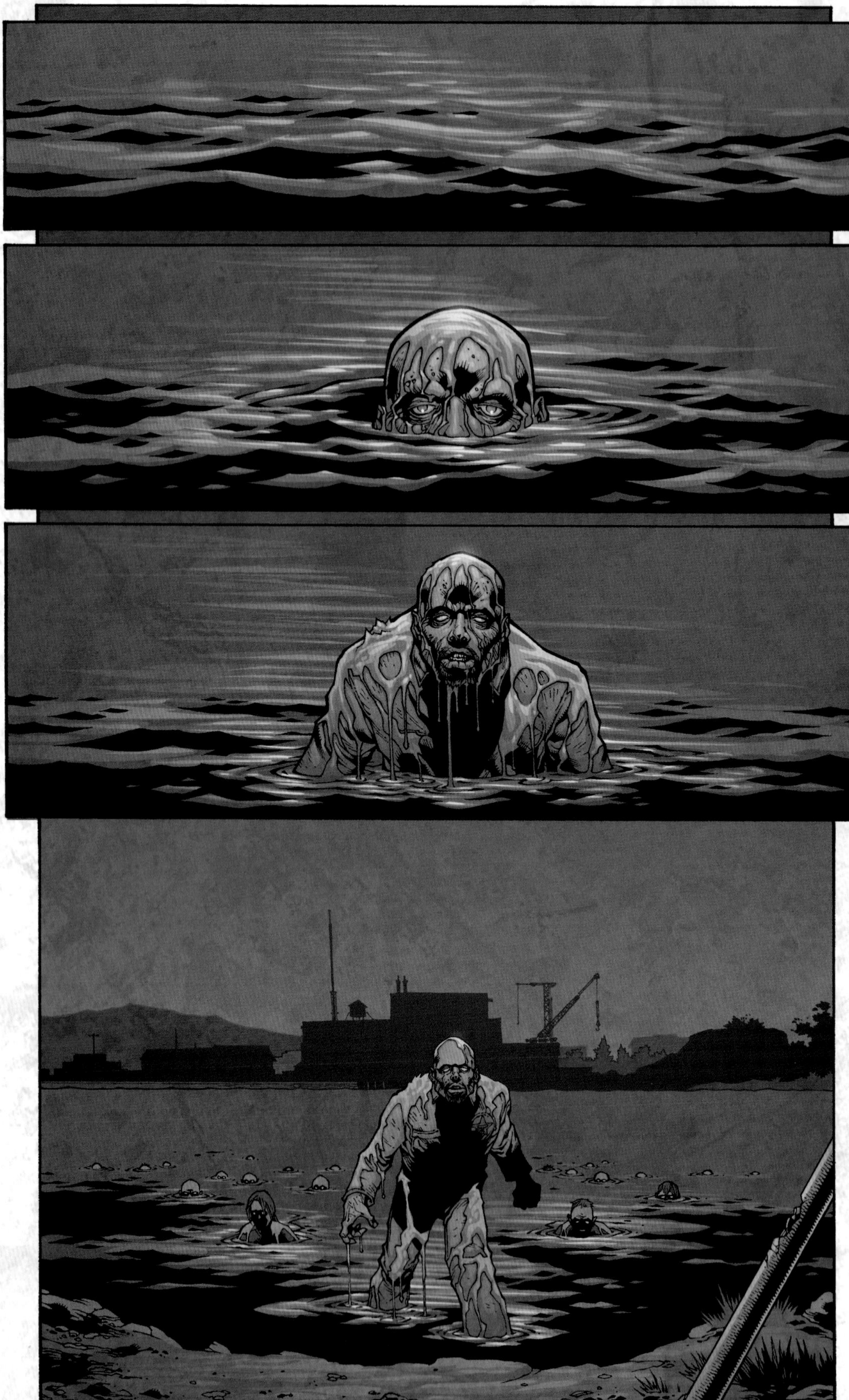

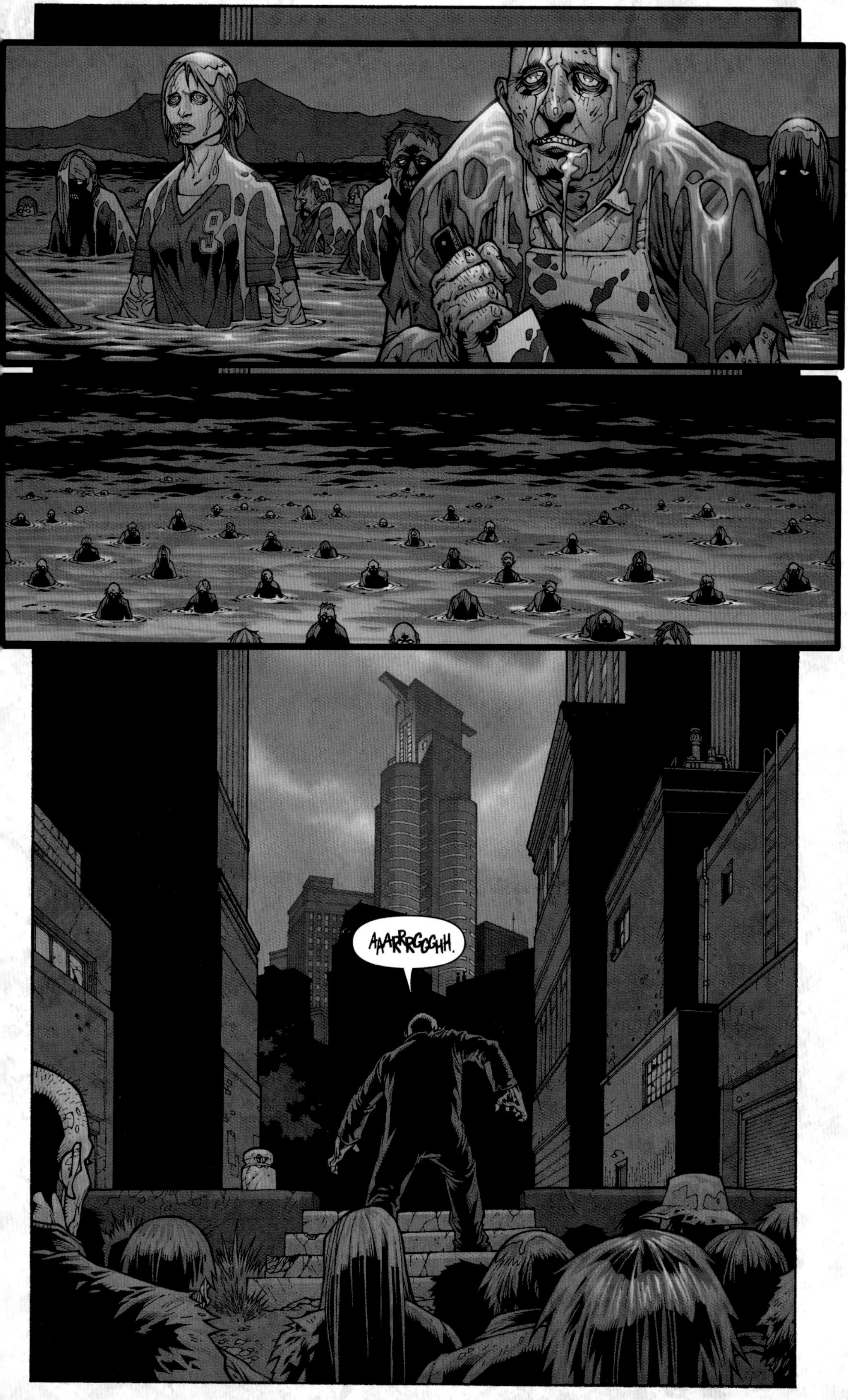
AAARRRGGGHH.

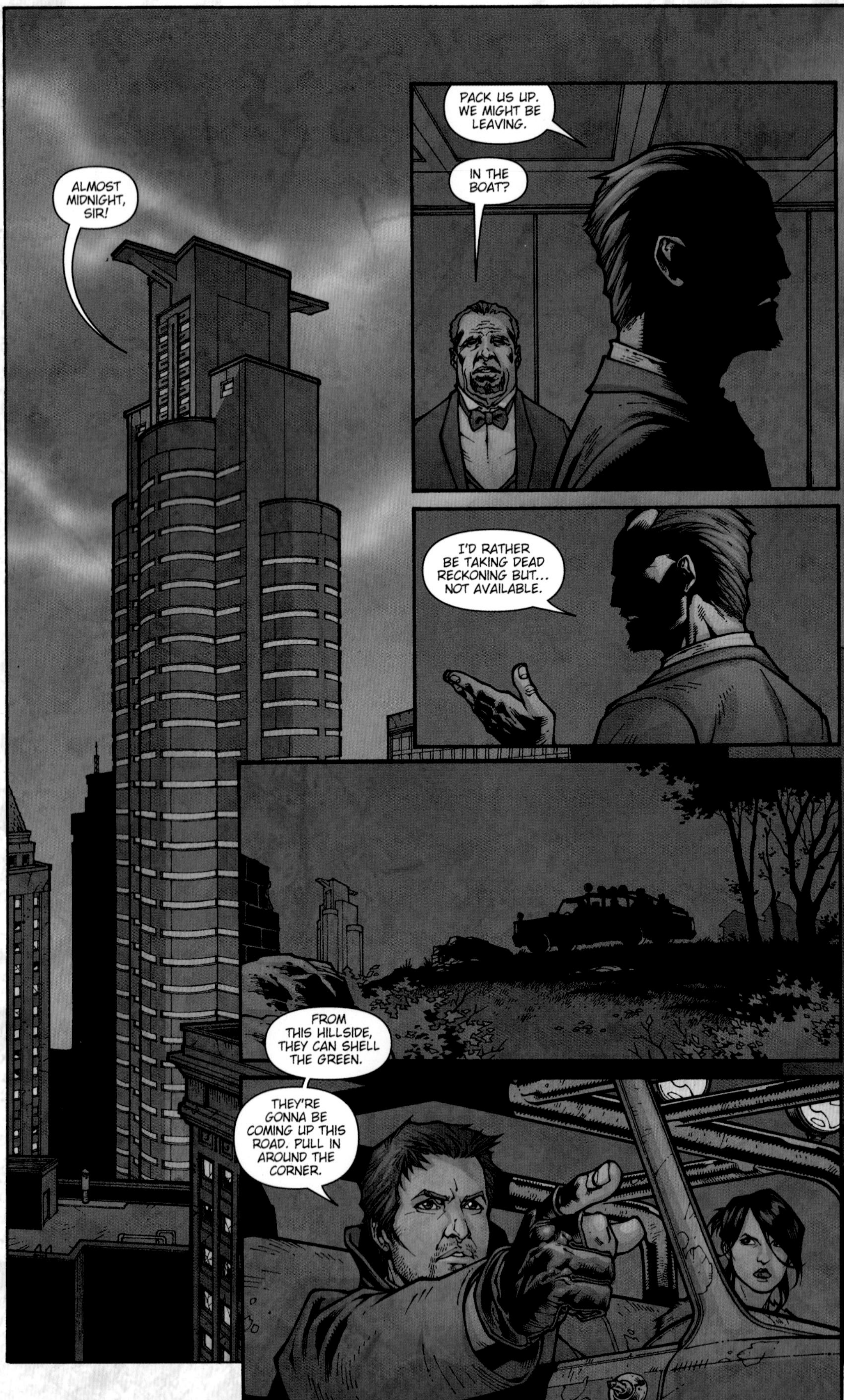
ALMOST MIDNIGHT, SIR!
PACK US UP. WE MIGHT BE LEAVING.
IN THE BOAT?
I'D RATHER BE TAKING DEAD RECKONING BUT... NOT AVAILABLE.
FROM THIS HILLSIDE, THEY CAN SHELL THE GREEN.
THEY'RE GONNA BE COMING UP THIS ROAD. PULL IN AROUND THE CORNER.

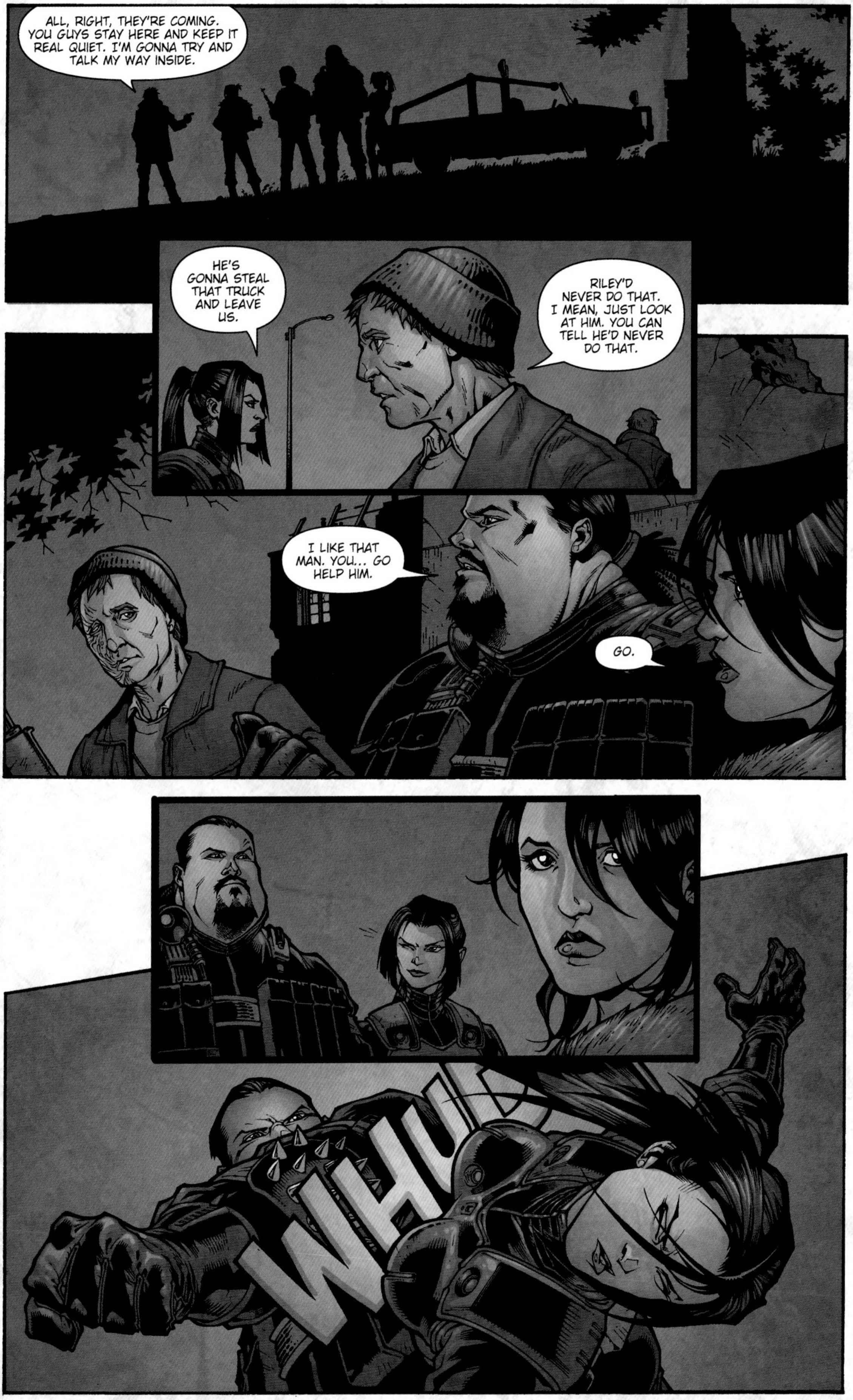
ALL, RIGHT, THEY'RE COMING. YOU GUYS STAY HERE AND KEEP IT REAL QUIET. I'M GONNA TRY AND TALK MY WAY INSIDE.
HE'S GONNA STEAL THAT TRUCK AND LEAVE US.
RILEY'D NEVER DO THAT. I MEAN, JUST LOOK AT HIM. YOU CAN TELL HE'D NEVER DO THAT.
I LIKE THAT MAN. YOU... GO HELP HIM.
GO.
WHUD

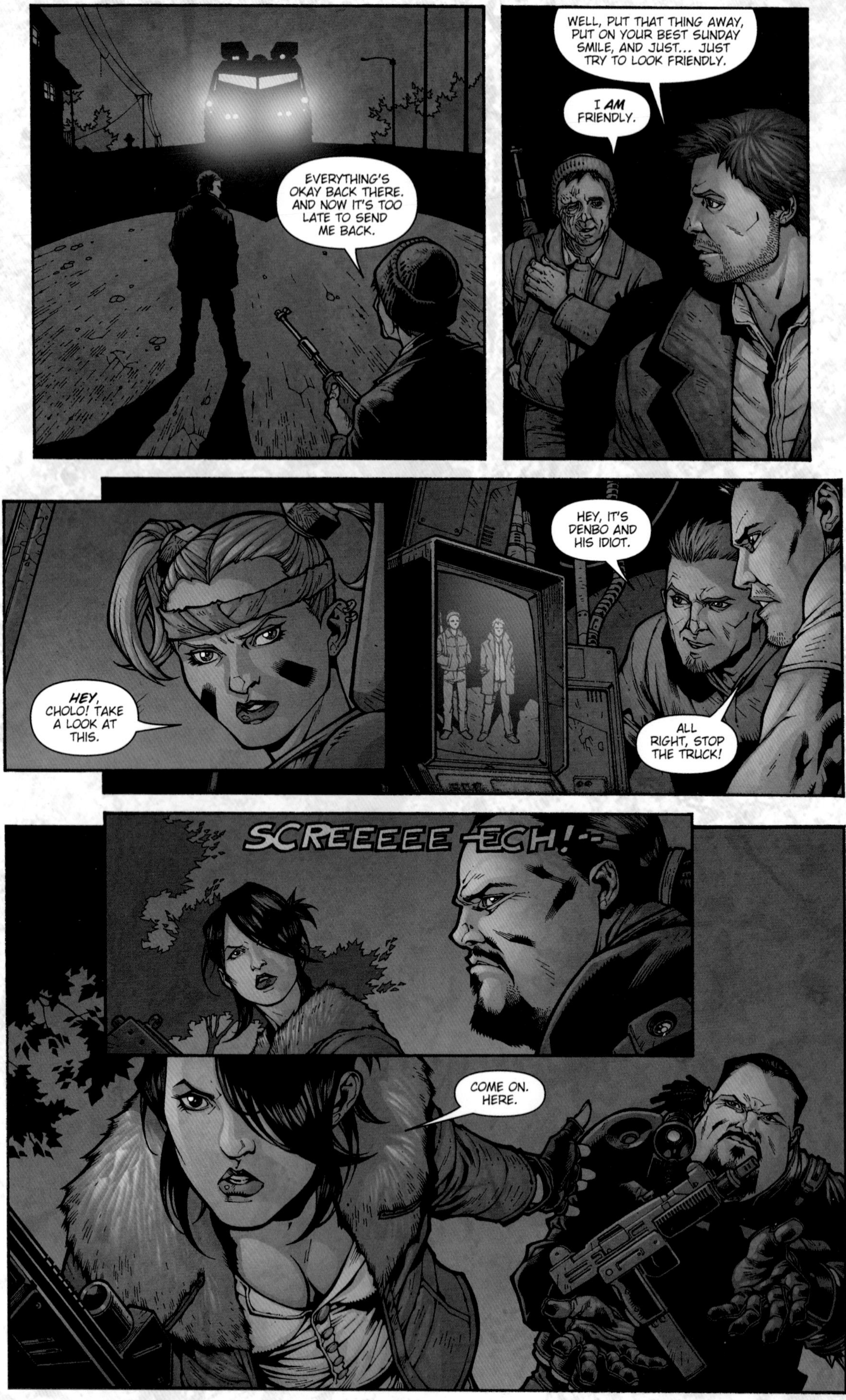
EVERYTHING'S OKAY BACK THERE. AND NOW IT'S TOO LATE TO SEND ME BACK.
WELL, PUT THAT THING AWAY, PUT ON YOUR BEST SUNDAY SMILE, AND JUST... JUST TRY TO LOOK FRIENDLY.
I *AM* FRIENDLY.
HEY, CHOLO! TAKE A LOOK AT THIS.
HEY, IT'S DENBO AND HIS IDIOT.
ALL RIGHT, STOP THE TRUCK!
SCREEEEEE-ECH!--
COME ON. HERE.

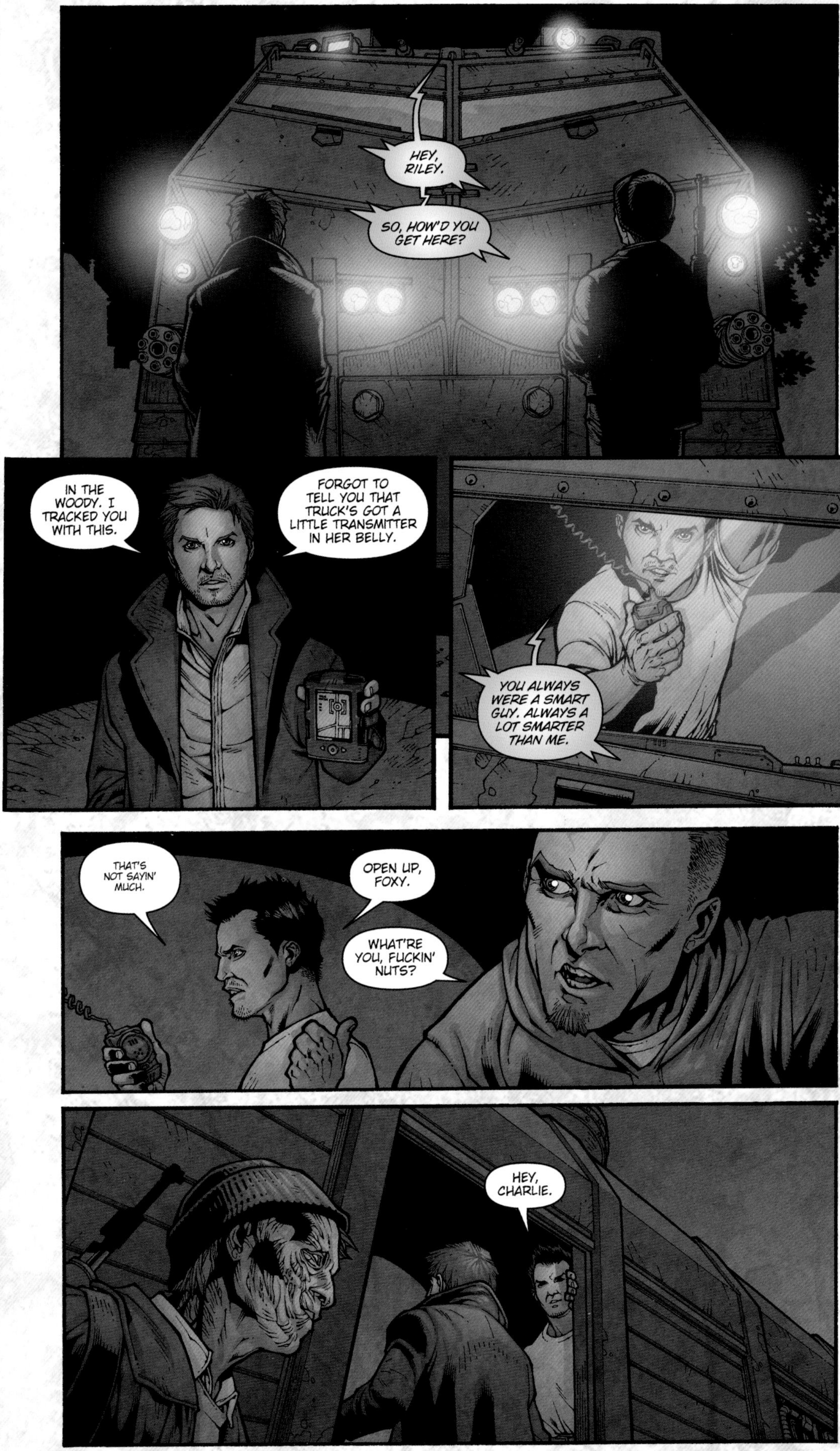
HEY, RILEY.
SO, HOW'D YOU GET HERE?
IN THE WOODY. I TRACKED YOU WITH THIS.
FORGOT TO TELL YOU THAT TRUCK'S GOT A LITTLE TRANSMITTER IN HER BELLY.
YOU ALWAYS WERE A SMART GUY. ALWAYS A LOT SMARTER THAN ME.
THAT'S NOT SAYIN' MUCH.
OPEN UP, FOXY.
WHAT'RE YOU, FUCKIN' NUTS?
HEY, CHARLIE.

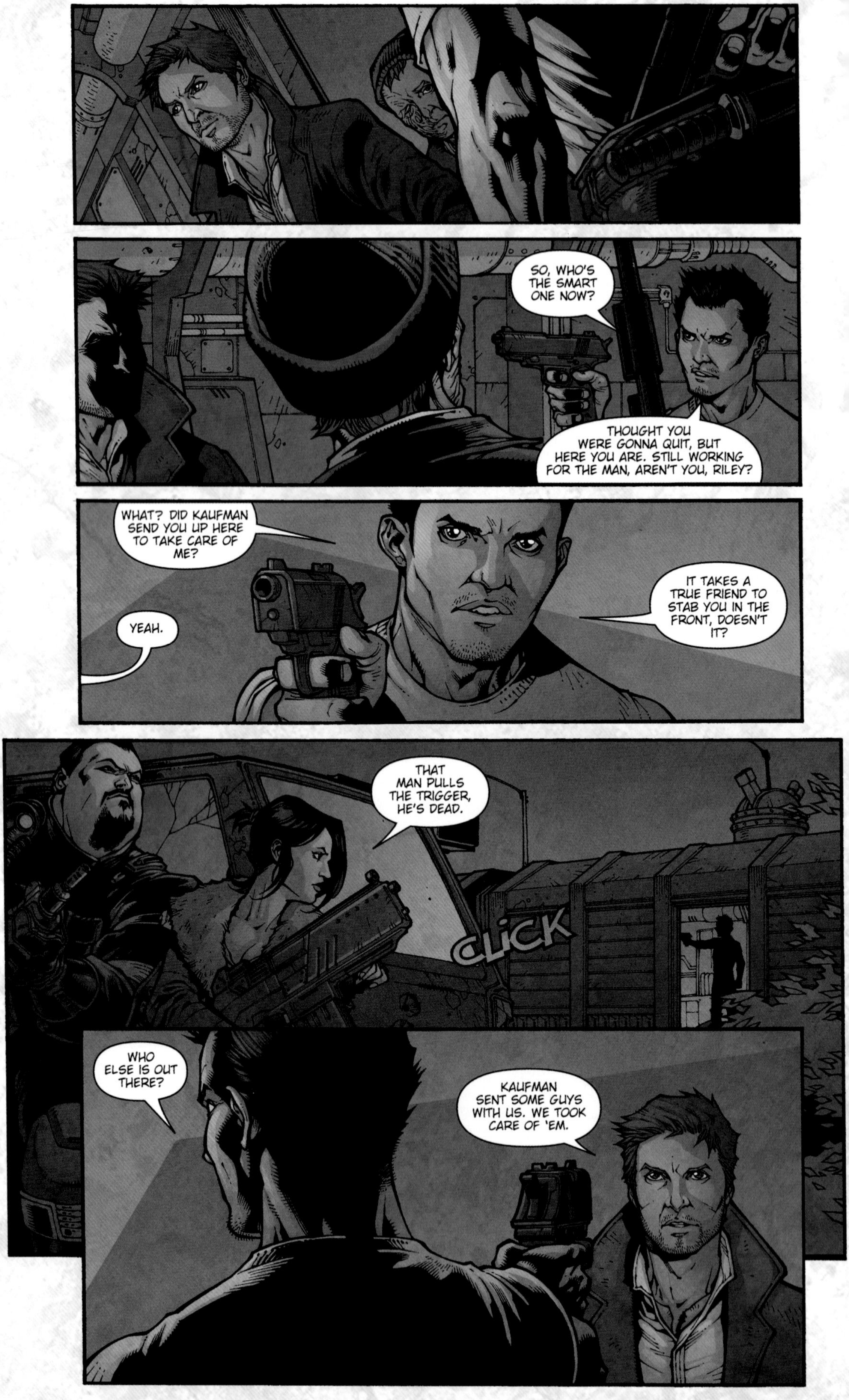

SO, WHO'S THE SMART ONE NOW?
THOUGHT YOU WERE GONNA QUIT, BUT HERE YOU ARE. STILL WORKING FOR THE MAN, AREN'T YOU, RILEY?
WHAT? DID KAUFMAN SEND YOU UP HERE TO TAKE CARE OF ME?
YEAH.
IT TAKES A TRUE FRIEND TO STAB YOU IN THE FRONT, DOESN'T IT?
THAT MAN PULLS THE TRIGGER, HE'S DEAD.
CLICK
WHO ELSE IS OUT THERE?
KAUFMAN SENT SOME GUYS WITH US. WE TOOK CARE OF 'EM.

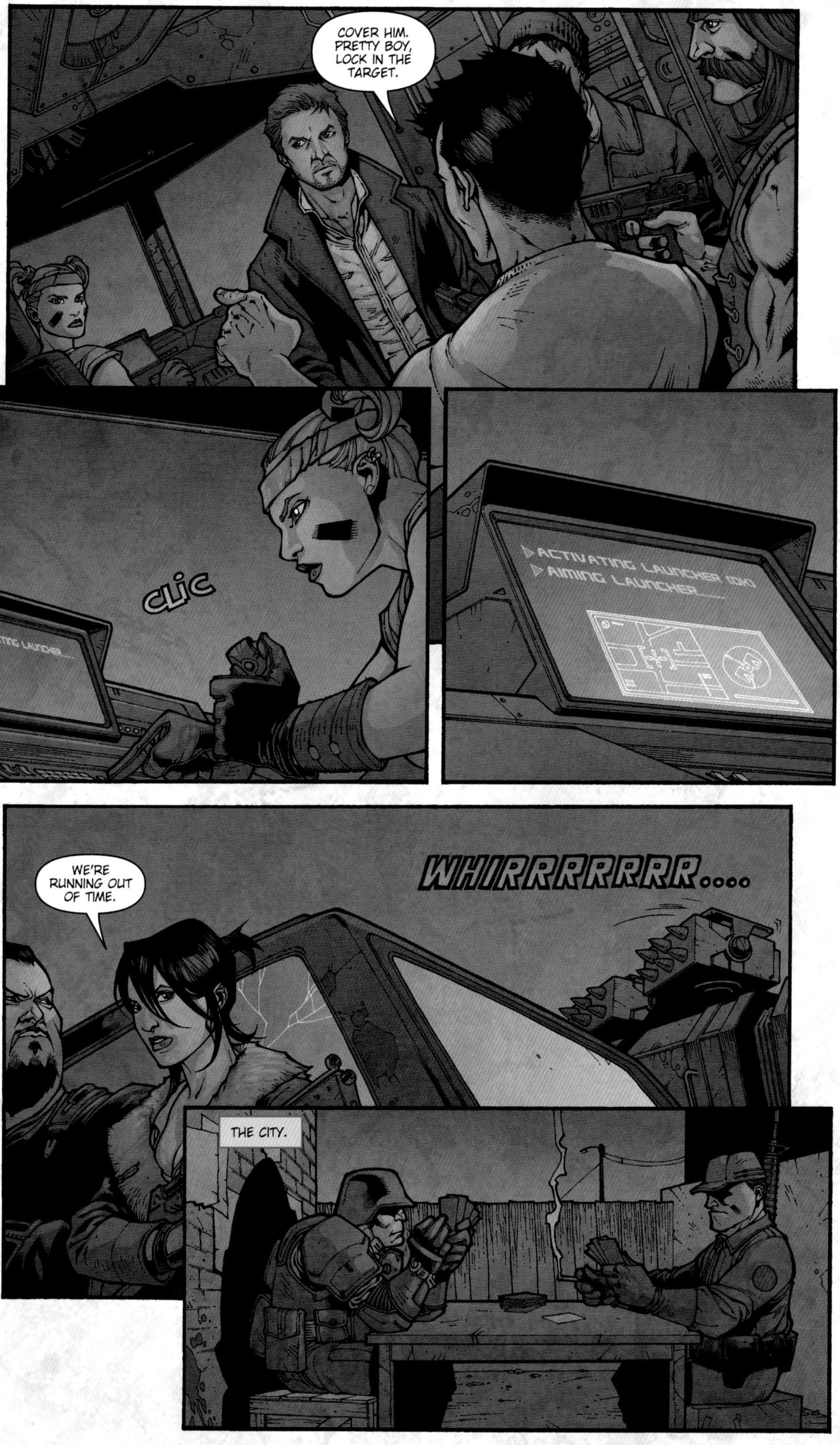
COVER HIM. PRETTY BOY, LOCK IN THE TARGET.
CLIC
ACTIVATING LAUNCHER....
ACTIVATING LAUNCHER (OK)
AIMING LAUNCHER.......
WE'RE RUNNING OUT OF TIME.
WHIRRRRRRRR....
THE CITY.

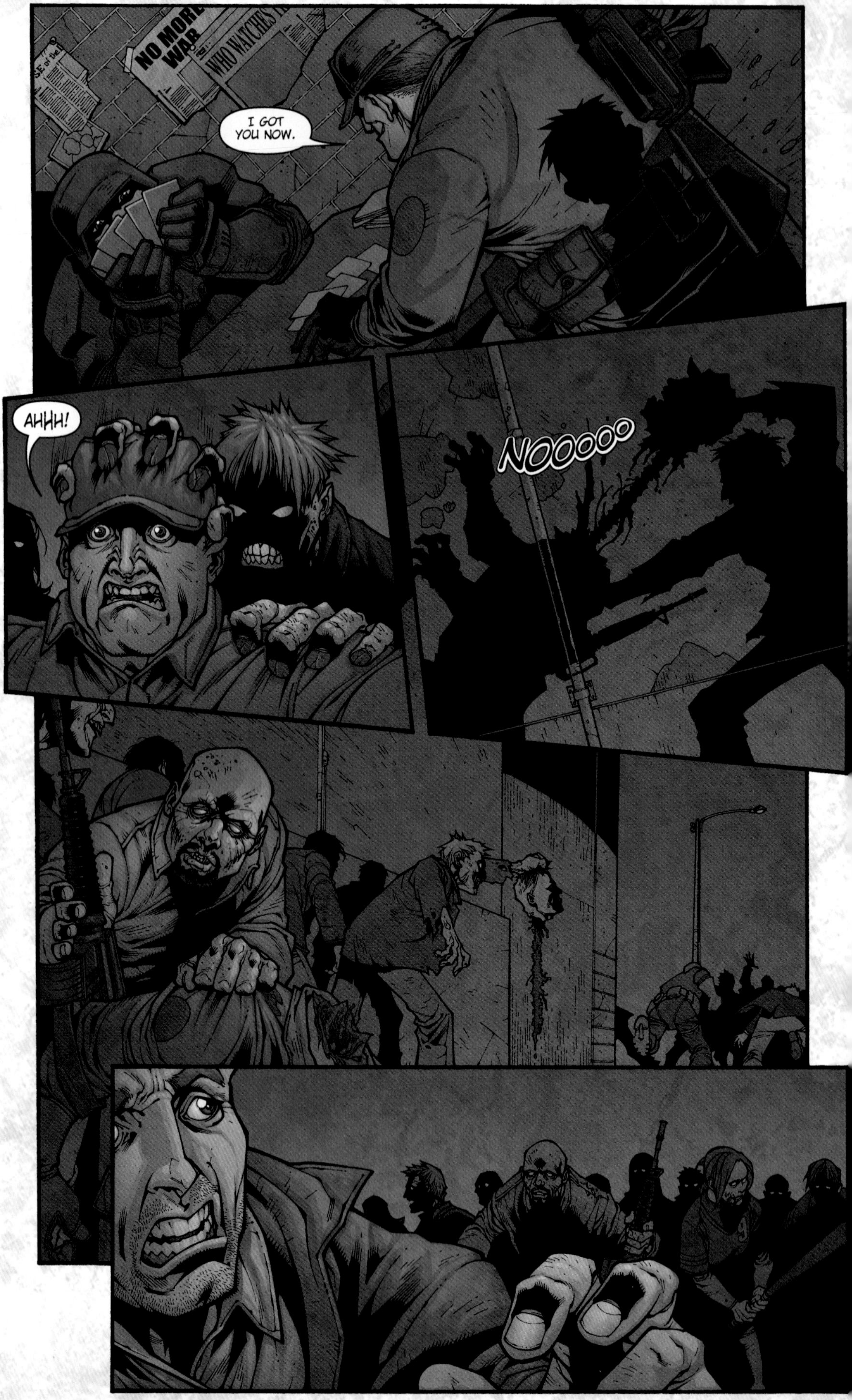
NO MORE WAR
WHO WATCHES
I GOT YOU NOW.
AHHH!
NOOOOO

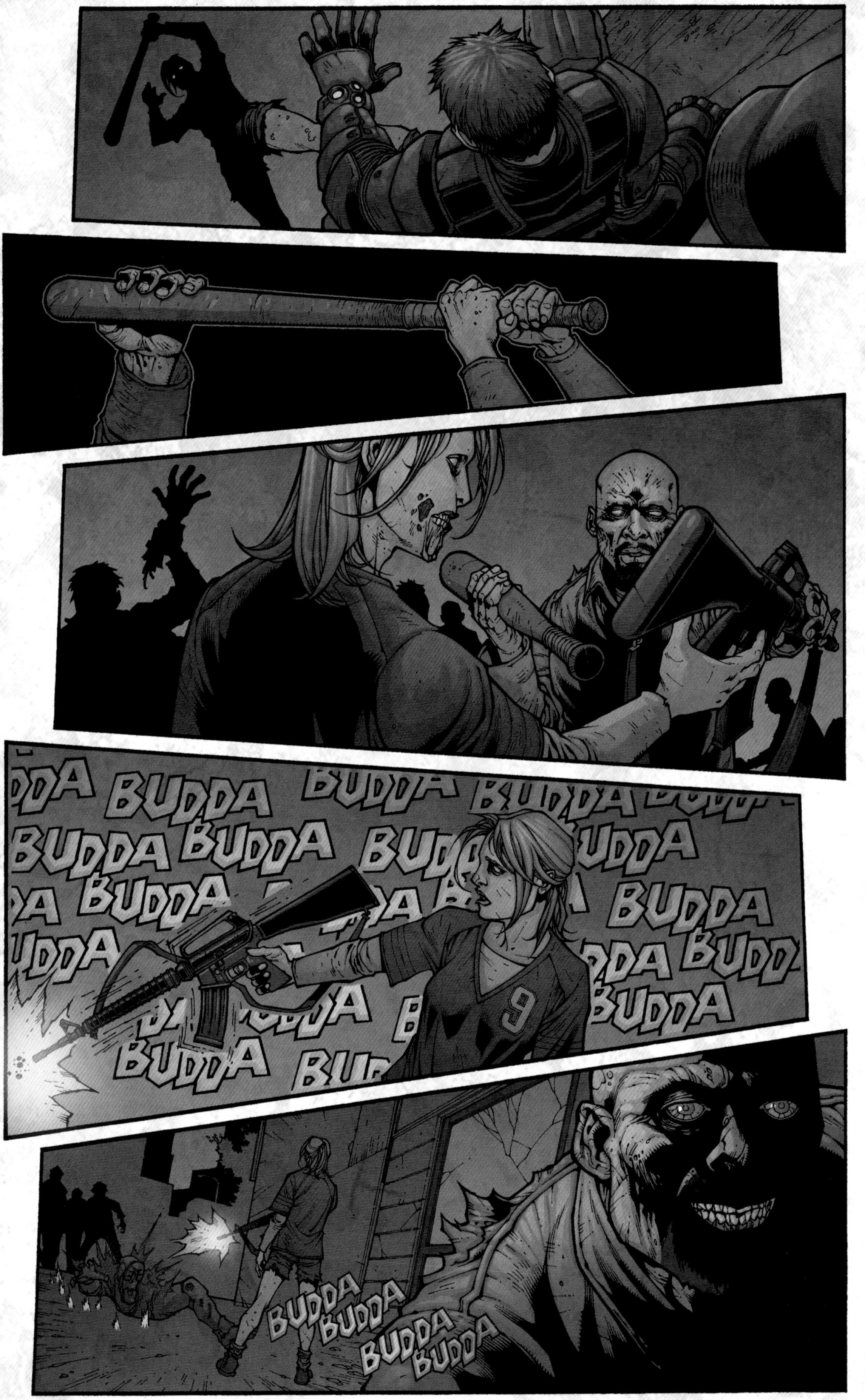
BUDDA BUDDA BUDDA BUDDA
BUDDA BUDDA BUDDA
BUDDA BUDDA
BUDDA BUDDA
BUDDA
BUDDA
BUDDA
BUDDA
BUDDA
BUDDA

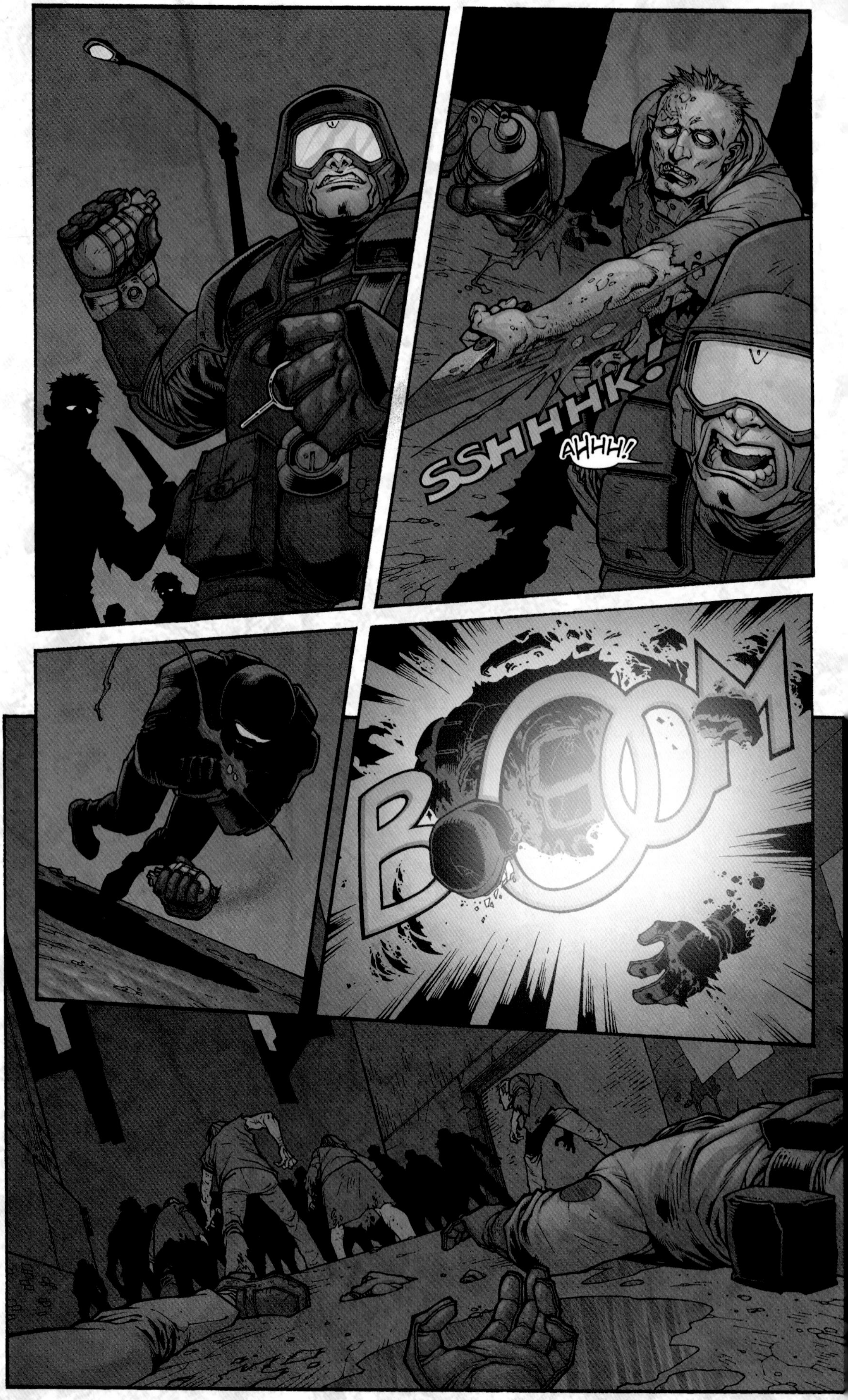
SSHHHHK!
AHHH!
BOOM

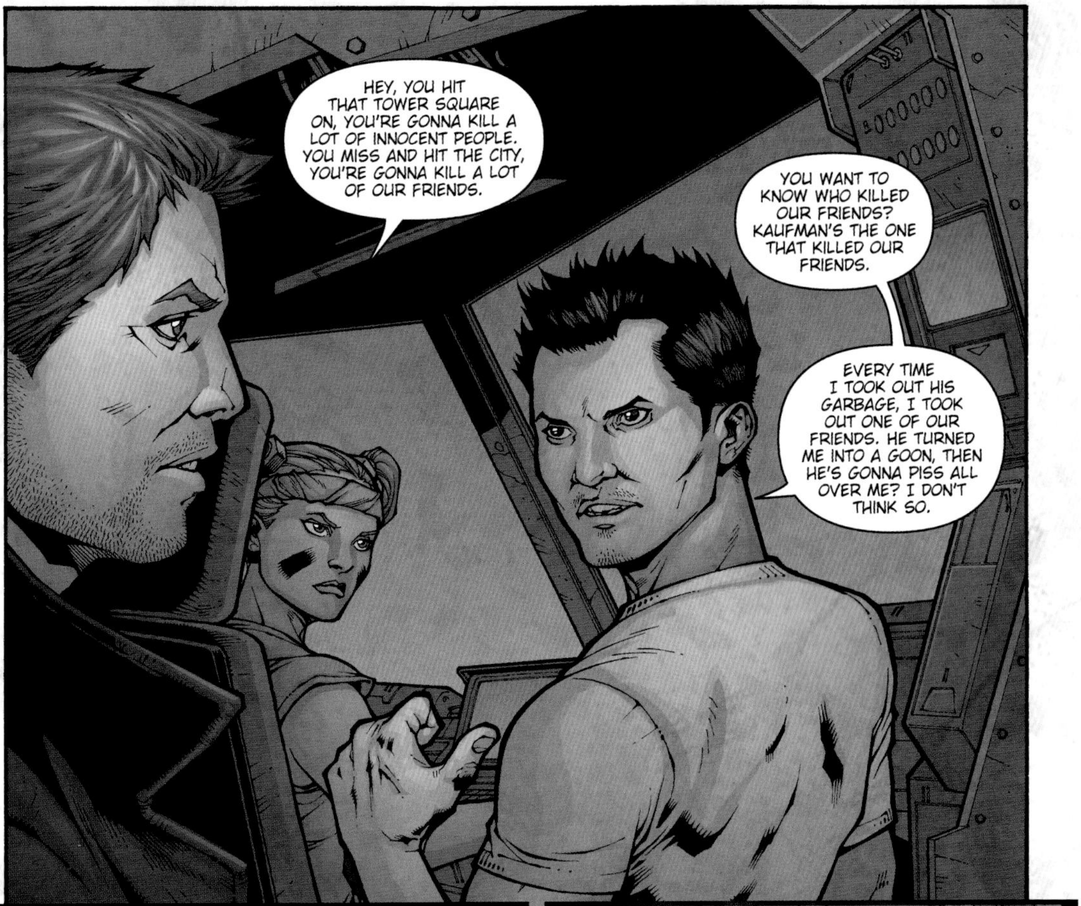
HEY, YOU HIT THAT TOWER SQUARE ON, YOU'RE GONNA KILL A LOT OF INNOCENT PEOPLE. YOU MISS AND HIT THE CITY, YOU'RE GONNA KILL A LOT OF OUR FRIENDS.
YOU WANT TO KNOW WHO KILLED OUR FRIENDS? KAUFMAN'S THE ONE THAT KILLED OUR FRIENDS.
EVERY TIME I TOOK OUT HIS GARBAGE, I TOOK OUT ONE OF OUR FRIENDS. HE TURNED ME INTO A GOON, THEN HE'S GONNA PISS ALL OVER ME? I DON'T THINK SO.
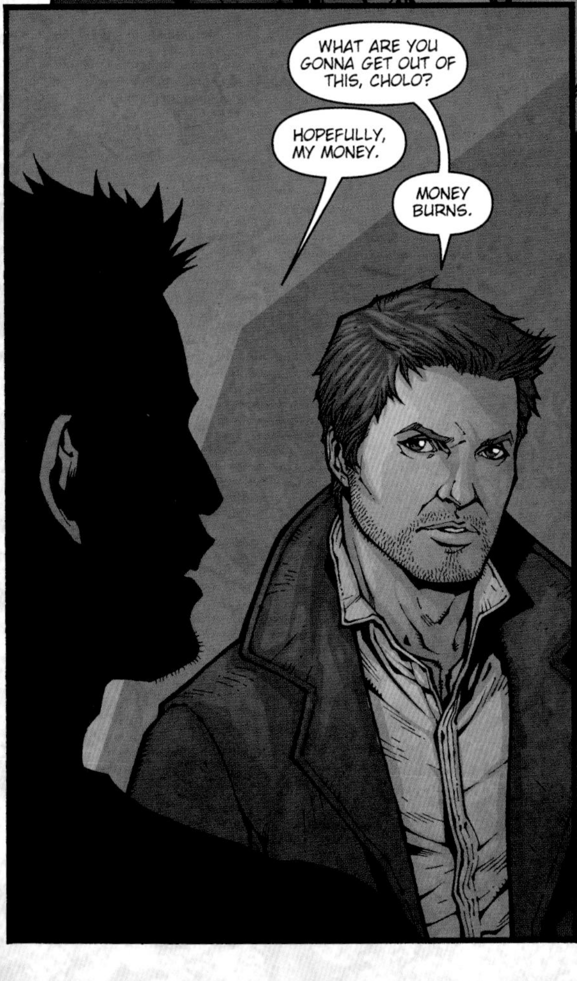
WHAT ARE YOU GONNA GET OUT OF THIS, CHOLO?
HOPEFULLY, MY MONEY.
MONEY BURNS.
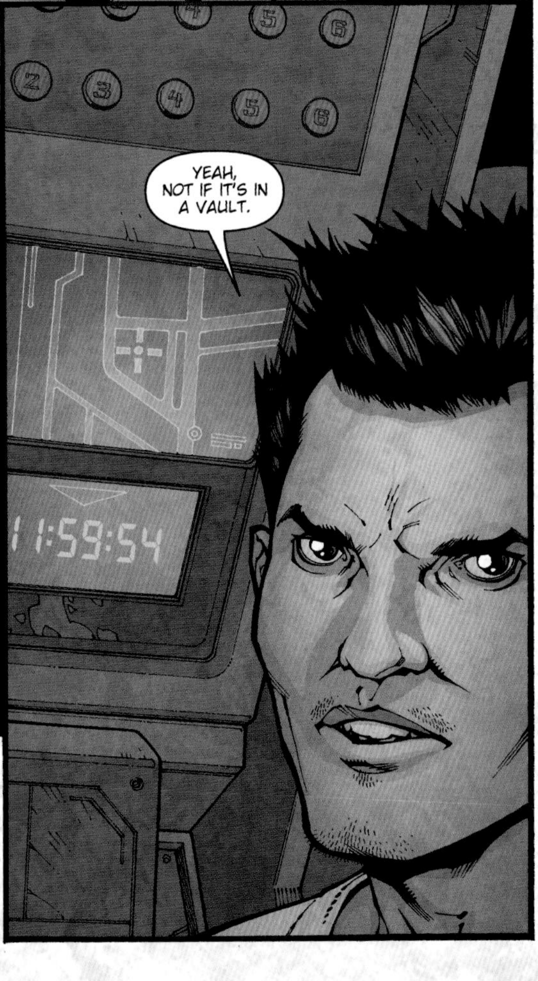
YEAH, NOT IF IT'S IN A VAULT.
11:59:54

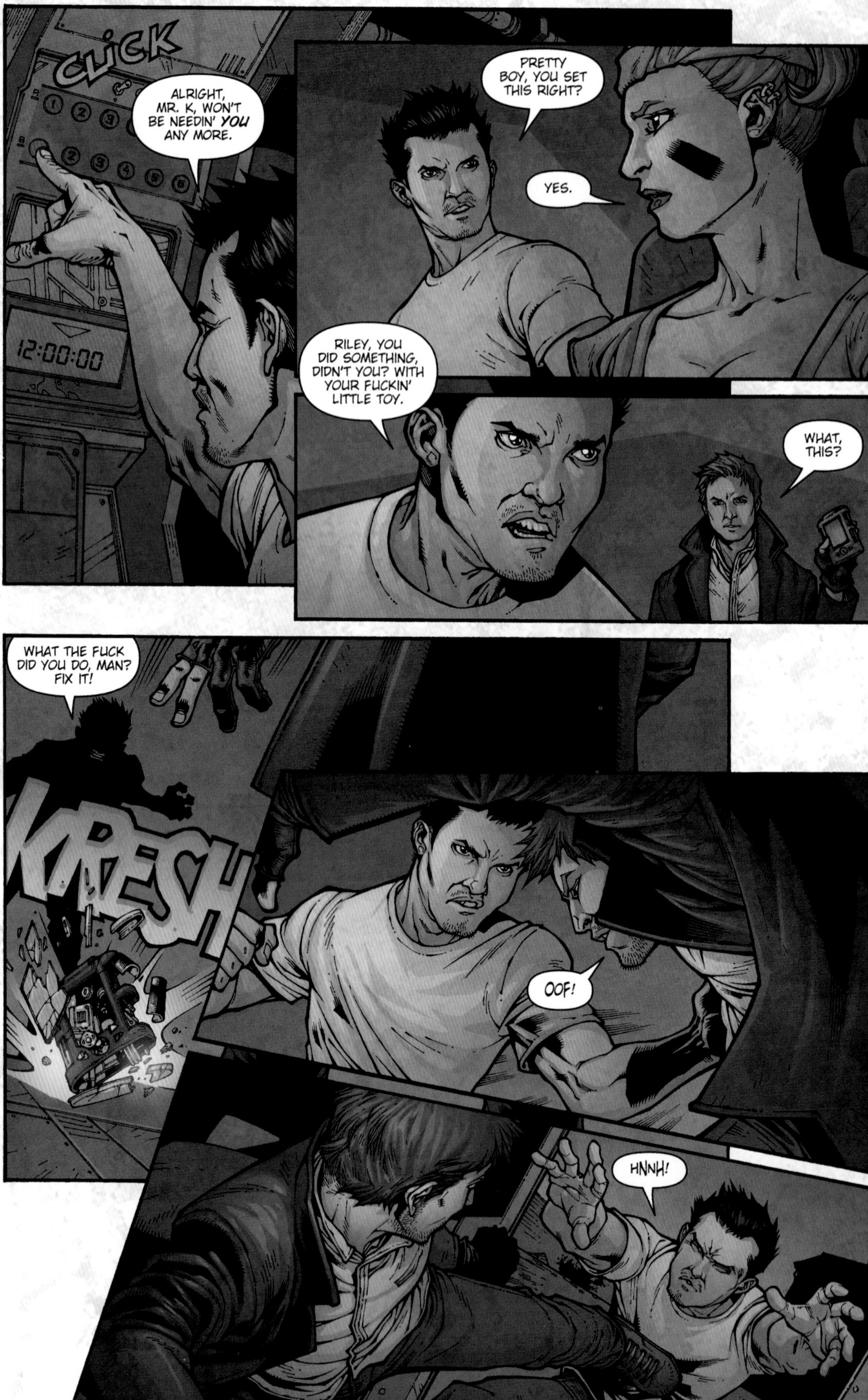
CLICK
ALRIGHT, MR. K, WON'T BE NEEDIN' *YOU* ANY MORE.
12:00:00
PRETTY BOY, YOU SET THIS RIGHT?
YES.
RILEY, YOU DID SOMETHING, DIDN'T YOU? WITH YOUR FUCKIN' LITTLE TOY.
WHAT, THIS?
WHAT THE FUCK DID YOU DO, MAN? FIX IT!
KRESH
OOF!
HNNH!

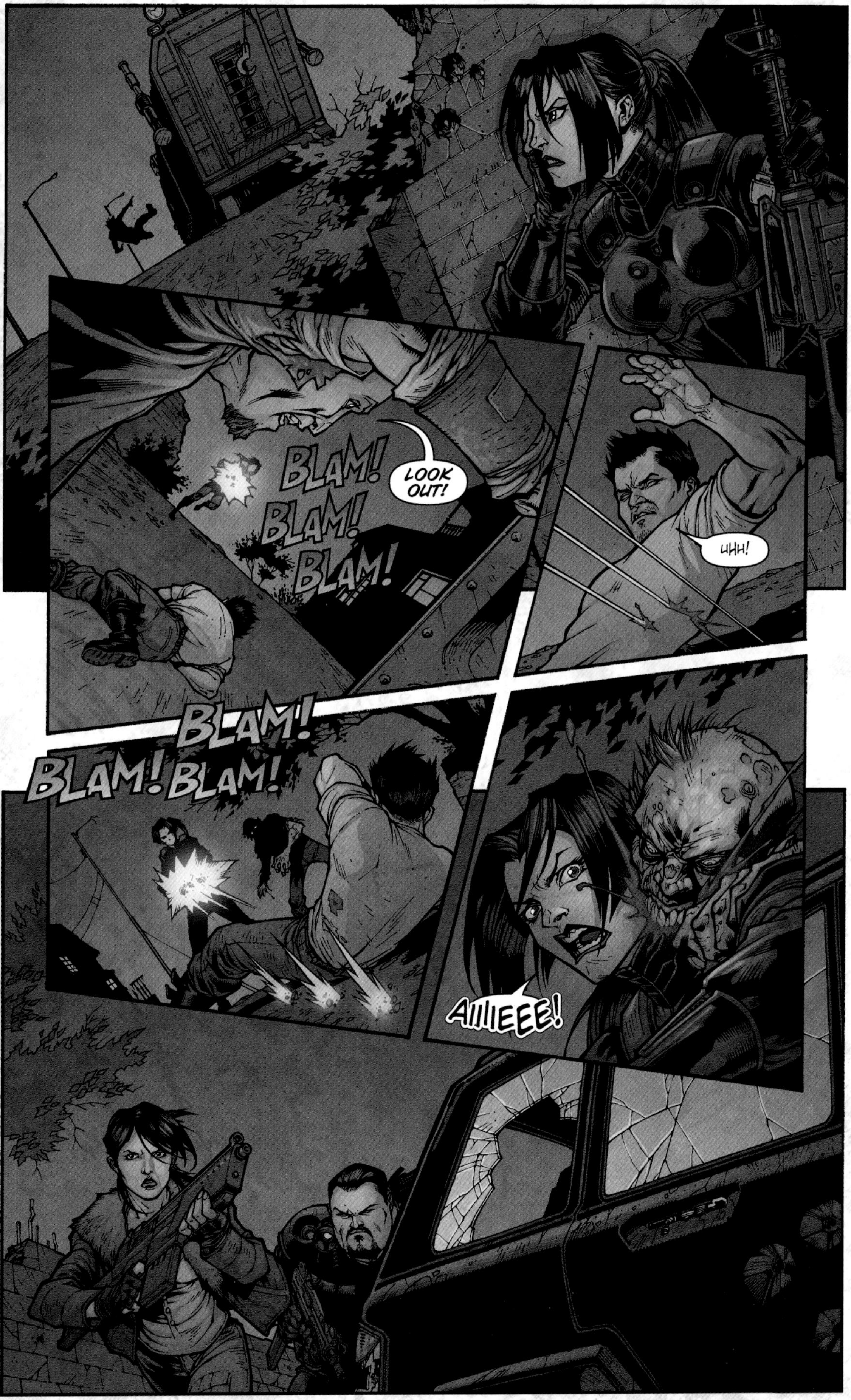
BLAM!
BLAM!
BLAM!
LOOK OUT!
UHH!
BLAM!
BLAM! BLAM!
AIIIIEEE!

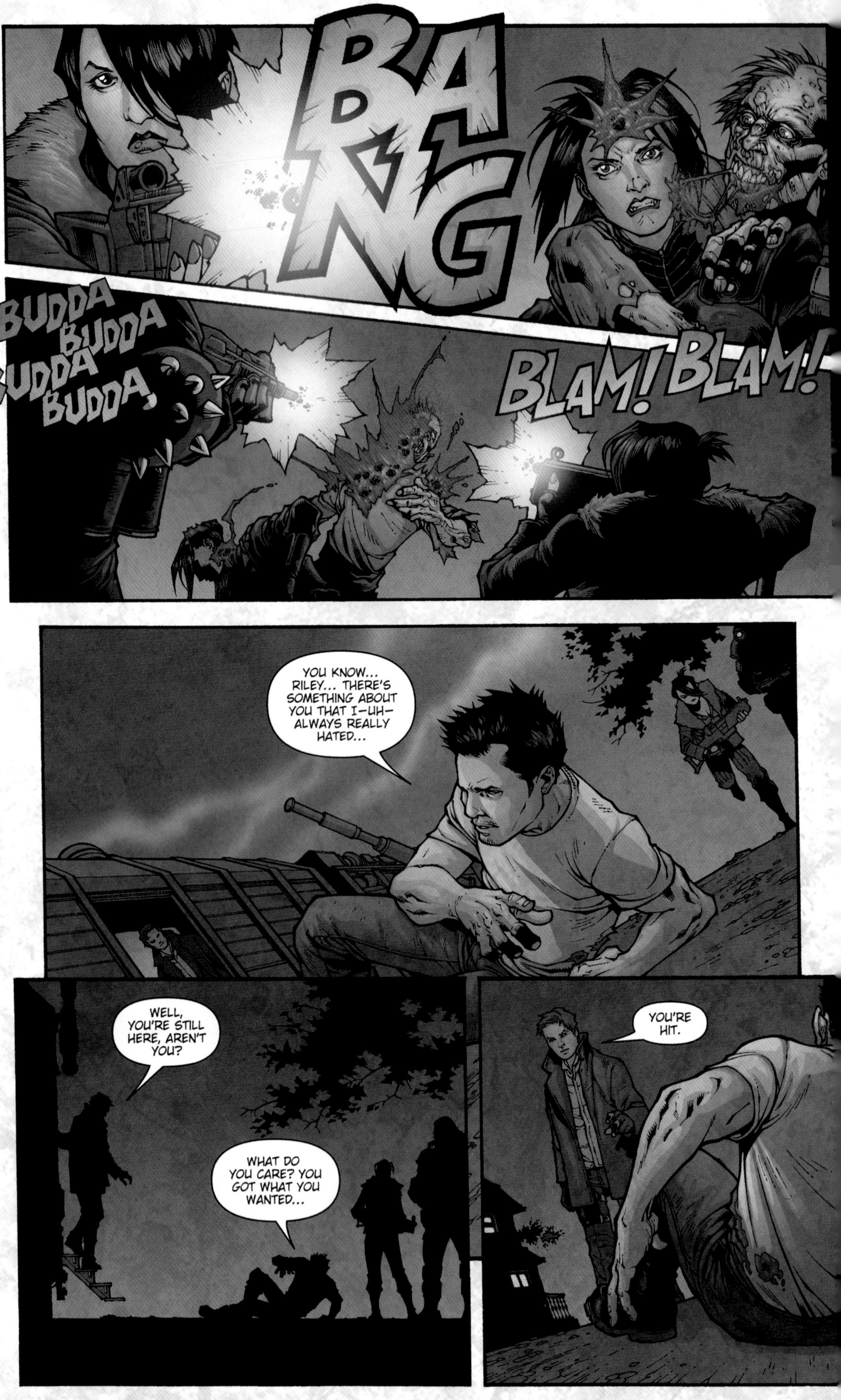
BANG
BUDDA BUDDA BUDDA BUDDA
BLAM! BLAM!
YOU KNOW... RILEY... THERE'S SOMETHING ABOUT YOU THAT I--UH--ALWAYS REALLY HATED...
WELL, YOU'RE STILL HERE, AREN'T YOU?
WHAT DO YOU CARE? YOU GOT WHAT YOU WANTED...
YOU'RE HIT.

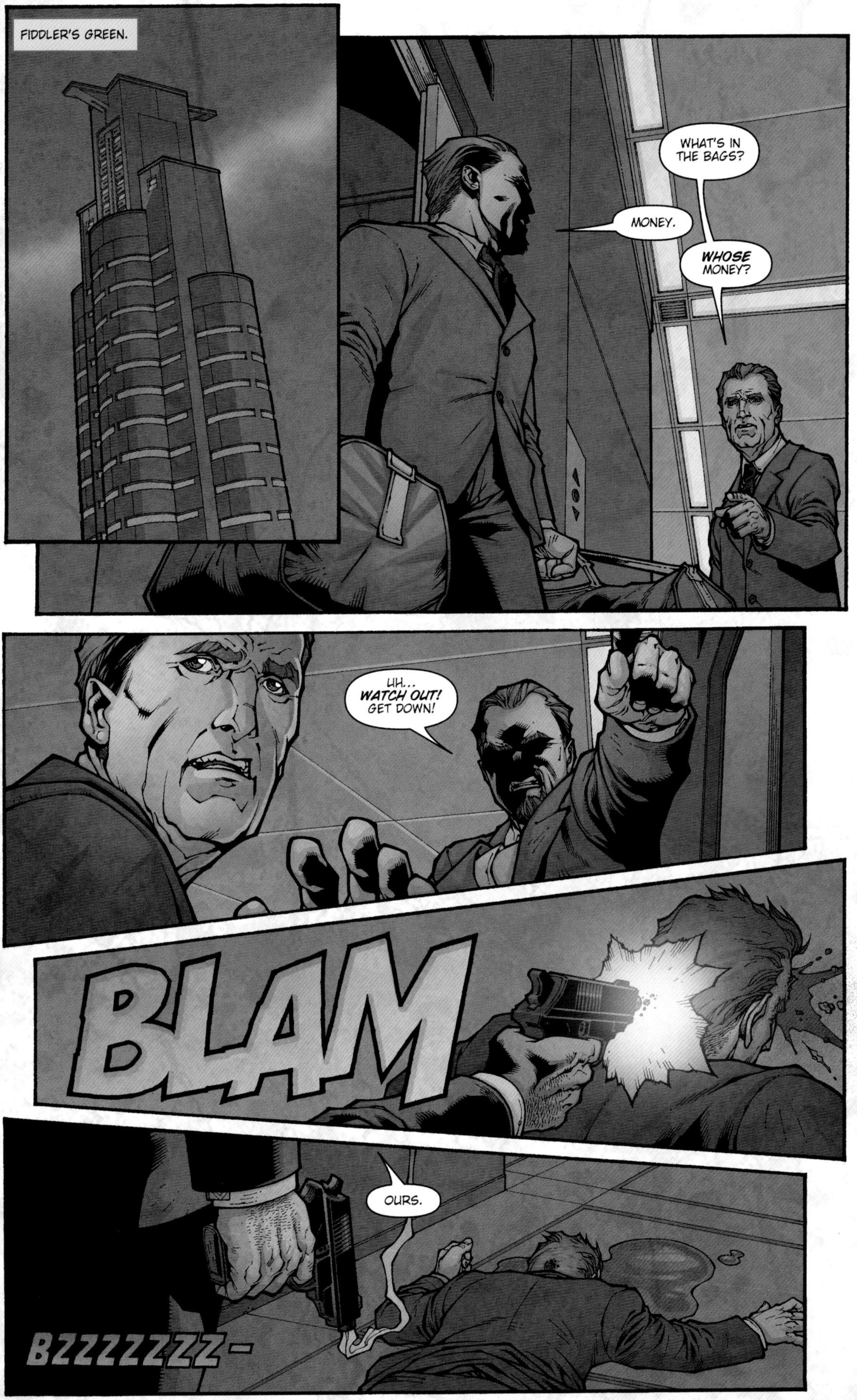

FIDDLER'S GREEN.
WHAT'S IN THE BAGS?
MONEY.
WHOSE MONEY?
UH... WATCH OUT! GET DOWN!
BLAM
OURS.
BZZZZZZZ-

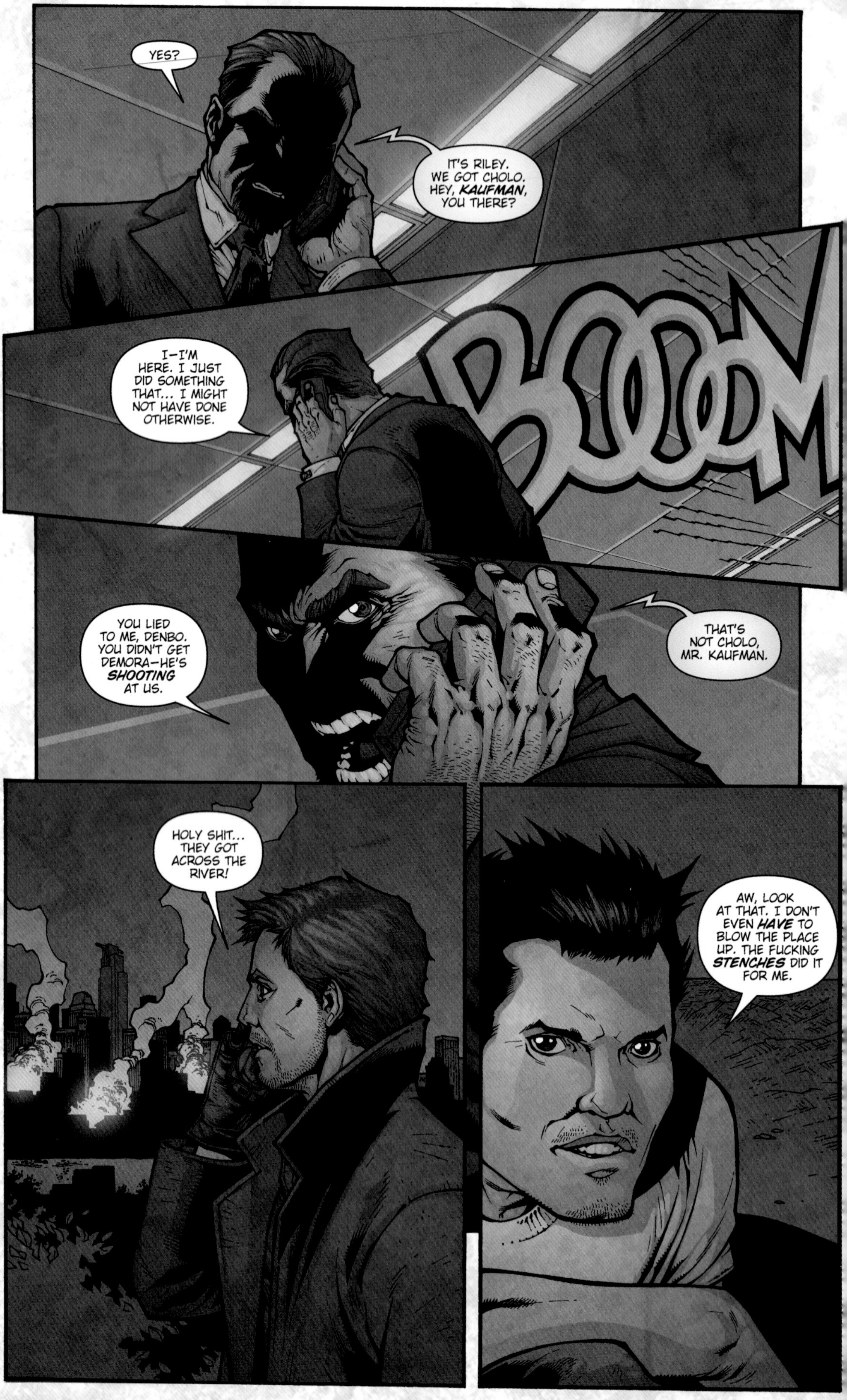
YES?
IT'S RILEY. WE GOT CHOLO. HEY, KAUFMAN, YOU THERE?
I-I'M HERE. I JUST DID SOMETHING THAT... I MIGHT NOT HAVE DONE OTHERWISE.
BOOOM
YOU LIED TO ME, DENBO. YOU DIDN'T GET DEMORA-HE'S SHOOTING AT US.
THAT'S NOT CHOLO, MR. KAUFMAN.
HOLY SHIT... THEY GOT ACROSS THE RIVER!
AW, LOOK AT THAT. I DON'T EVEN HAVE TO BLOW THE PLACE UP. THE FUCKING STENCHES DID IT FOR ME.

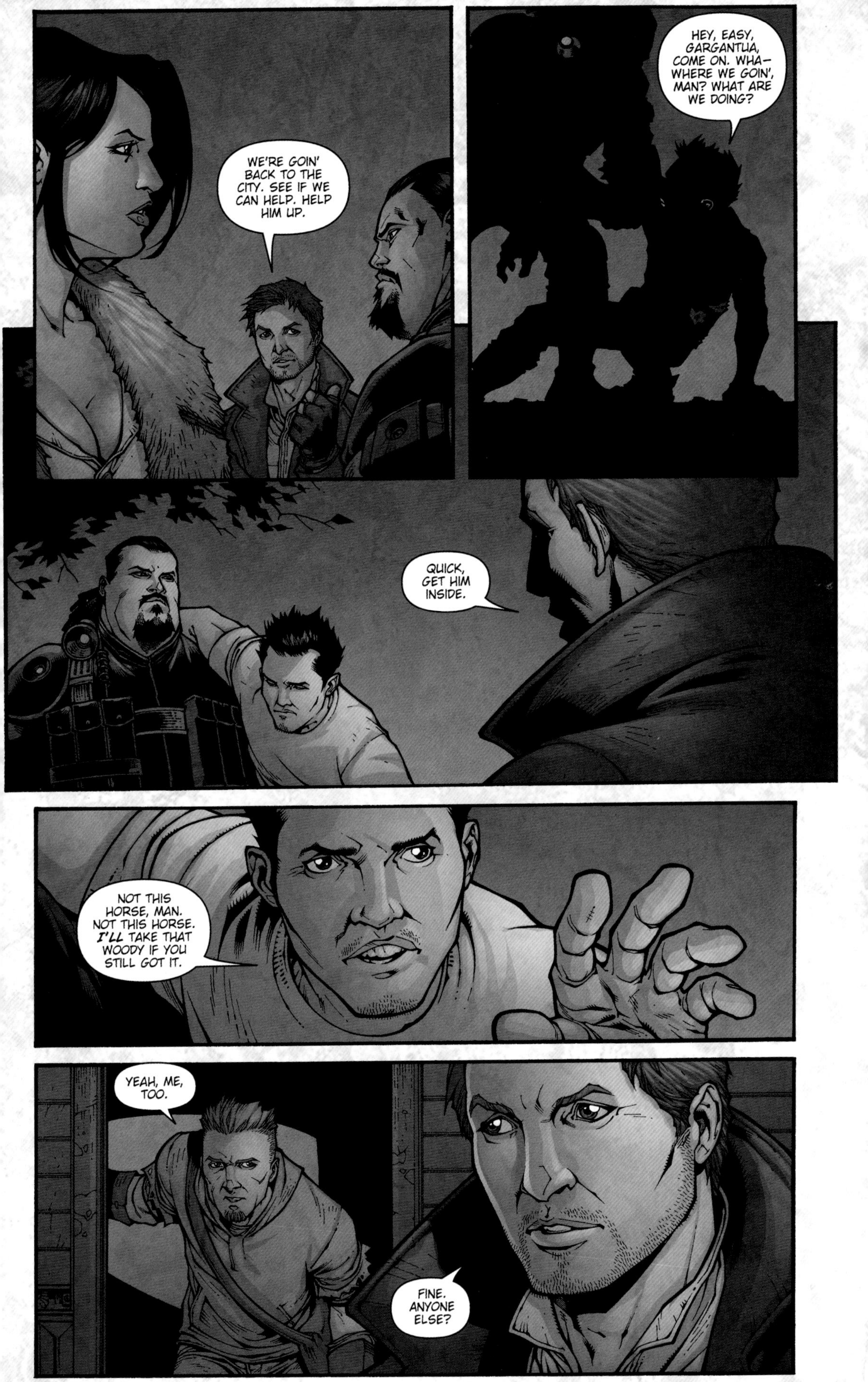
WE'RE GOIN' BACK TO THE CITY. SEE IF WE CAN HELP. HELP HIM UP.
HEY, EASY, GARGANTUA, COME ON. WHA-WHERE WE GOIN', MAN? WHAT ARE WE DOING?
QUICK, GET HIM INSIDE.
NOT THIS HORSE, MAN. NOT THIS HORSE. *I'LL* TAKE THAT WOODY IF YOU STILL GOT IT.
YEAH, ME, TOO.
FINE. ANYONE ELSE?

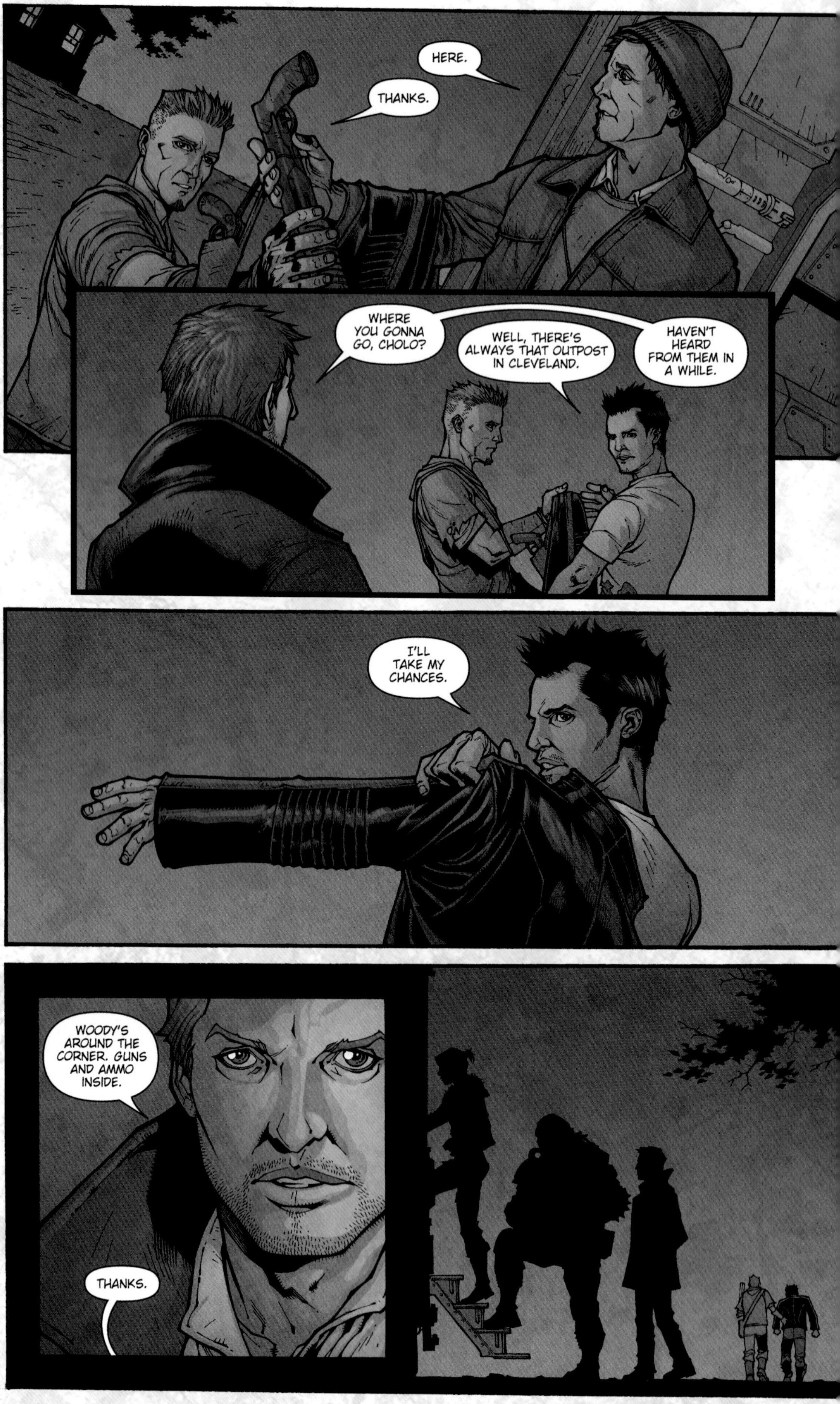
HERE.
THANKS.
WHERE YOU GONNA GO, CHOLO?
WELL, THERE'S ALWAYS THAT OUTPOST IN CLEVELAND.
HAVEN'T HEARD FROM THEM IN A WHILE.
I'LL TAKE MY CHANCES.
WOODY'S AROUND THE CORNER. GUNS AND AMMO INSIDE.
THANKS.

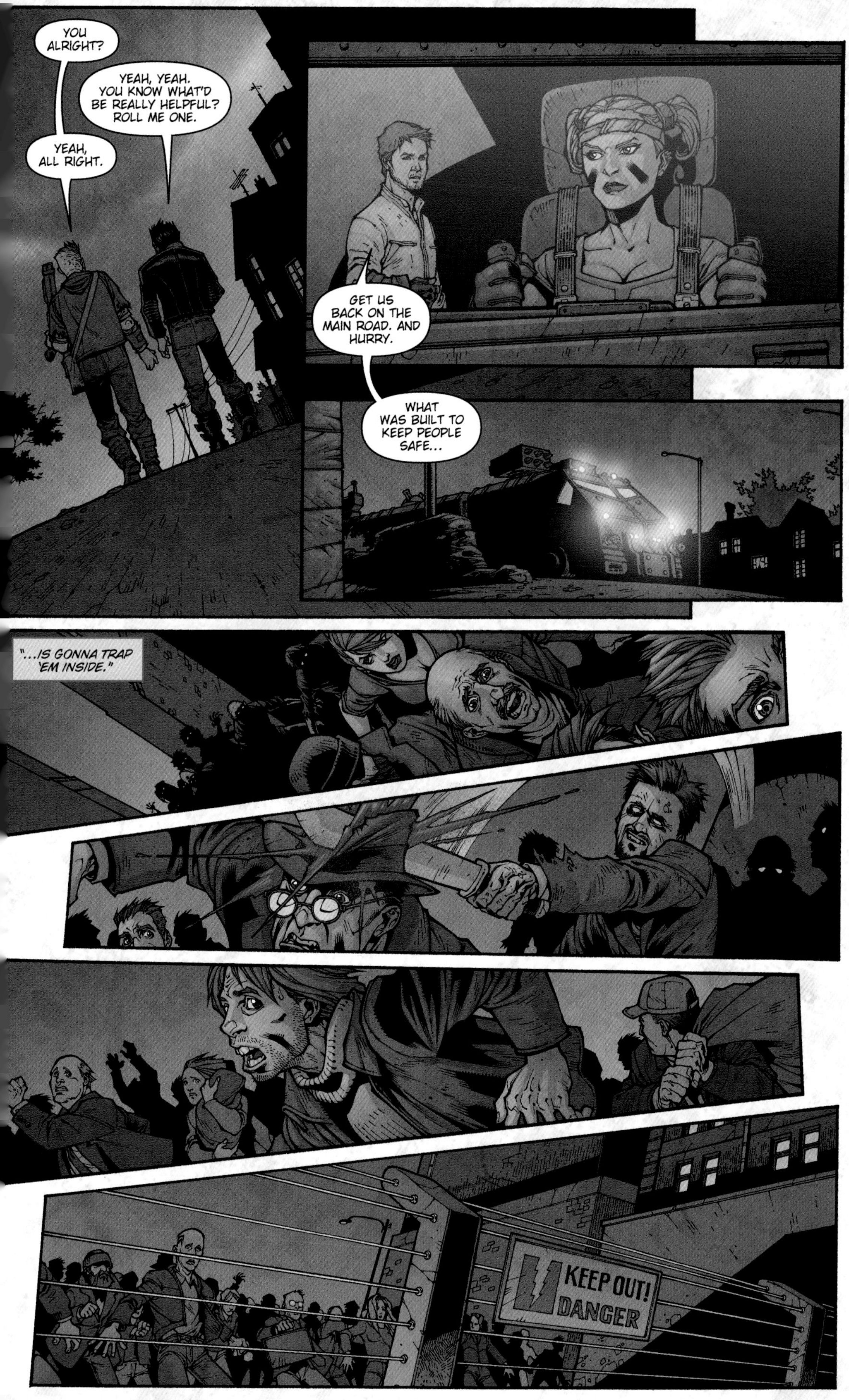
YOU ALRIGHT?
YEAH, YEAH. YOU KNOW WHAT'D BE REALLY HELPFUL? ROLL ME ONE.
YEAH, ALL RIGHT.
GET US BACK ON THE MAIN ROAD. AND HURRY.
WHAT WAS BUILT TO KEEP PEOPLE SAFE...
"...IS GONNA TRAP 'EM INSIDE."
KEEP OUT! DANGER

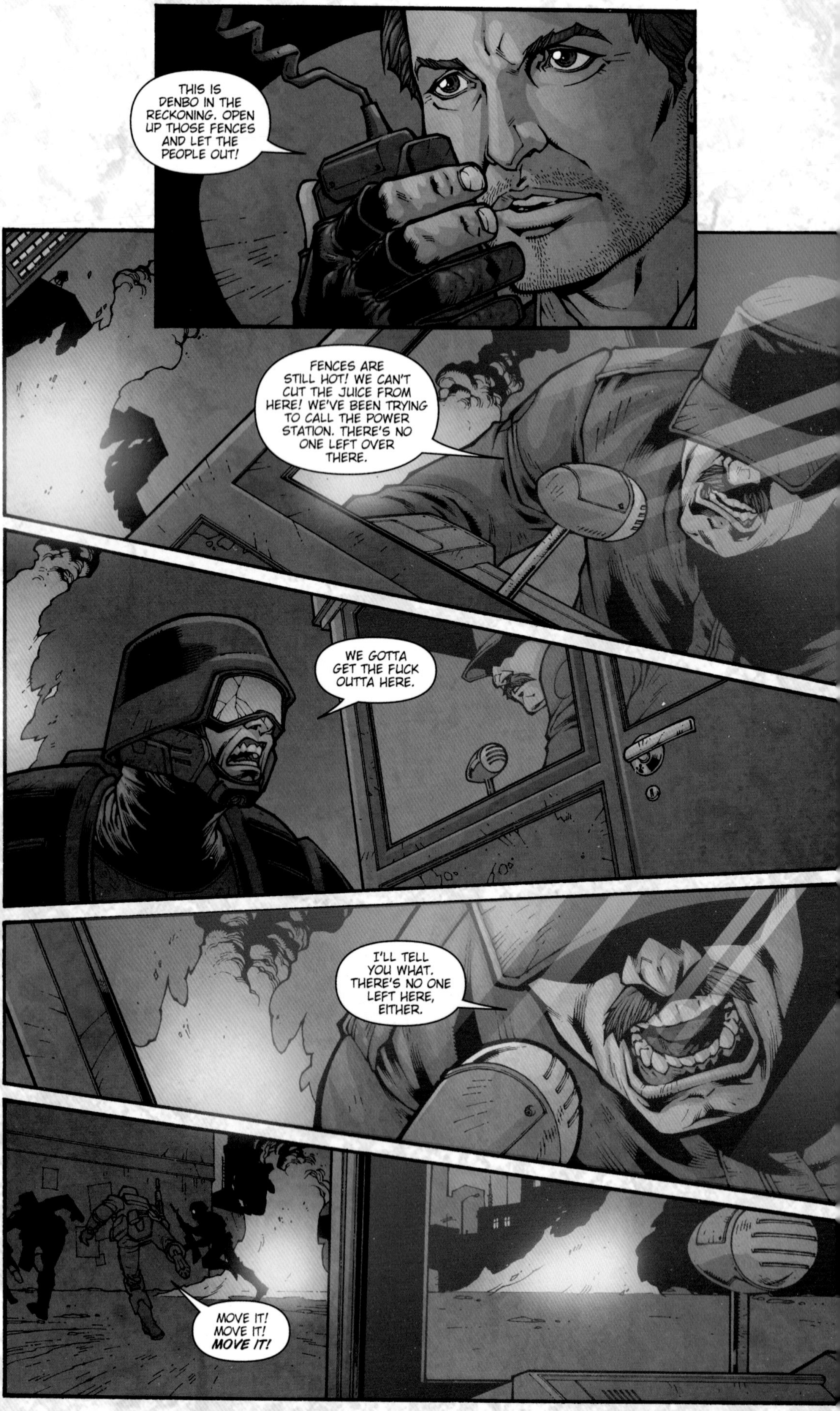
THIS IS DENBO IN THE RECKONING. OPEN UP THOSE FENCES AND LET THE PEOPLE OUT!
FENCES ARE STILL HOT! WE CAN'T CUT THE JUICE FROM HERE! WE'VE BEEN TRYING TO CALL THE POWER STATION. THERE'S NO ONE LEFT OVER THERE.
WE GOTTA GET THE FUCK OUTTA HERE.
I'LL TELL YOU WHAT. THERE'S NO ONE LEFT HERE, EITHER.
MOVE IT! MOVE IT! *MOVE IT!*

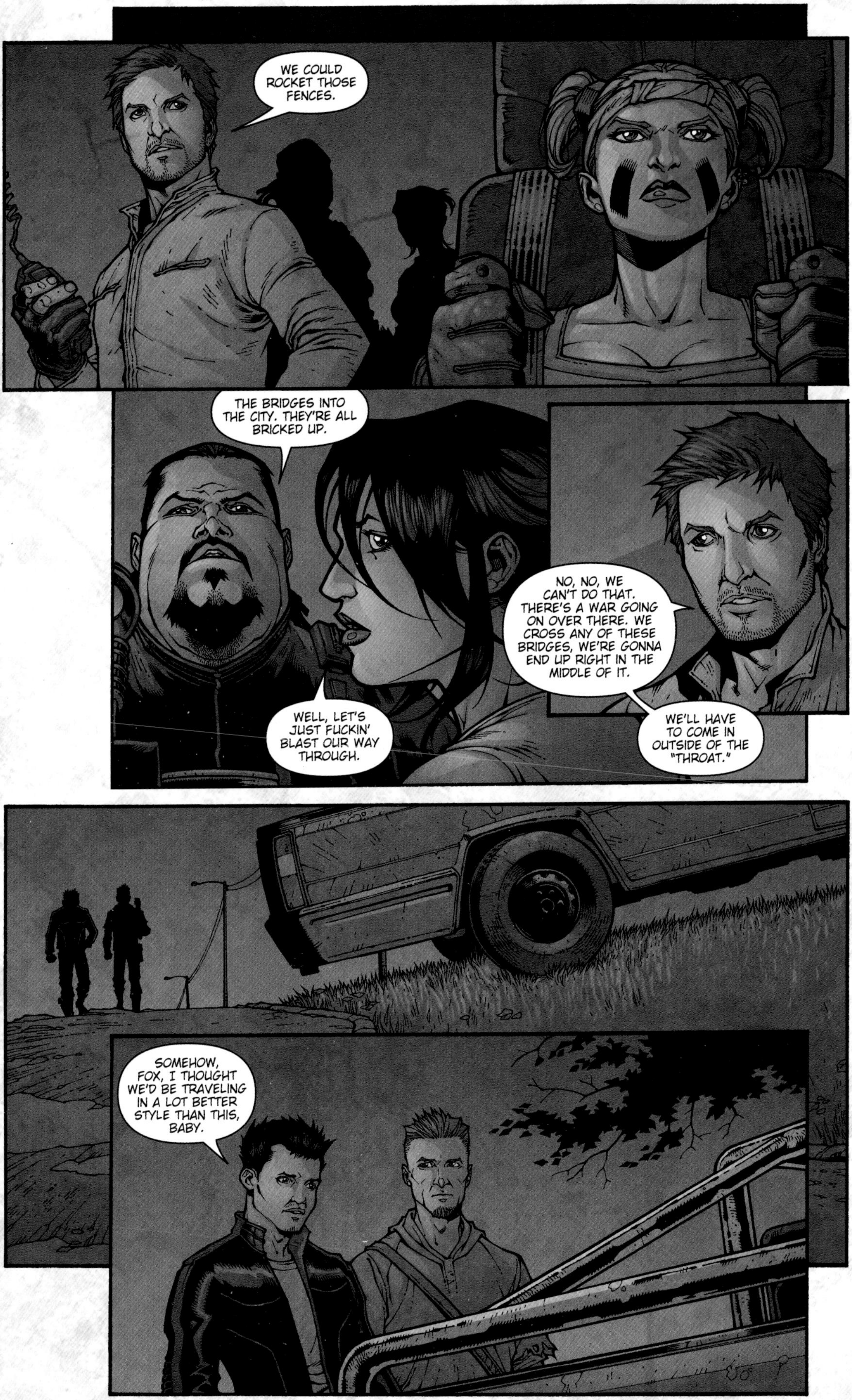
WE COULD ROCKET THOSE FENCES.
THE BRIDGES INTO THE CITY. THEY'RE ALL BRICKED UP.
WELL, LET'S JUST FUCKIN' BLAST OUR WAY THROUGH.
NO, NO, WE CAN'T DO THAT. THERE'S A WAR GOING ON OVER THERE. WE CROSS ANY OF THESE BRIDGES, WE'RE GONNA END UP RIGHT IN THE MIDDLE OF IT.
WE'LL HAVE TO COME IN OUTSIDE OF THE "THROAT."
SOMEHOW, FOX, I THOUGHT WE'D BE TRAVELING IN A LOT BETTER STYLE THAN THIS, BABY.

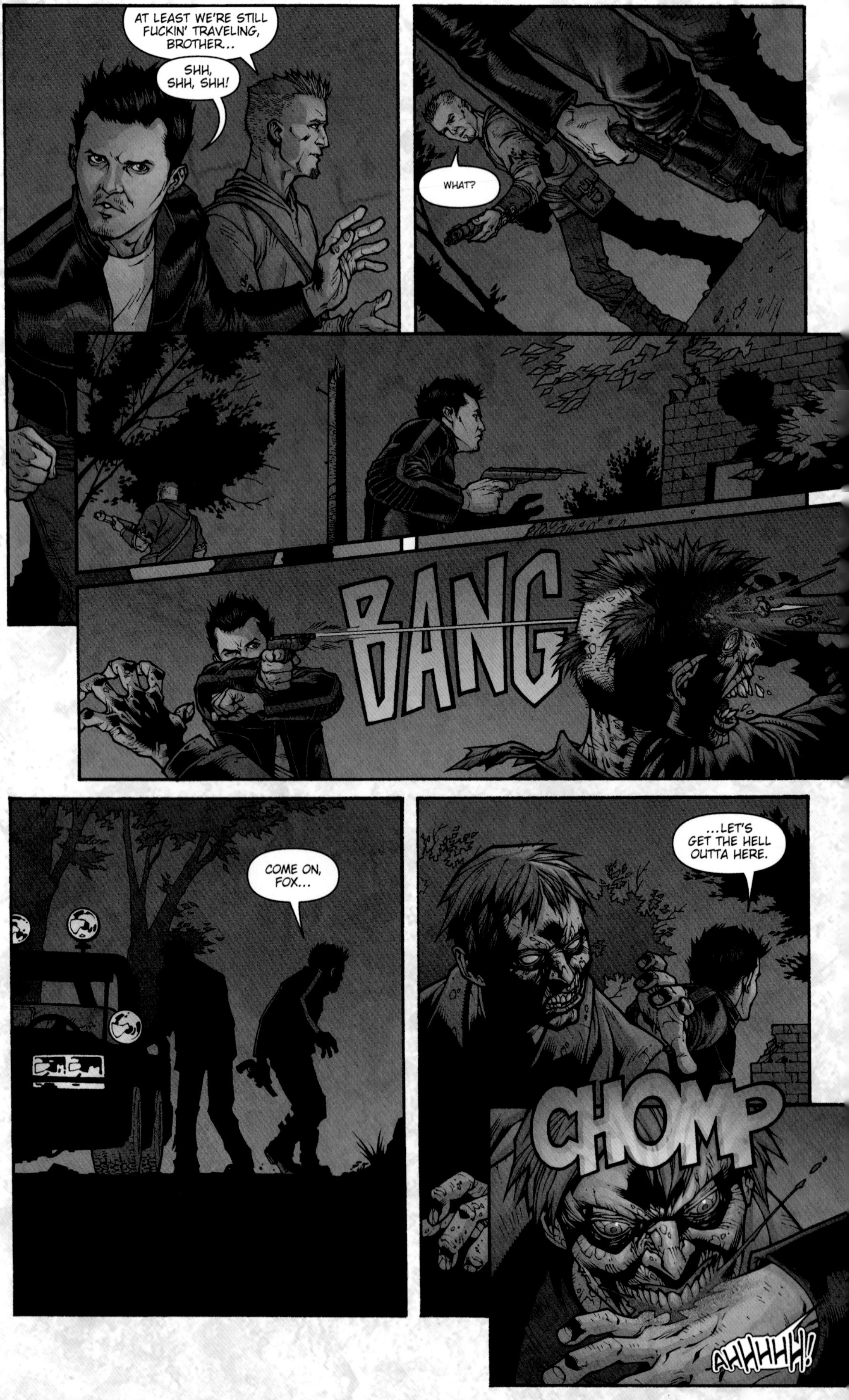
AT LEAST WE'RE STILL FUCKIN' TRAVELING, BROTHER...
SHH, SHH, SHH!
WHAT?
BANG
COME ON, FOX...
...LET'S GET THE HELL OUTTA HERE.
CHOMP
AHHHHH!

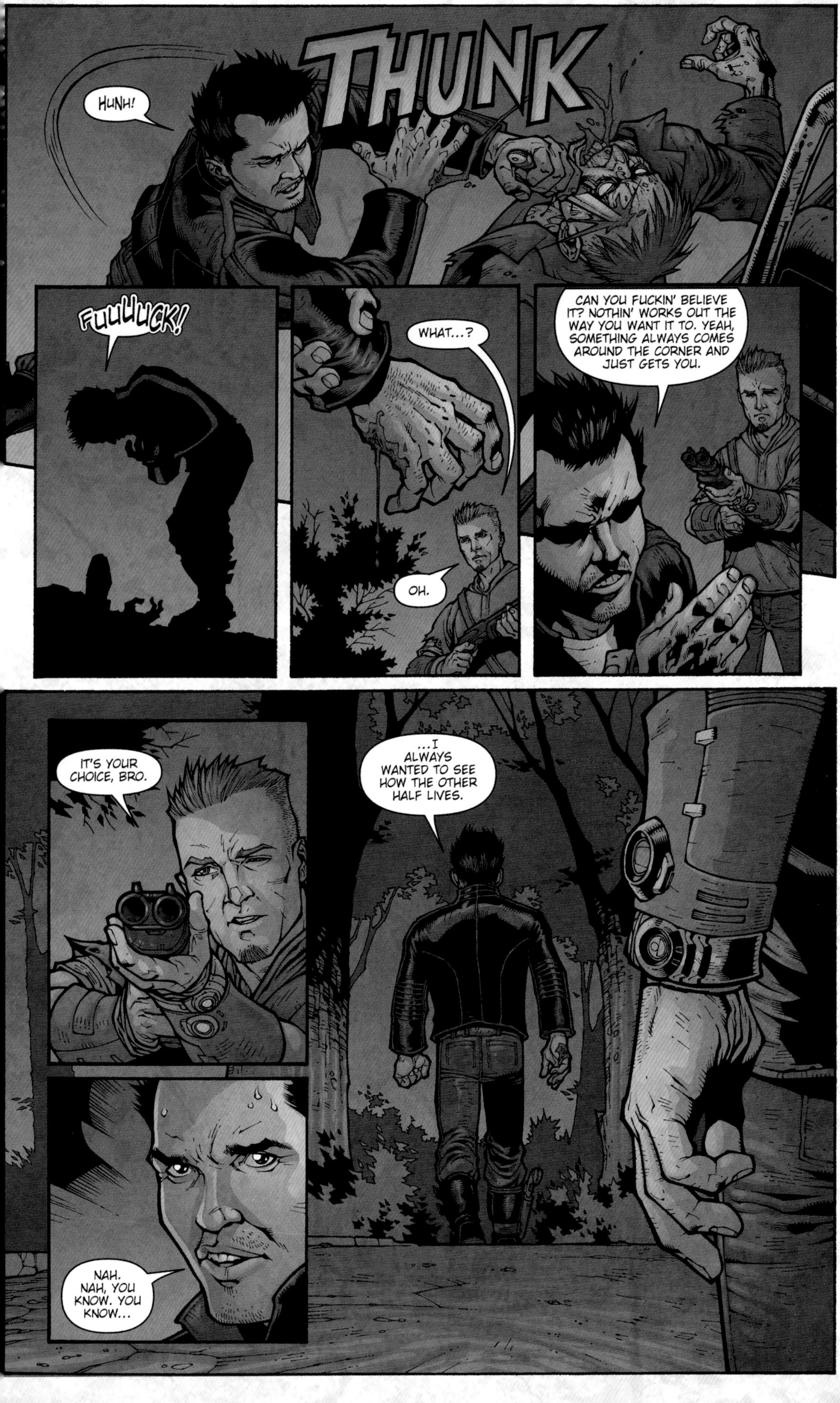
HUNH!
THUNK
FUUUUCK!
WHAT...?
OH.
CAN YOU FUCKIN' BELIEVE IT? NOTHIN' WORKS OUT THE WAY YOU WANT IT TO. YEAH, SOMETHING ALWAYS COMES AROUND THE CORNER AND JUST GETS YOU.
IT'S YOUR CHOICE, BRO.
NAH. NAH, YOU KNOW. YOU KNOW...
...I ALWAYS WANTED TO SEE HOW THE OTHER HALF LIVES.

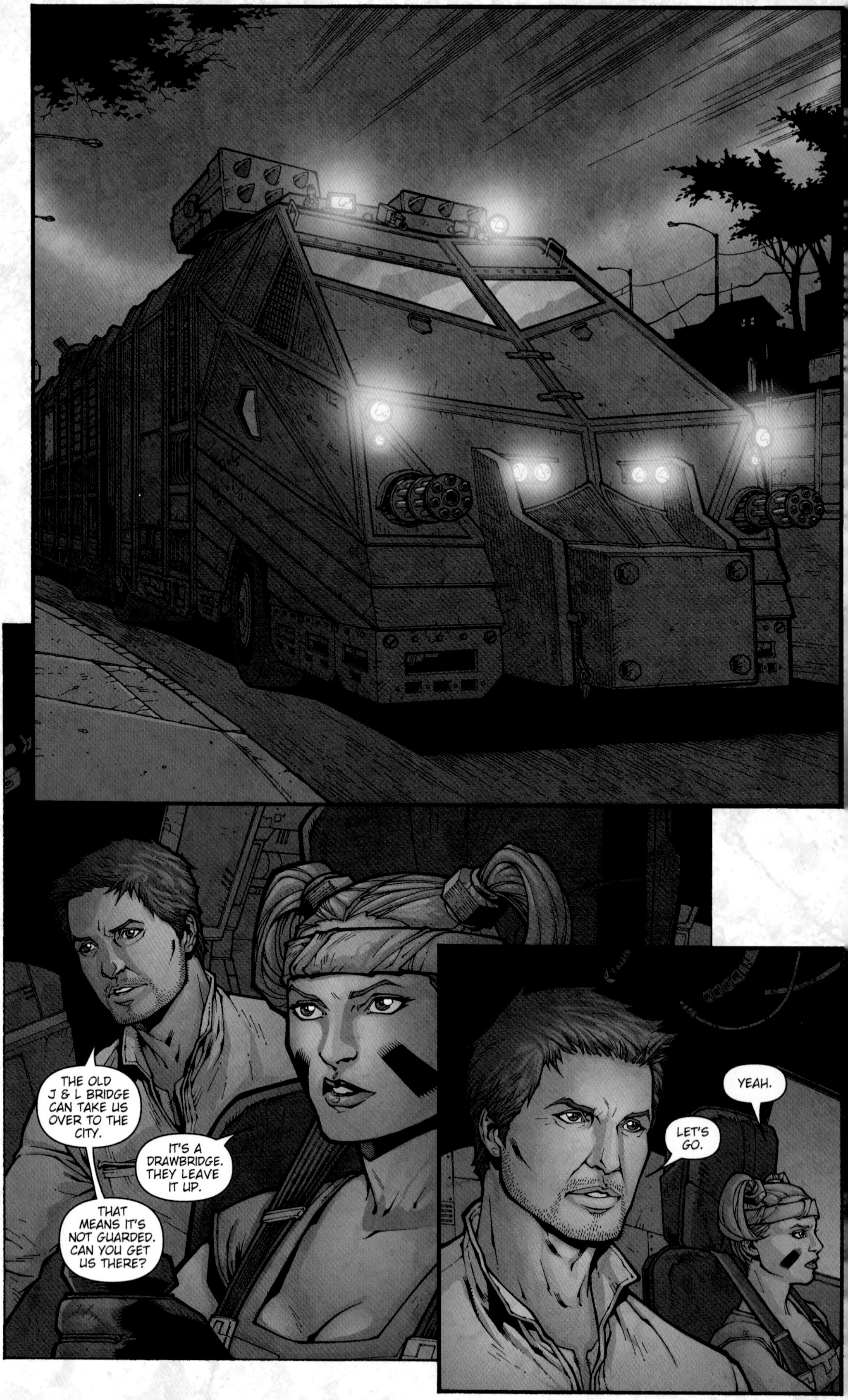
THE OLD J & L BRIDGE CAN TAKE US OVER TO THE CITY.
IT'S A DRAWBRIDGE. THEY LEAVE IT UP.
THAT MEANS IT'S NOT GUARDED. CAN YOU GET US THERE?
YEAH.
LET'S GO.

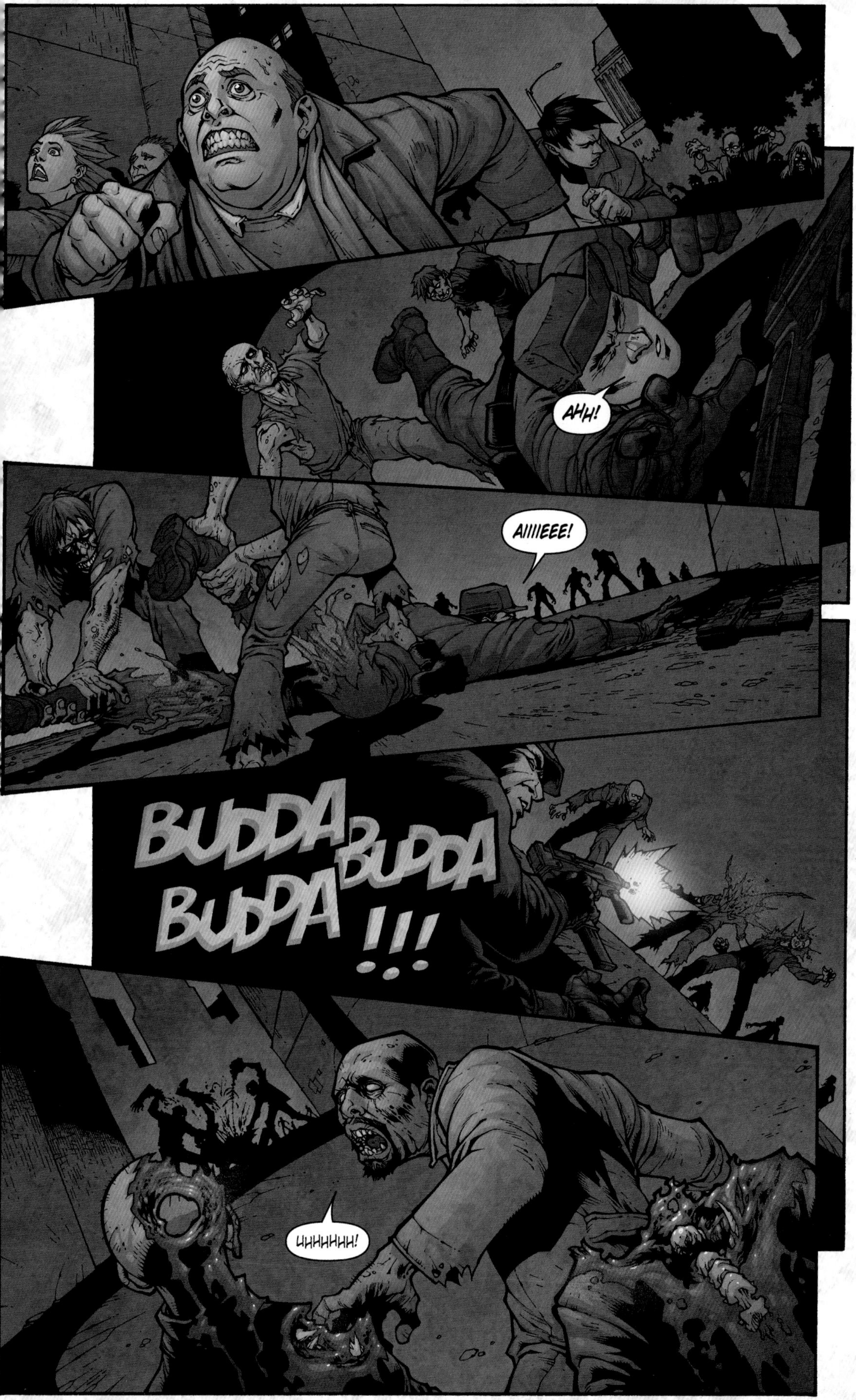

AHH!
AIIIIEEE!
BUDDA BUDDA BUDDA!!!
UHHHHHH!

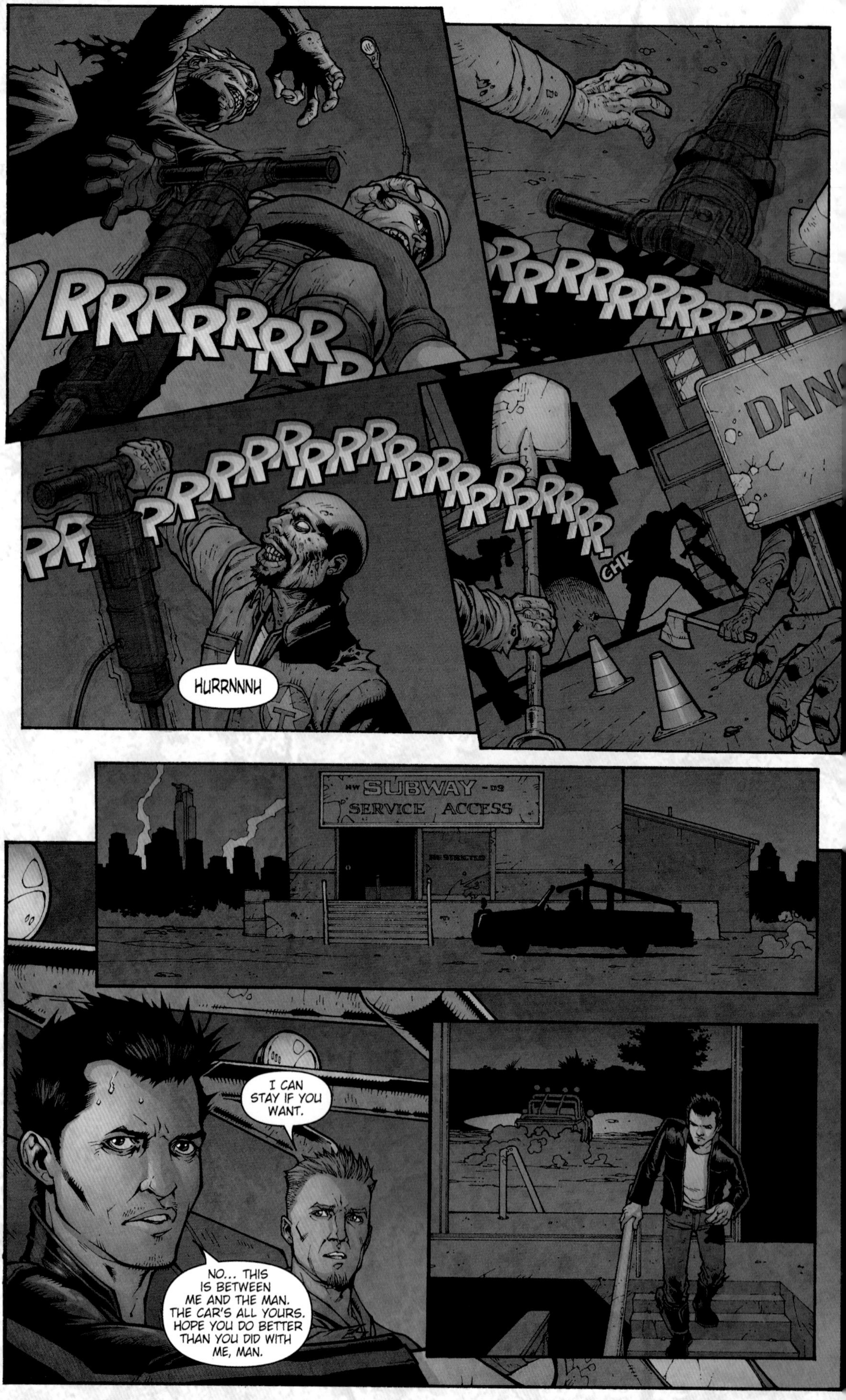
RRRRRRRD
RRRRRRRRRRRR
PRRRRRRRRRRRRRRRRRRR.
HURRNNNH
CHK
SUBWAY
SERVICE ACCESS
RESTRICTED
I CAN STAY IF YOU WANT.
NO... THIS IS BETWEEN ME AND THE MAN. THE CAR'S ALL YOURS. HOPE YOU DO BETTER THAN YOU DID WITH ME, MAN.

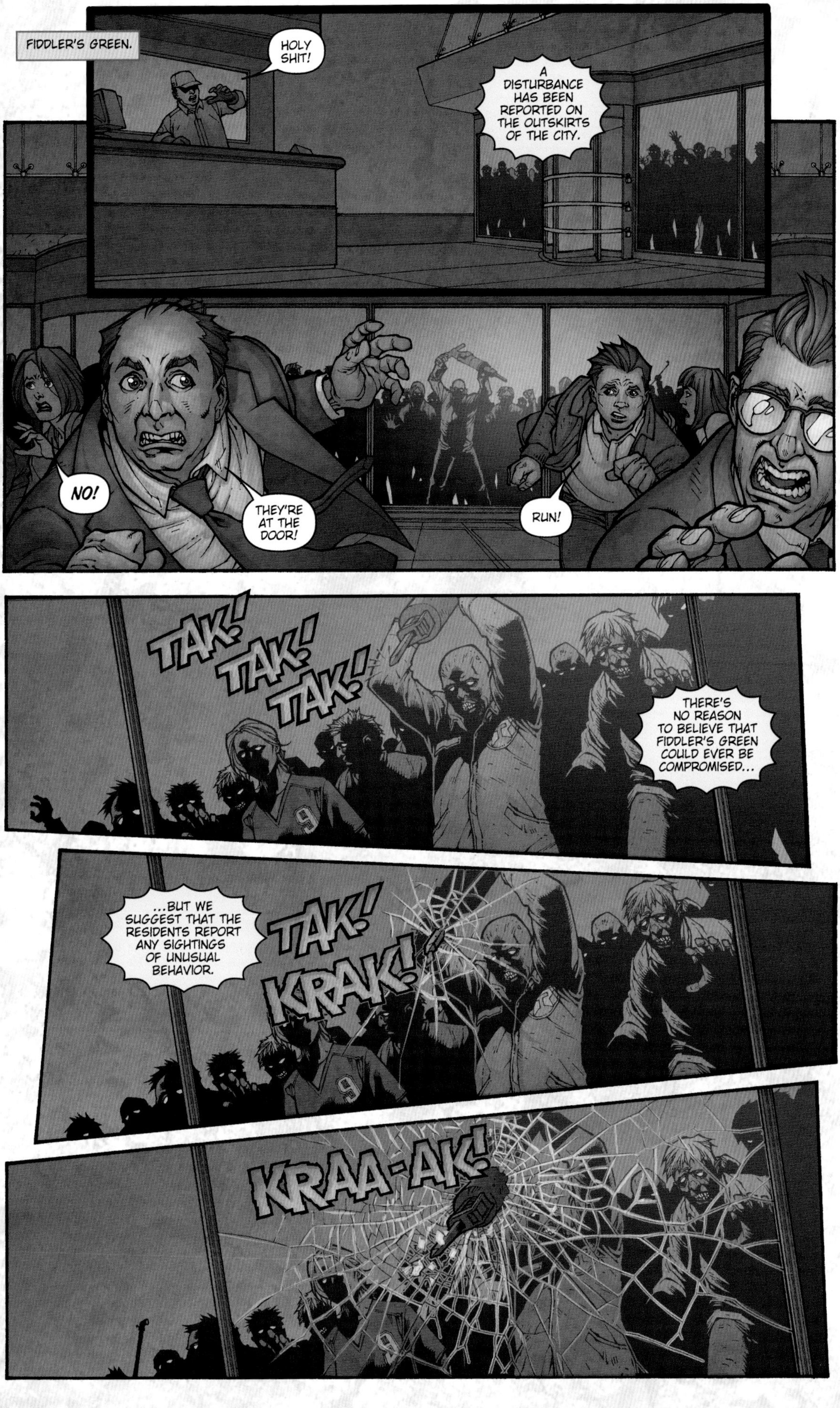
FIDDLER'S GREEN.
HOLY SHIT!
A DISTURBANCE HAS BEEN REPORTED ON THE OUTSKIRTS OF THE CITY.
NO!
THEY'RE AT THE DOOR!
RUN!
TAK! TAK! TAK!
THERE'S NO REASON TO BELIEVE THAT FIDDLER'S GREEN COULD EVER BE COMPROMISED...
...BUT WE SUGGEST THAT THE RESIDENTS REPORT ANY SIGHTINGS OF UNUSUAL BEHAVIOR.
TAK! KRAK!
KRAA-AK!

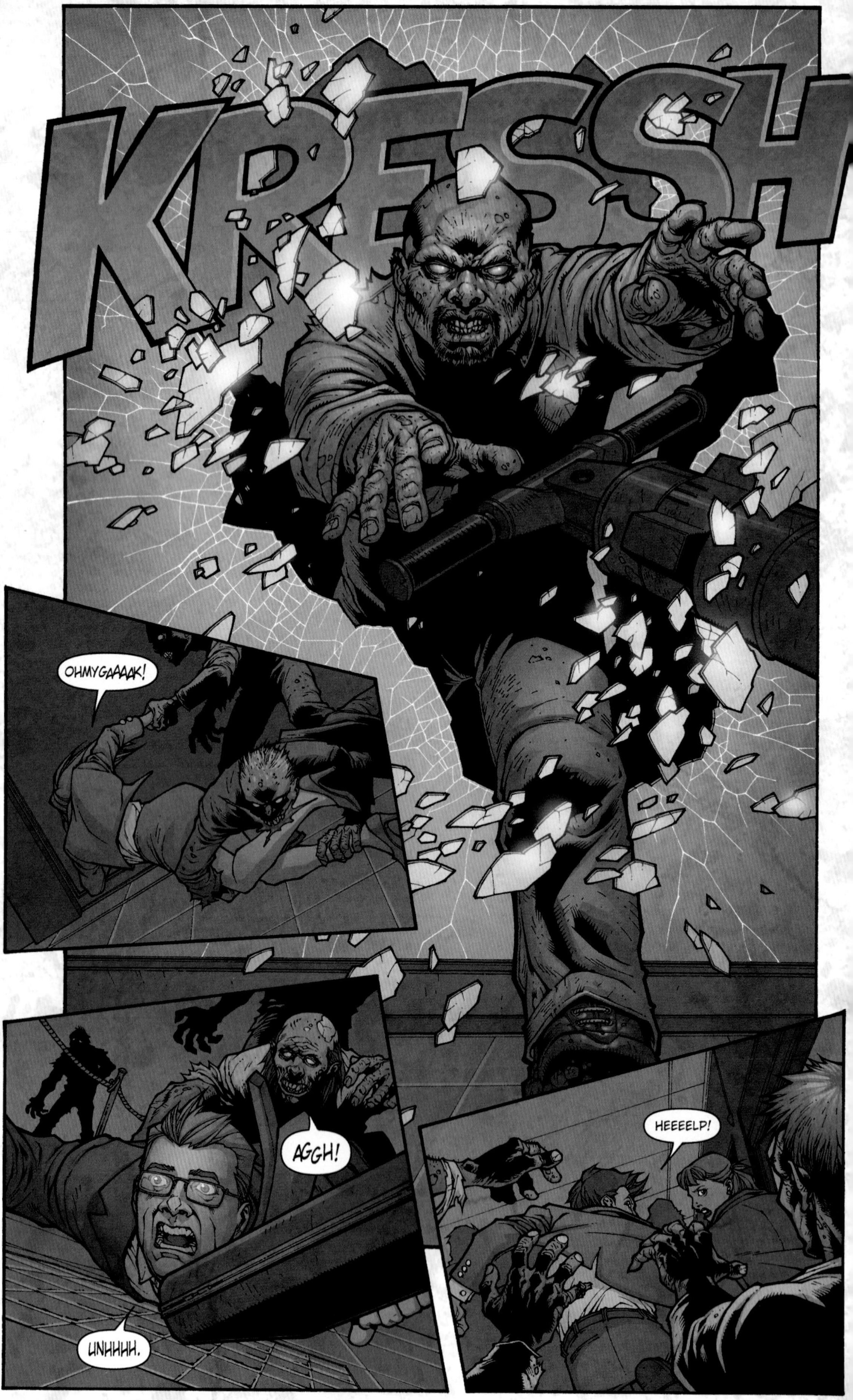
KRESSH
OHMYGAAAAK!
AGGH!
UNHHHH.
HEEEELP!

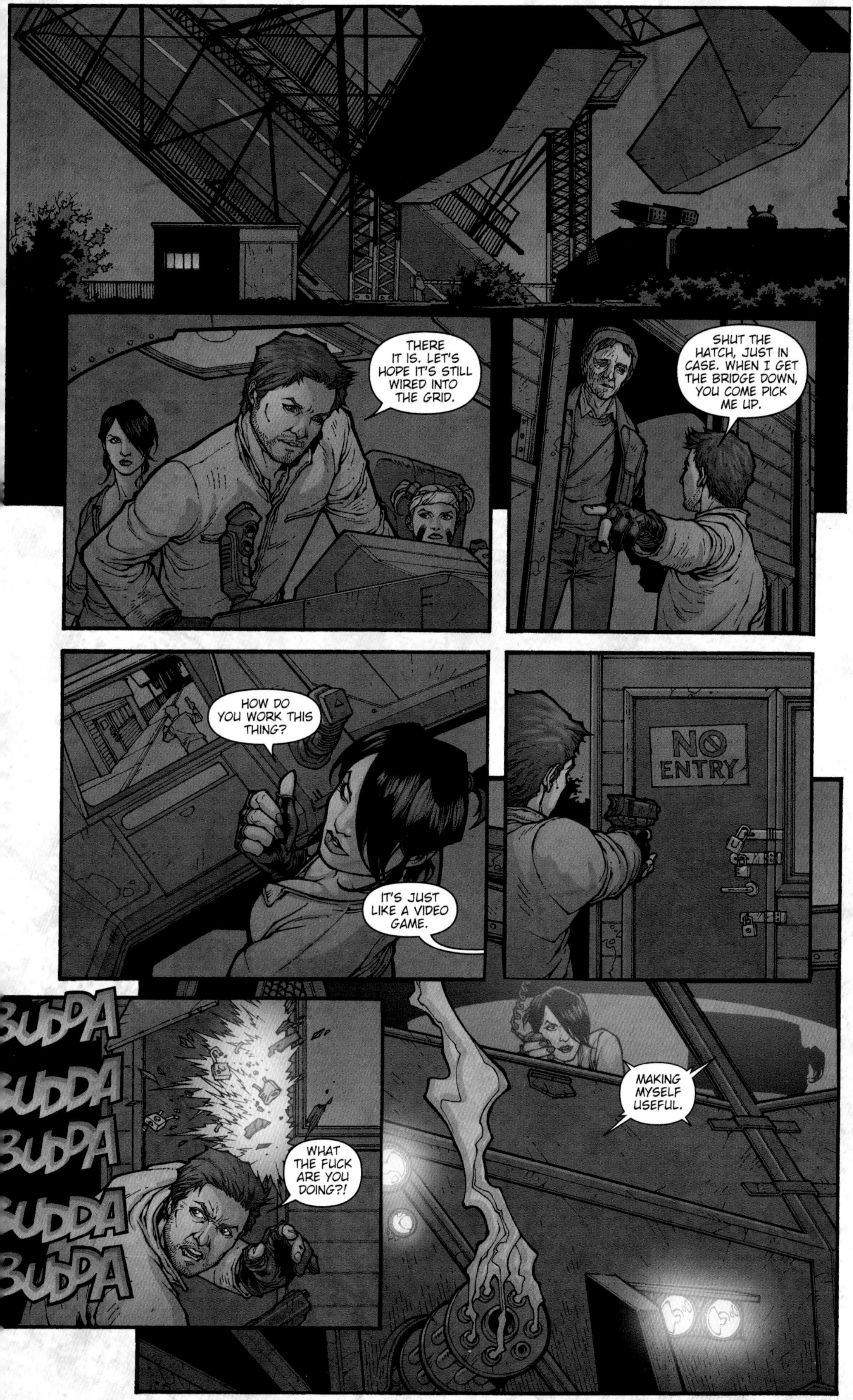
THERE IT IS. LET'S HOPE IT'S STILL WIRED INTO THE GRID.
SHUT THE HATCH, JUST IN CASE. WHEN I GET THE BRIDGE DOWN, YOU COME PICK ME UP.
HOW DO YOU WORK THIS THING?
IT'S JUST LIKE A VIDEO GAME.
NO ENTRY
BUDDA
BUDDA
BUDDA
BUDDA
BUDDA
WHAT THE FUCK ARE YOU DOING?!
MAKING MYSELF USEFUL.

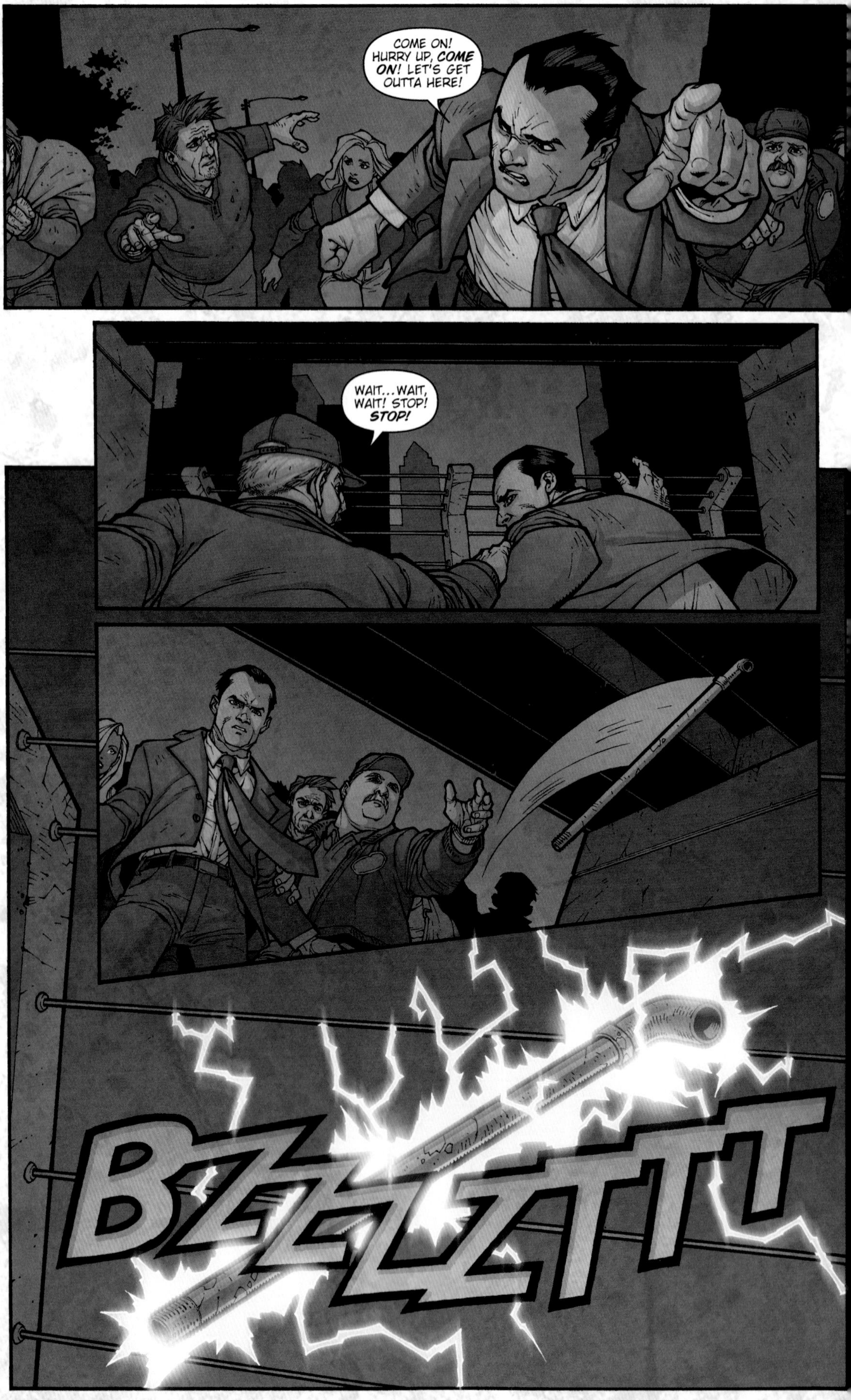
COME ON! HURRY UP, COME ON! LET'S GET OUTTA HERE!
WAIT...WAIT, WAIT! STOP! STOP!
BZZZTTT

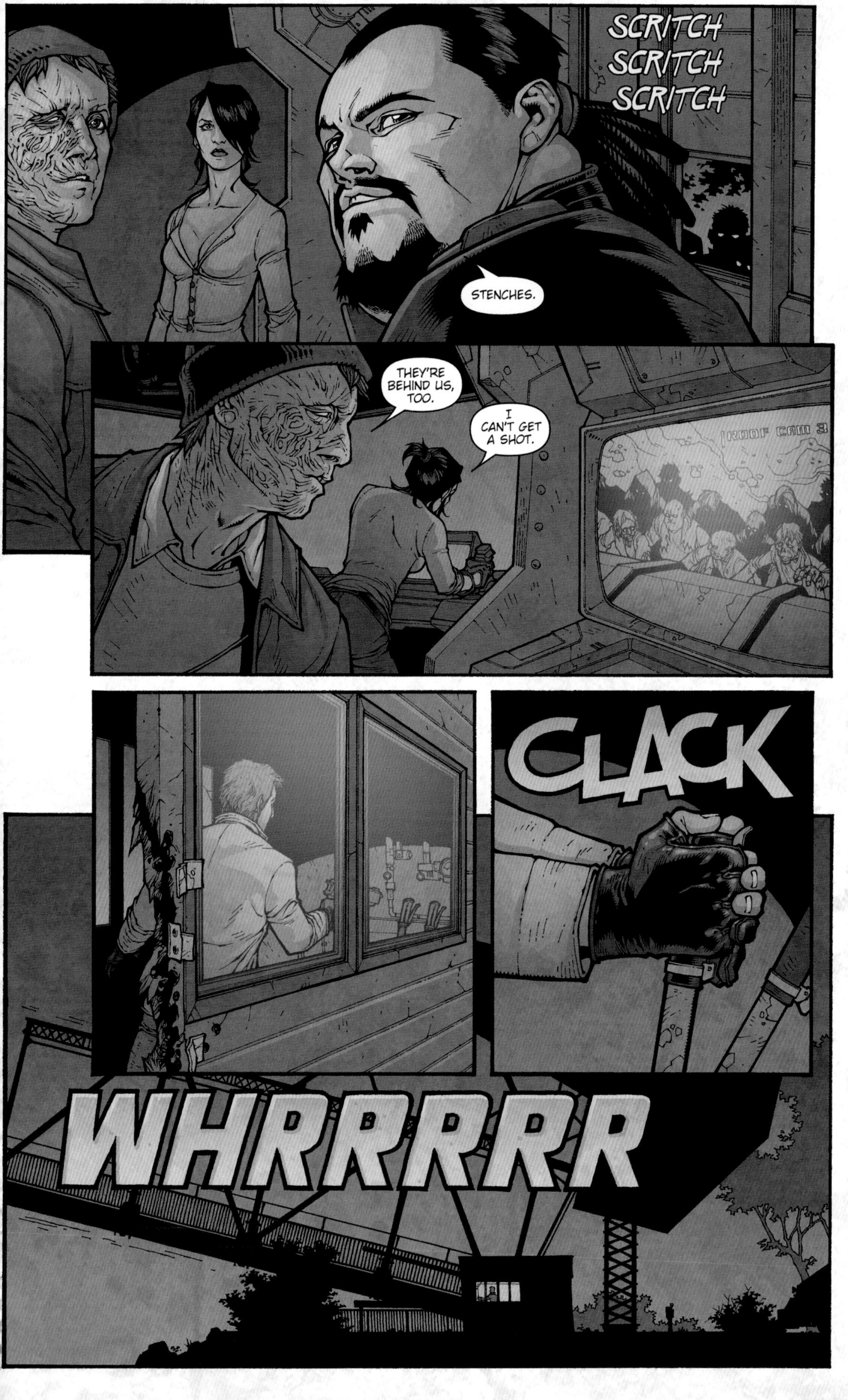
SCRITCH
SCRITCH
SCRITCH
STENCHES.
THEY'RE BEHIND US, TOO.
I CAN'T GET A SHOT.
ROOF CAM 3
CLACK
WHRRRRRR

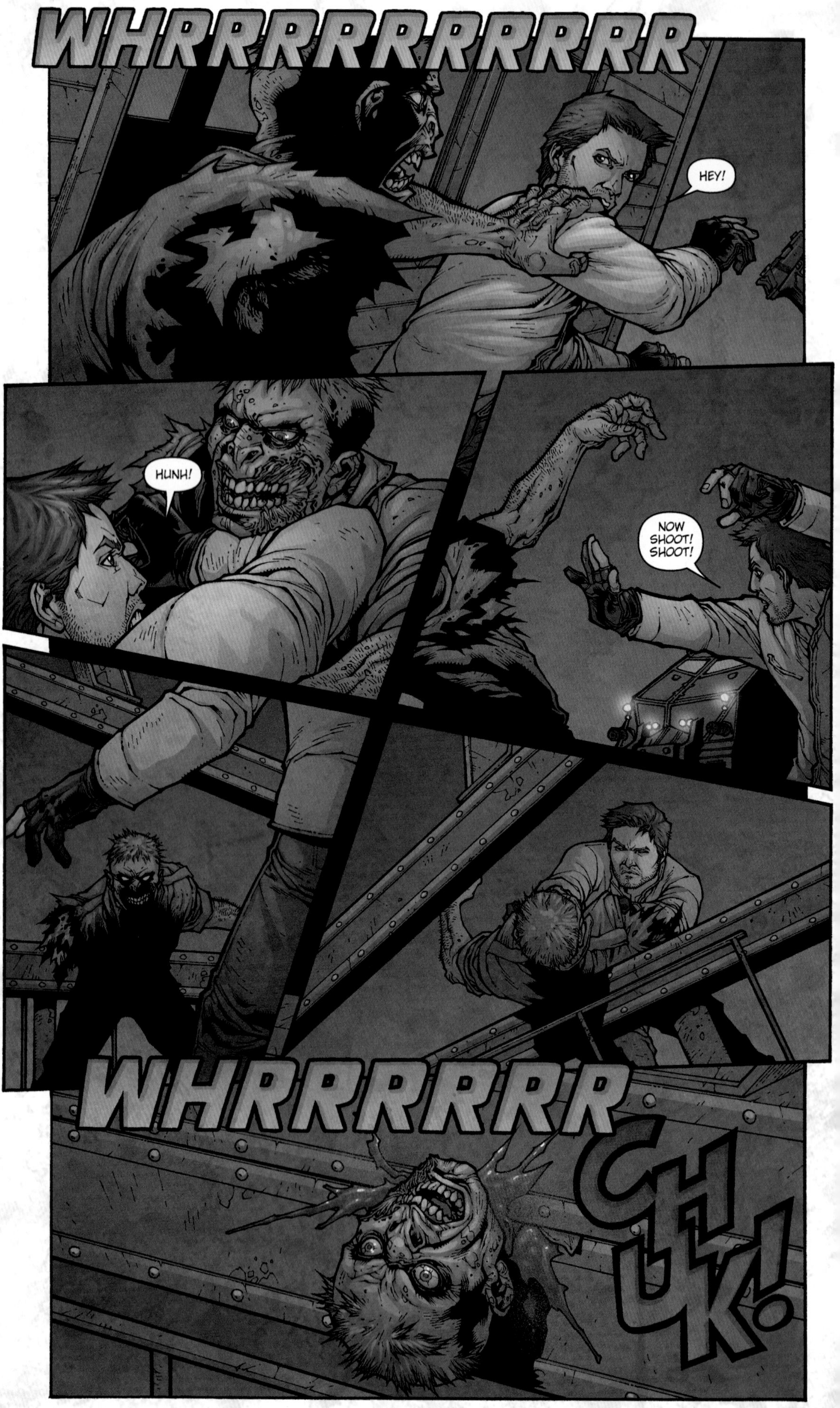
WHRRRRRRRRRR
HEY!
HUNH!
NOW SHOOT! SHOOT!
WHRRRRRRRR
CHUK!

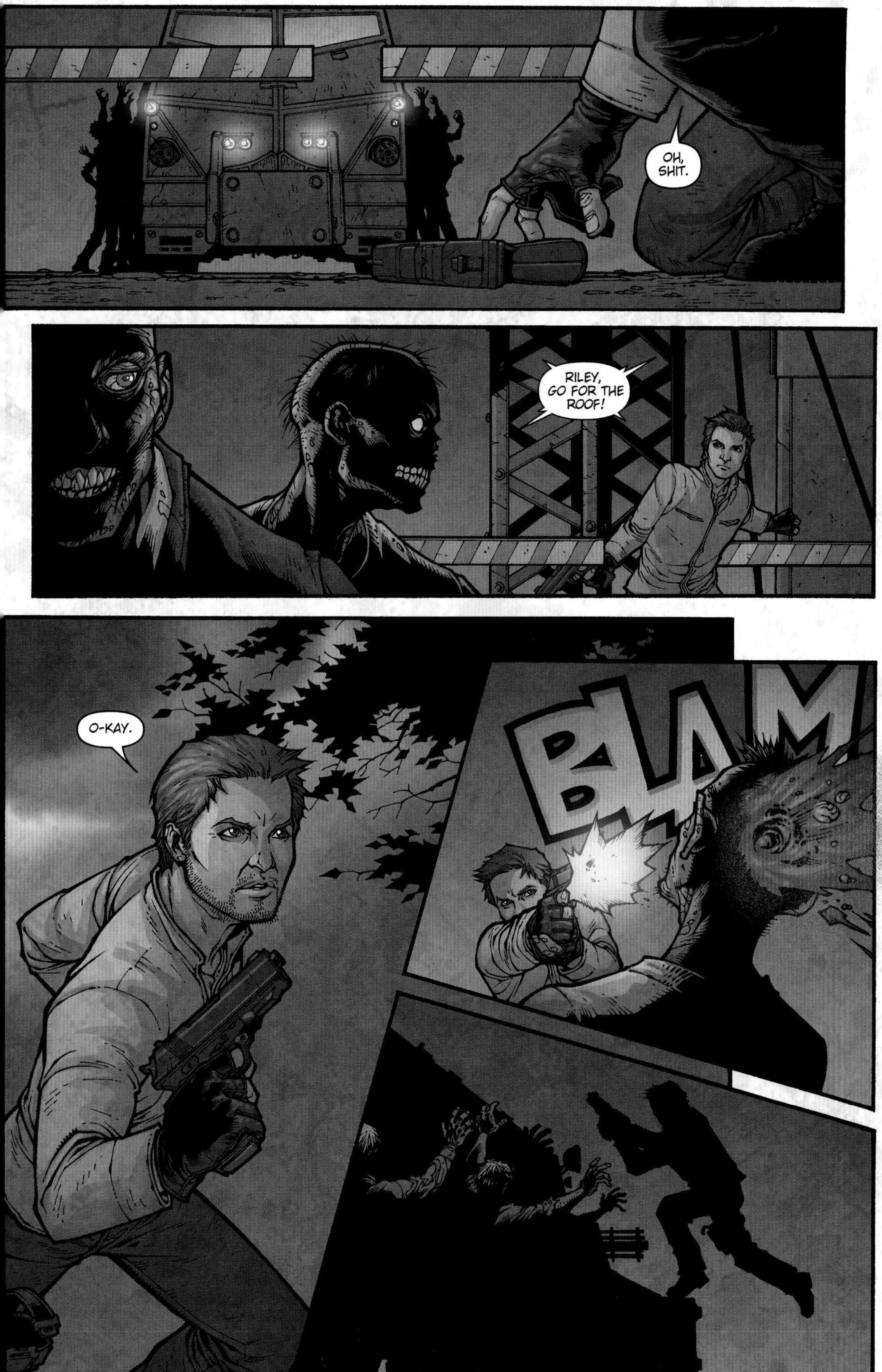
OH, SHIT.
RILEY, GO FOR THE ROOF!
O-KAY.
BLAM

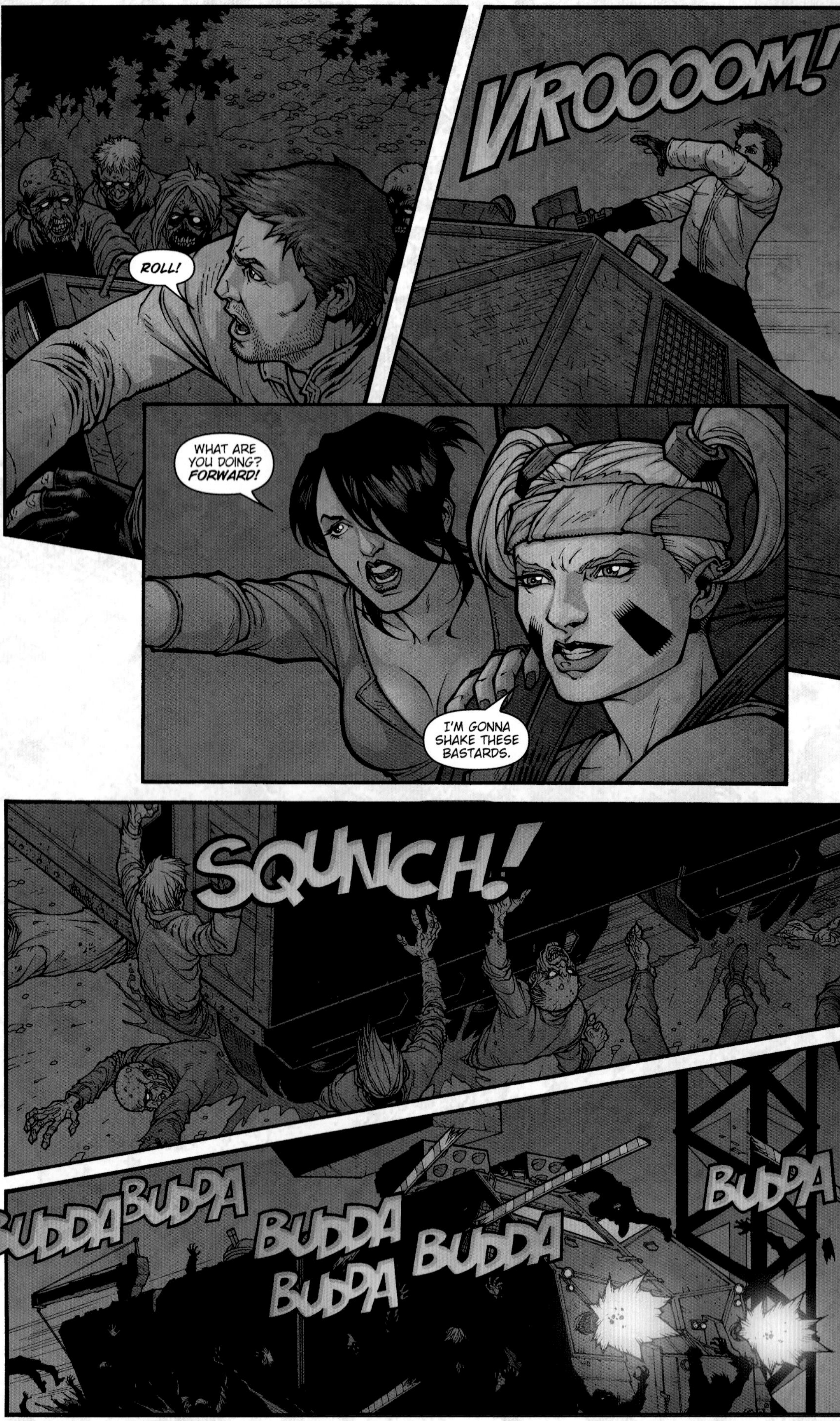
ROLL!
VROOOOM!
WHAT ARE YOU DOING? FORWARD!
I'M GONNA SHAKE THESE BASTARDS.
SQUNCH!
BUDDA BUDDA
BUDDA
BUDDA BUDDA
BUDDA

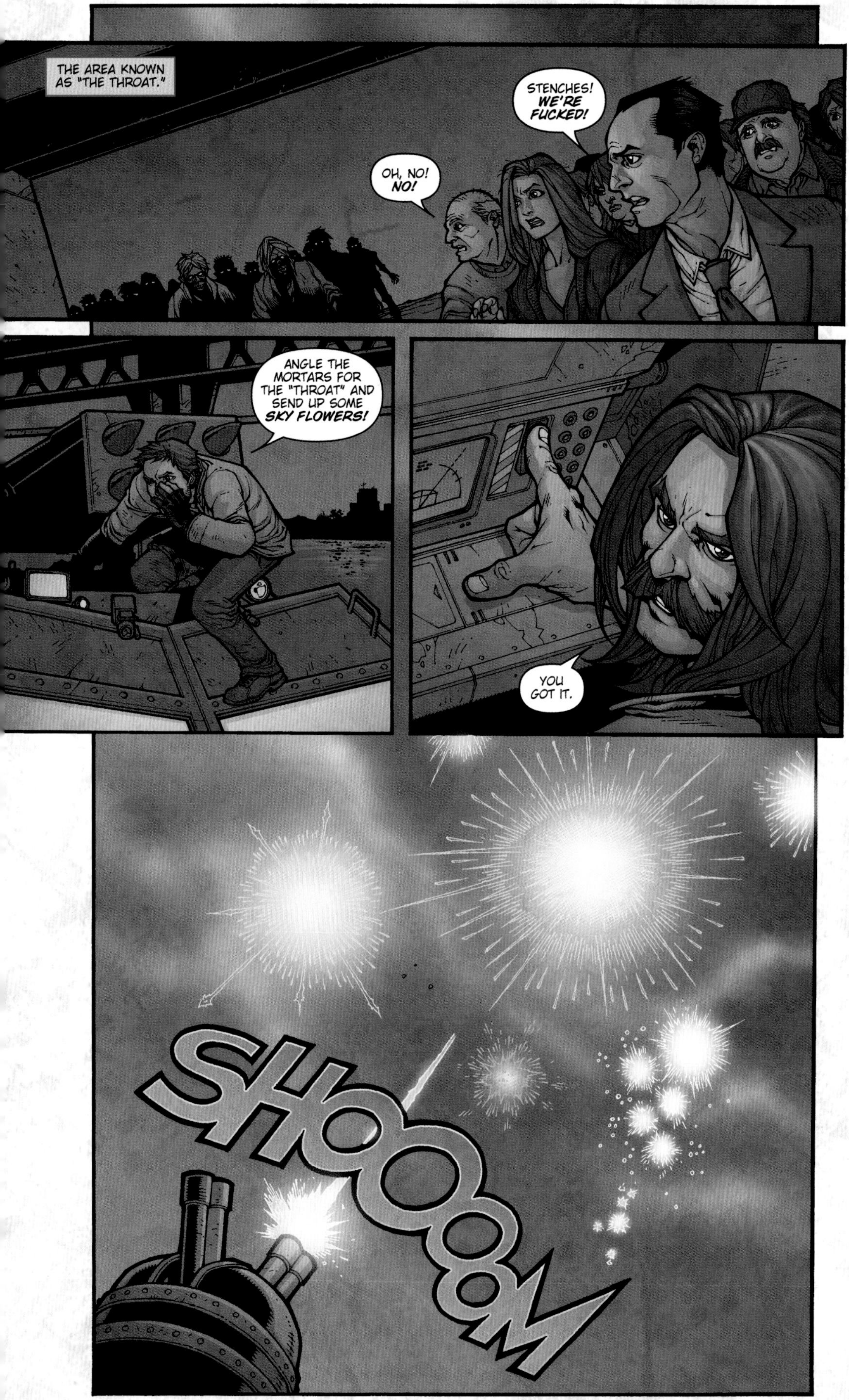

THE AREA KNOWN AS "THE THROAT."
STENCHES! *WE'RE FUCKED!*
OH, NO! *NO!*
ANGLE THE MORTARS FOR THE "THROAT" AND SEND UP SOME *SKY FLOWERS!*
YOU GOT IT.
SHOOOOM

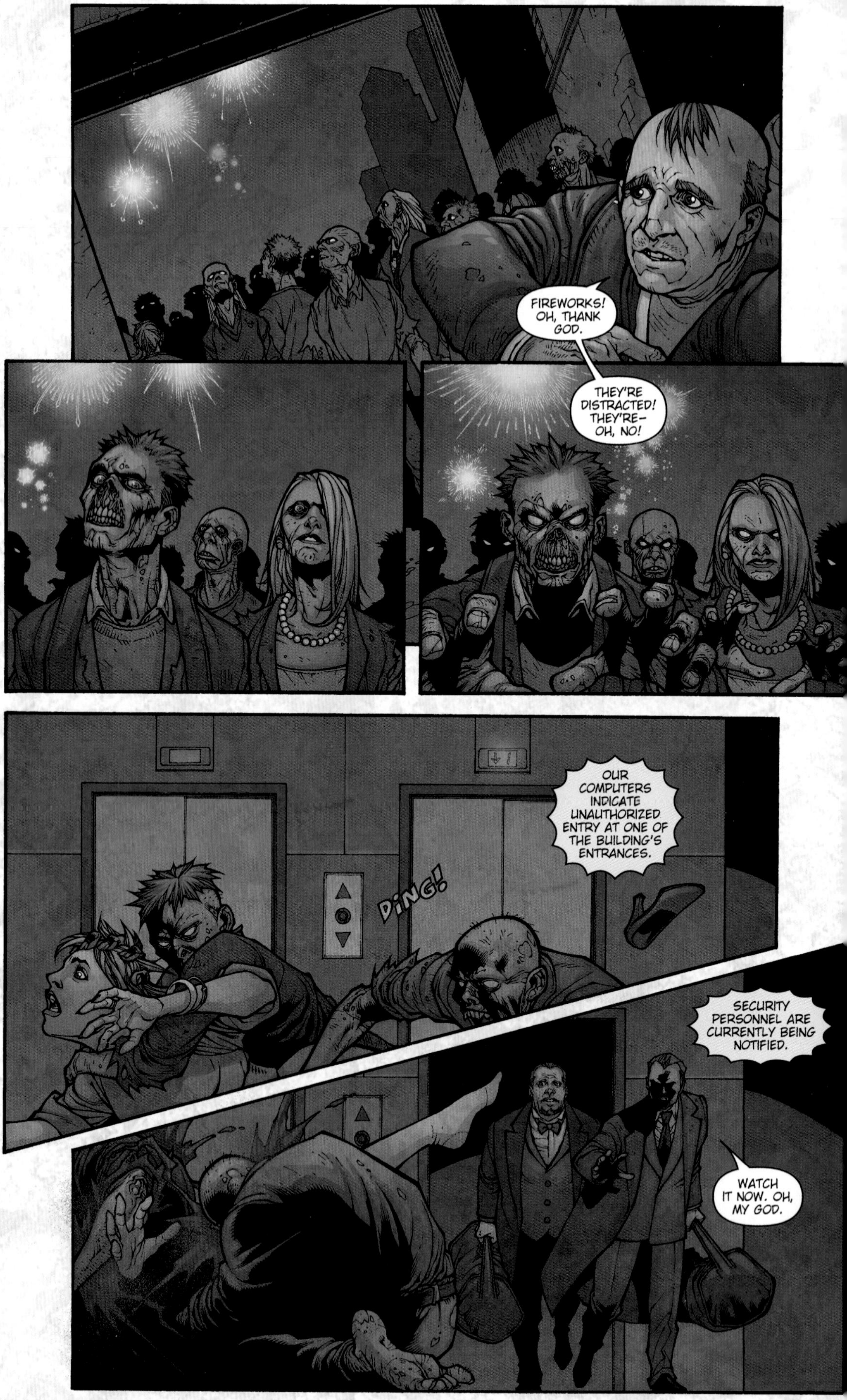
FIREWORKS! OH, THANK GOD.
THEY'RE DISTRACTED! THEY'RE— OH, NO!
OUR COMPUTERS INDICATE UNAUTHORIZED ENTRY AT ONE OF THE BUILDING'S ENTRANCES.
DiNG!
SECURITY PERSONNEL ARE CURRENTLY BEING NOTIFIED.
WATCH IT NOW. OH, MY GOD.

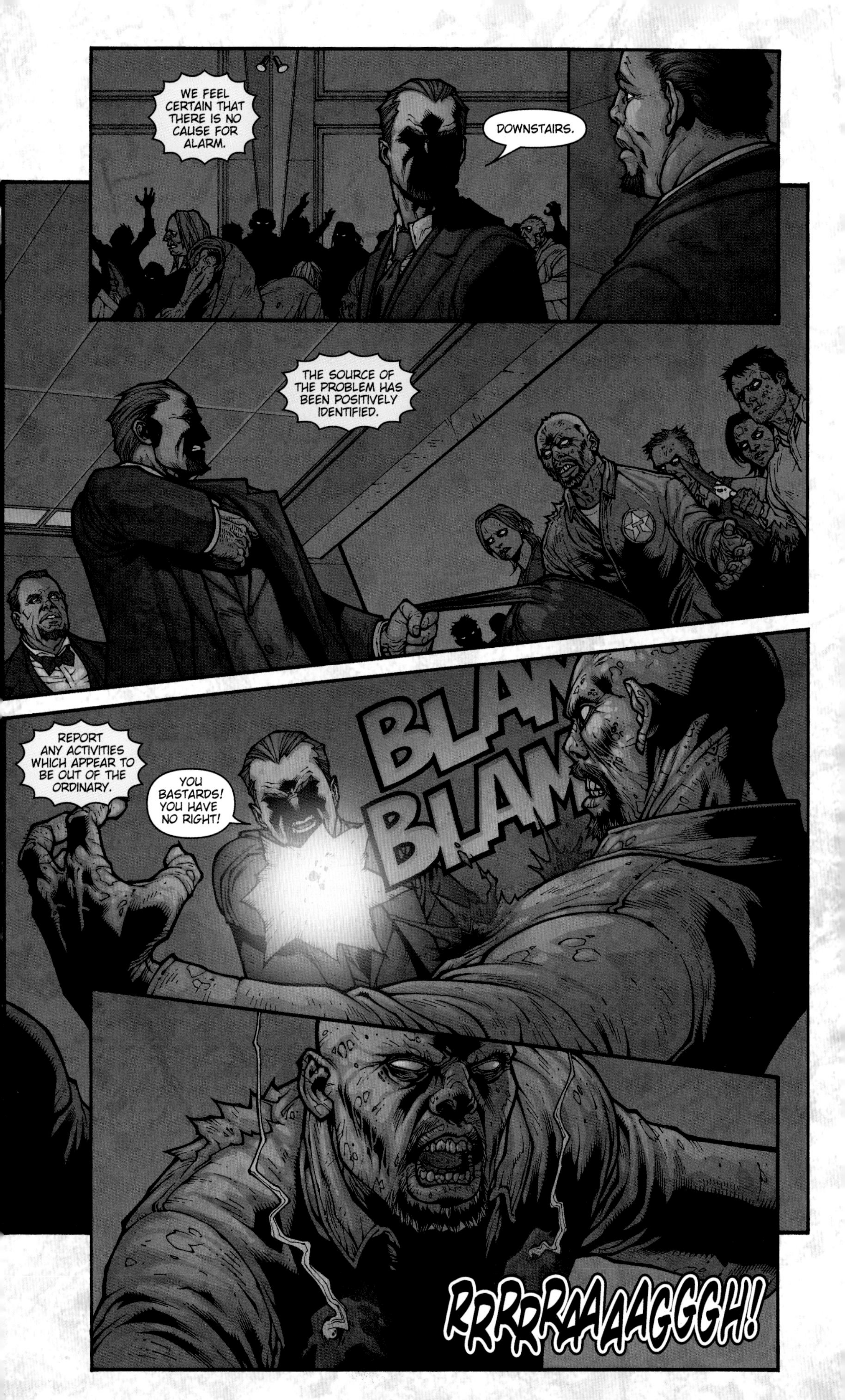
WE FEEL CERTAIN THAT THERE IS NO CAUSE FOR ALARM.
DOWNSTAIRS.
THE SOURCE OF THE PROBLEM HAS BEEN POSITIVELY IDENTIFIED.
REPORT ANY ACTIVITIES WHICH APPEAR TO BE OUT OF THE ORDINARY.
YOU BASTARDS! YOU HAVE NO RIGHT!
BLAM
BLAM
RRRRRAAAAGGGH!

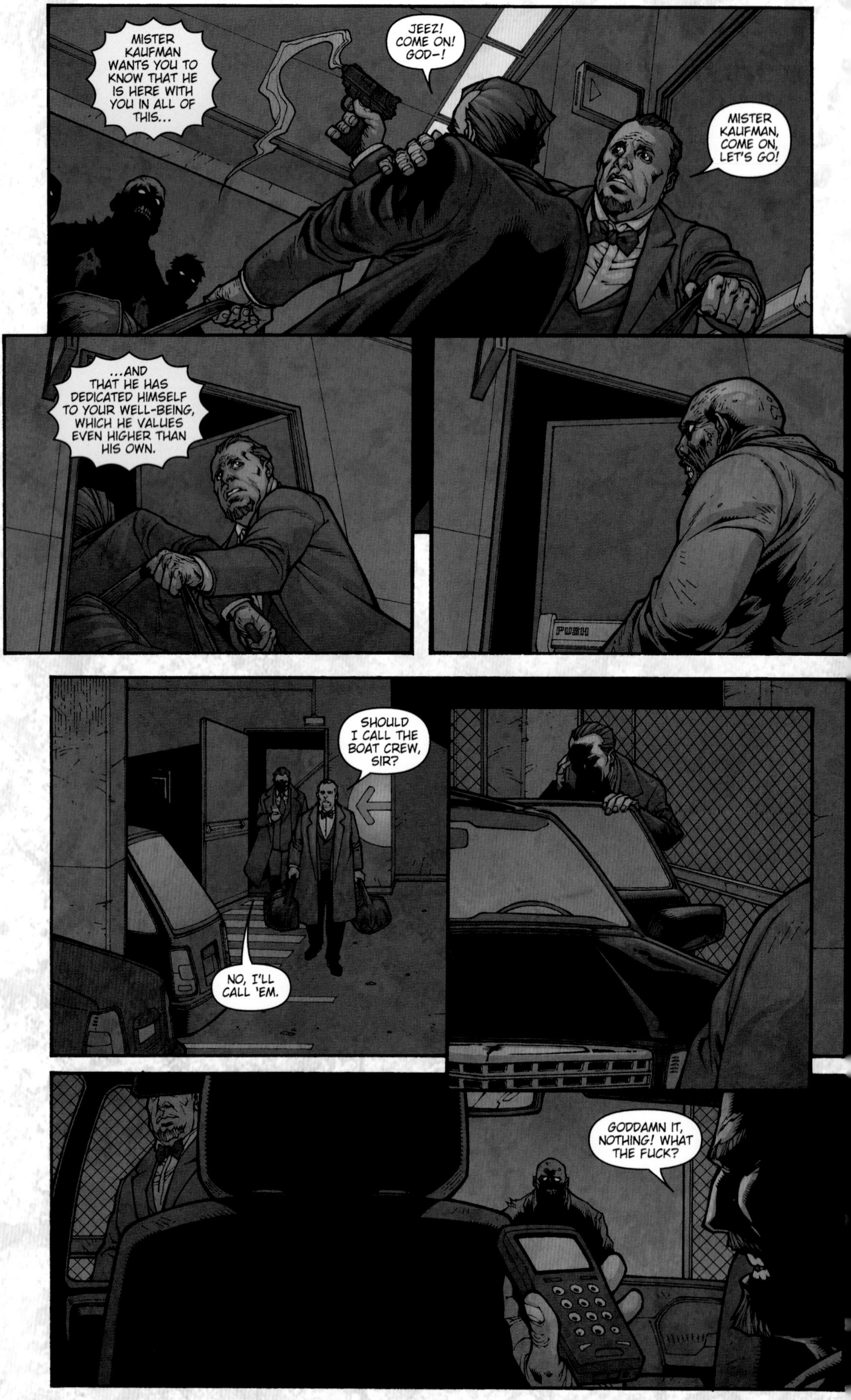
MISTER KAUFMAN WANTS YOU TO KNOW THAT HE IS HERE WITH YOU IN ALL OF THIS...
JEEZ! COME ON! GOD–!
MISTER KAUFMAN, COME ON, LET'S GO!
...AND THAT HE HAS DEDICATED HIMSELF TO YOUR WELL-BEING, WHICH HE VALUES EVEN HIGHER THAN HIS OWN.
PUSH
SHOULD I CALL THE BOAT CREW, SIR?
NO, I'LL CALL 'EM.
GODDAMN IT, NOTHING! WHAT THE FUCK?

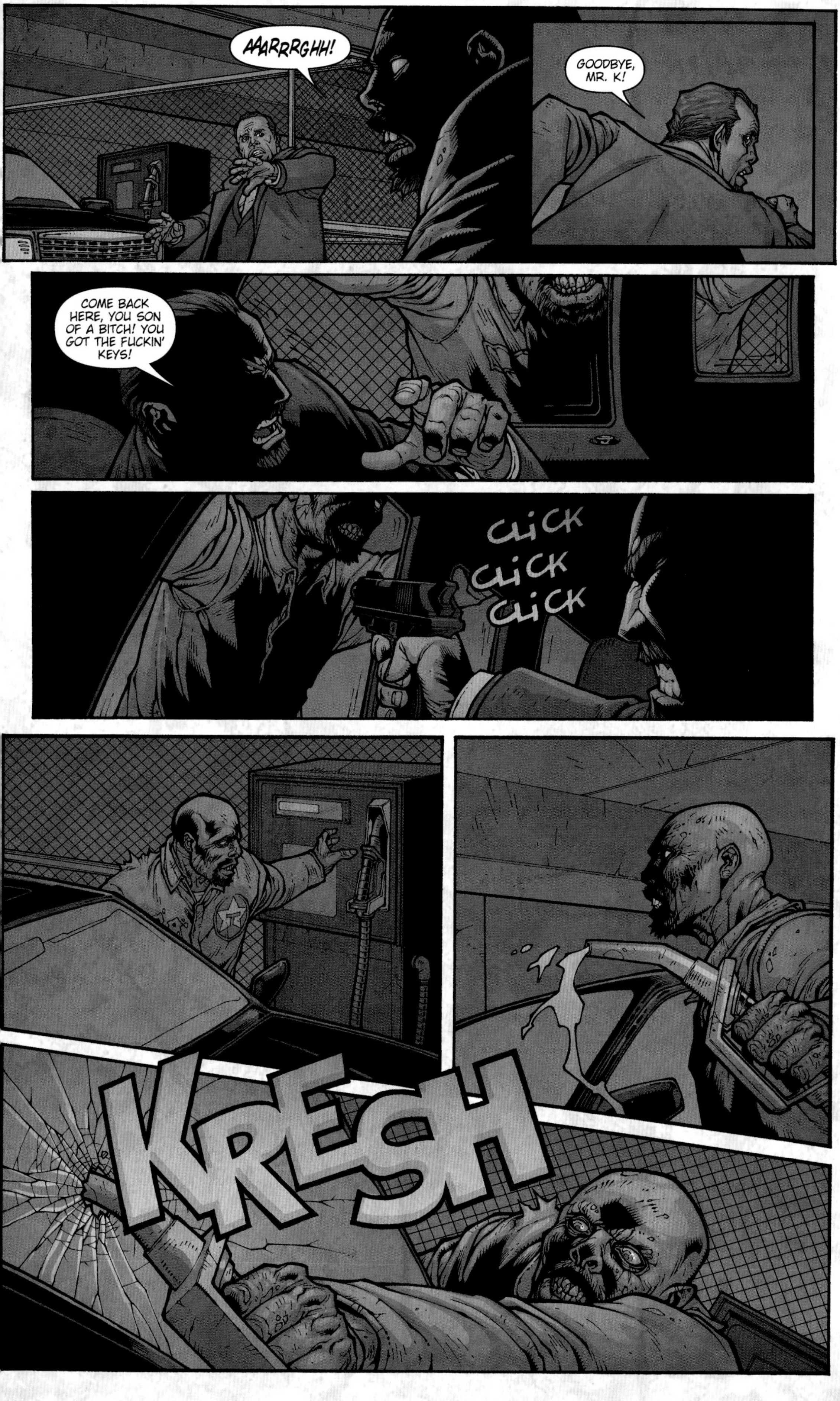
AAARRRGHH!
GOODBYE, MR. K!
COME BACK HERE, YOU SON OF A BITCH! YOU GOT THE FUCKIN' KEYS!
CLICK
CLICK
CLICK
KRESH

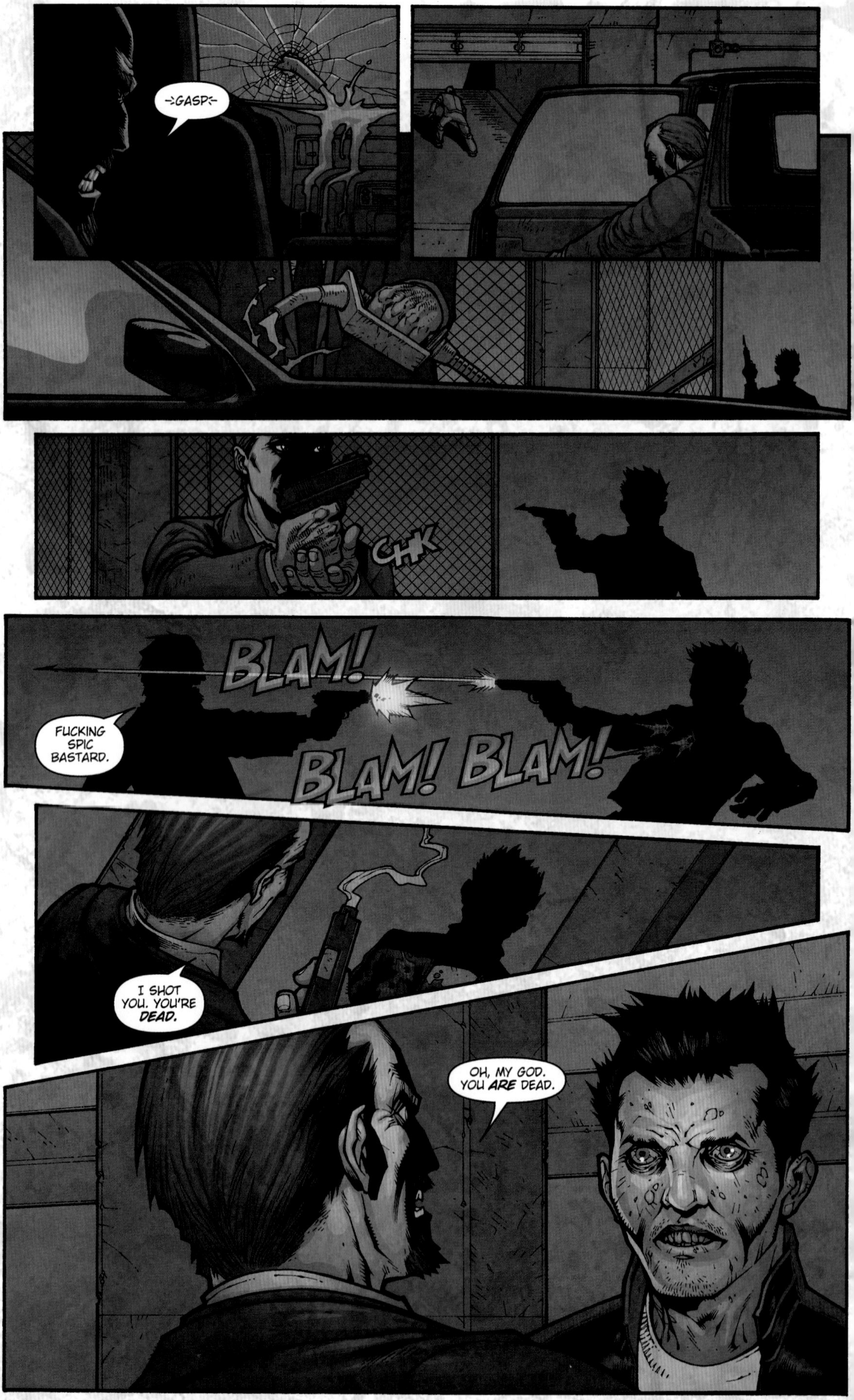
-GASP-
CHK
BLAM!
FUCKING SPIC BASTARD.
BLAM! BLAM!
I SHOT YOU. YOU'RE DEAD.
OH, MY GOD. YOU ARE DEAD.

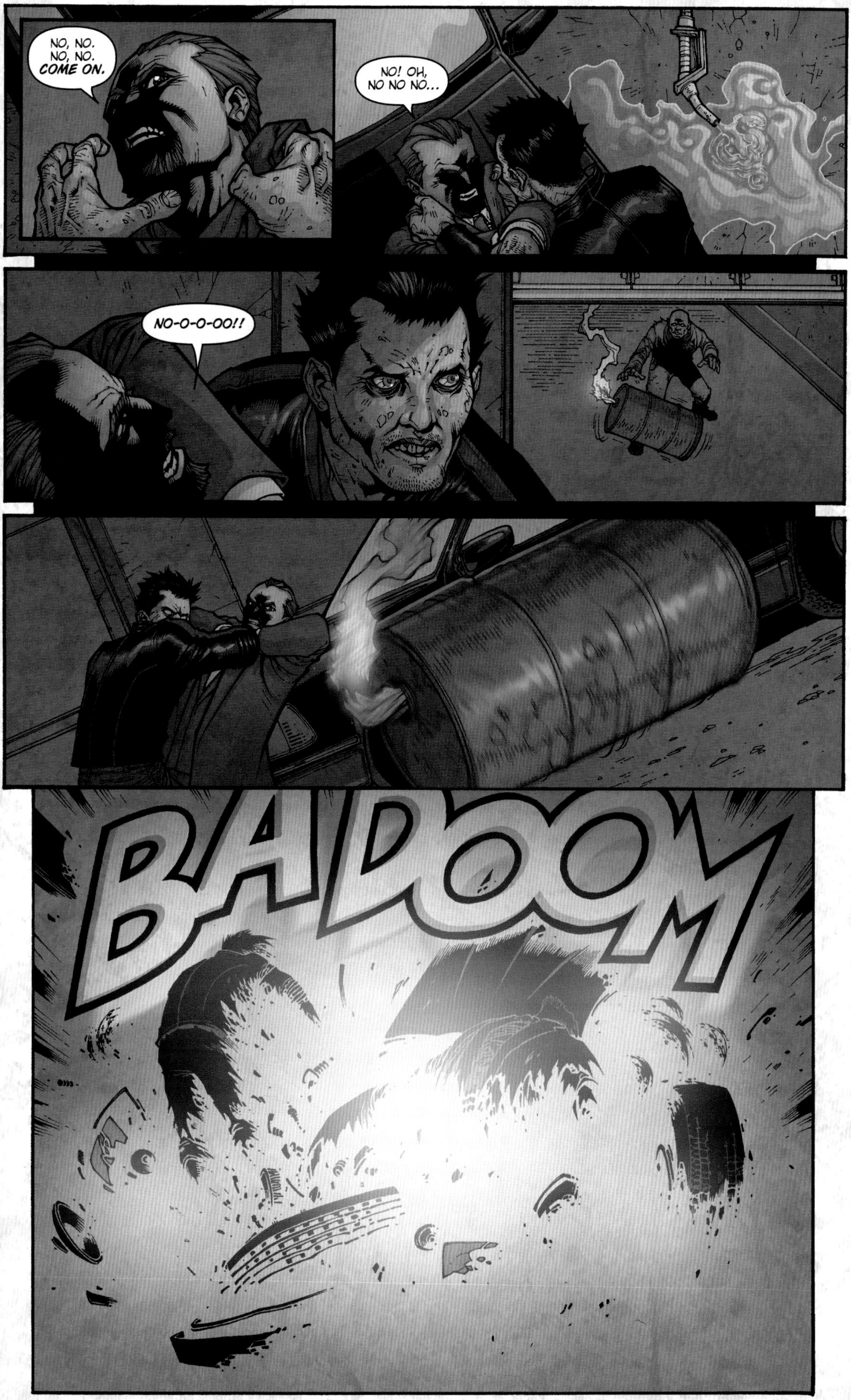
NO, NO.
NO, NO.
COME ON.
NO! OH, NO NO NO...
NO-O-O-OO!!
BADOOM

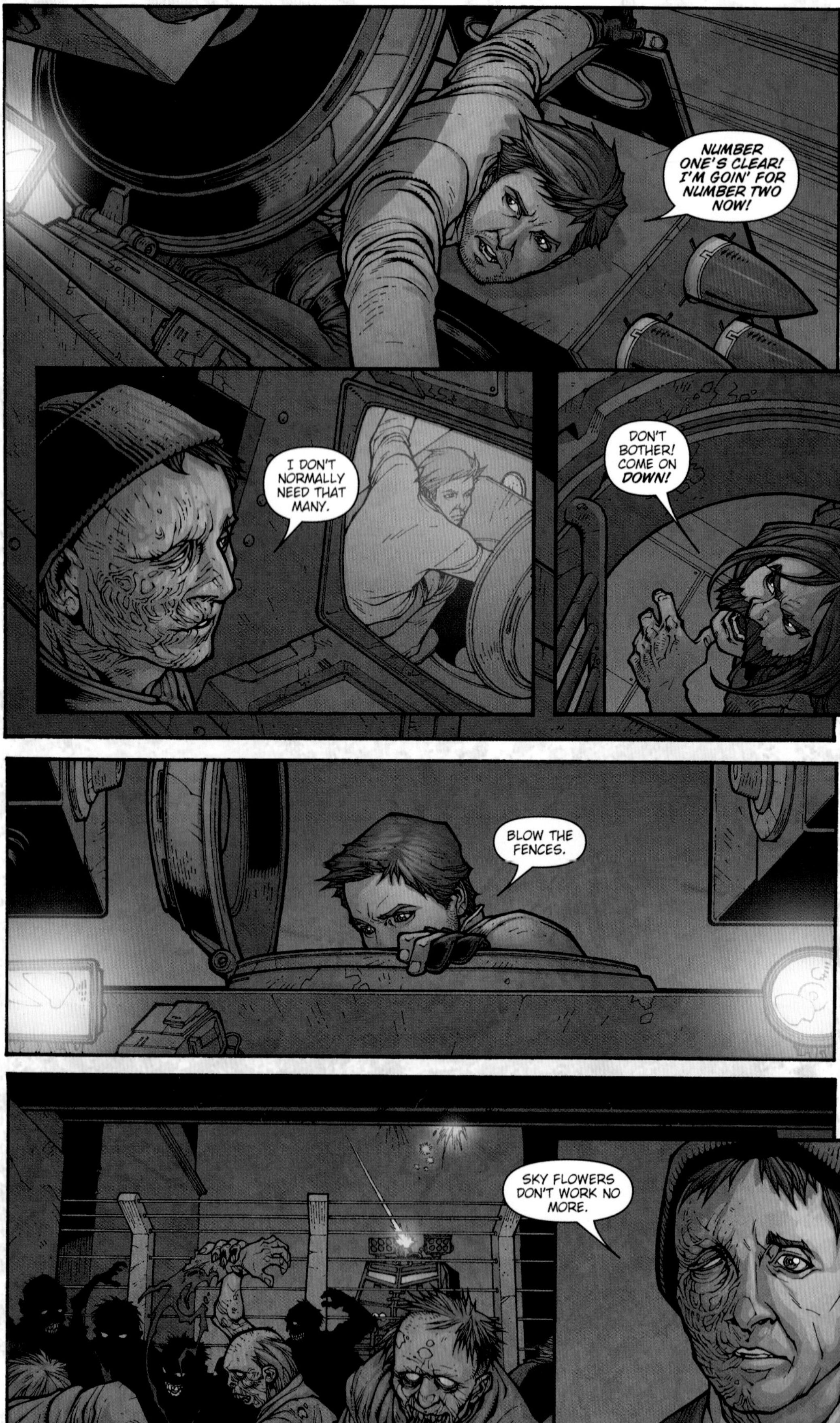
NUMBER ONE'S CLEAR! I'M GOIN' FOR NUMBER TWO NOW!
I DON'T NORMALLY NEED THAT MANY.
DON'T BOTHER! COME ON ***DOWN!***
BLOW THE FENCES.
SKY FLOWERS DON'T WORK NO MORE.

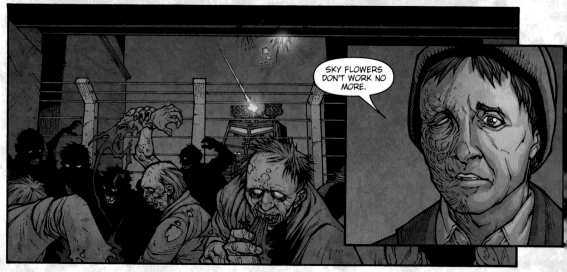

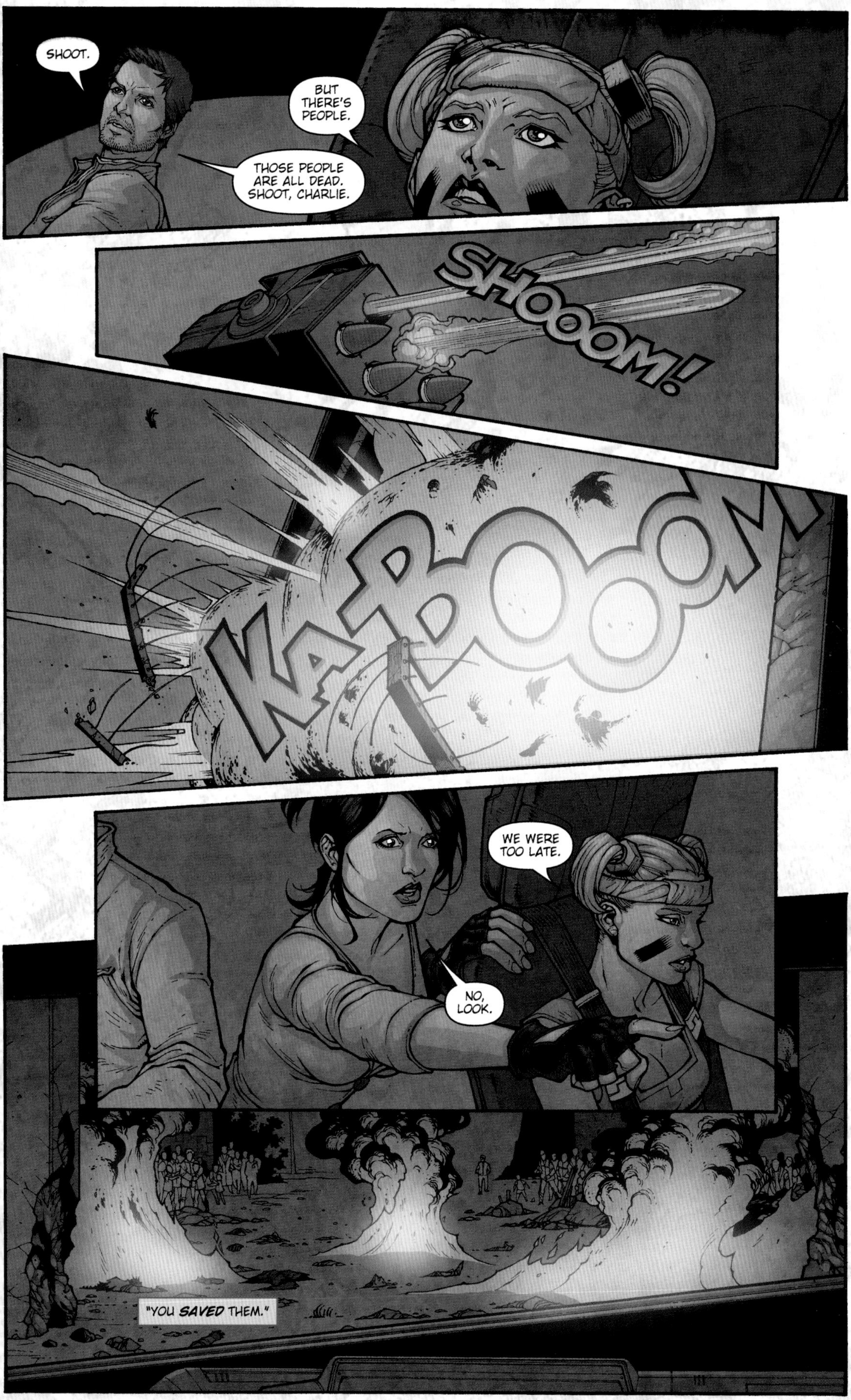

SHOOT.
BUT THERE'S PEOPLE.
THOSE PEOPLE ARE ALL DEAD. SHOOT, CHARLIE.
SHOOOOM!
KA-BOOOM!
WE WERE TOO LATE.
NO, LOOK.
"YOU SAVED THEM."

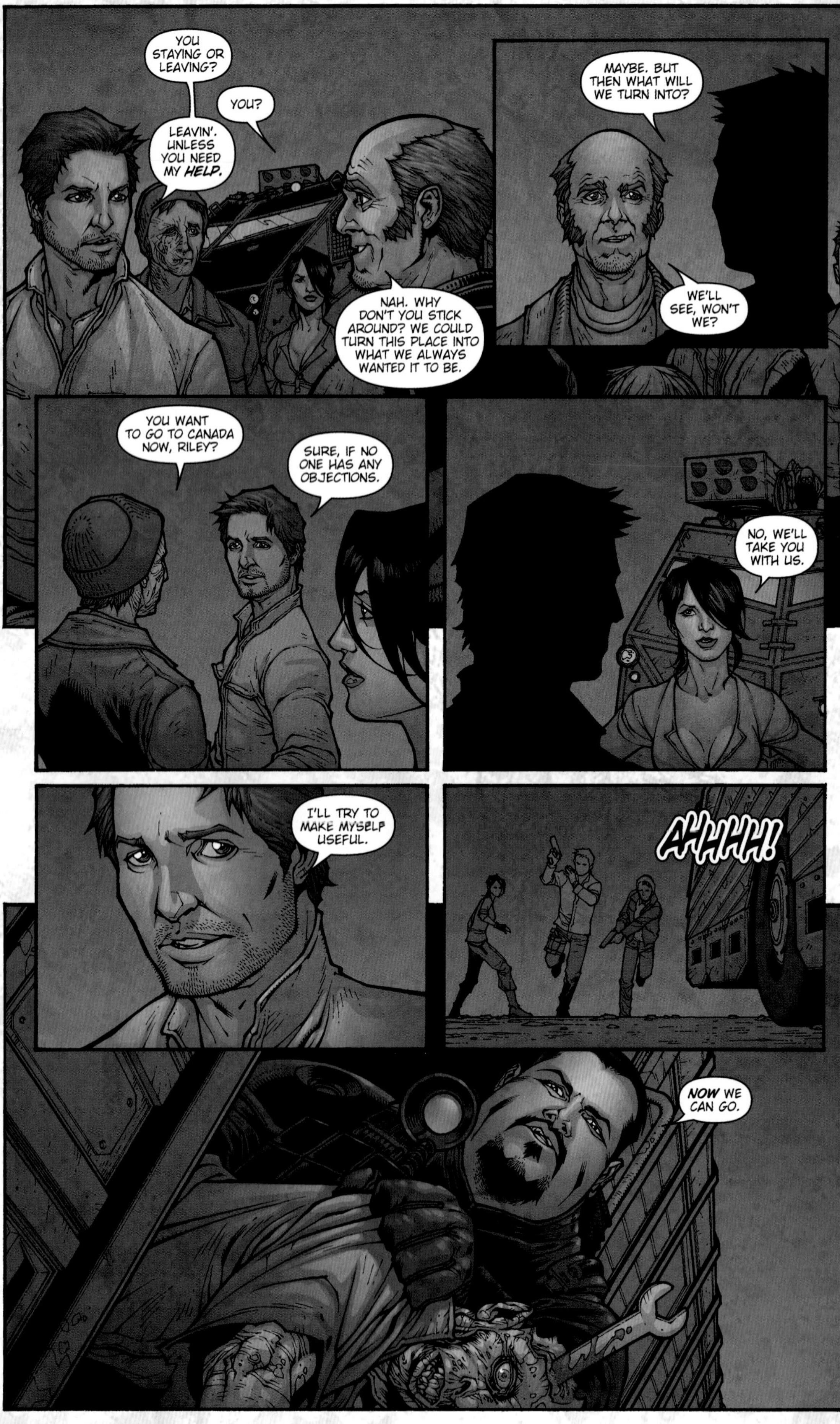

YOU STAYING OR LEAVING?
YOU?
LEAVIN'. UNLESS YOU NEED MY **HELP.**
NAH. WHY DON'T YOU STICK AROUND? WE COULD TURN THIS PLACE INTO WHAT WE ALWAYS WANTED IT TO BE.
MAYBE. BUT THEN WHAT WILL WE TURN INTO?
WE'LL SEE, WON'T WE?
YOU WANT TO GO TO CANADA NOW, RILEY?
SURE, IF NO ONE HAS ANY OBJECTIONS.
NO, WE'LL TAKE YOU WITH US.
I'LL TRY TO MAKE MYSELF USEFUL.
AHHHH!
NOW WE CAN GO.

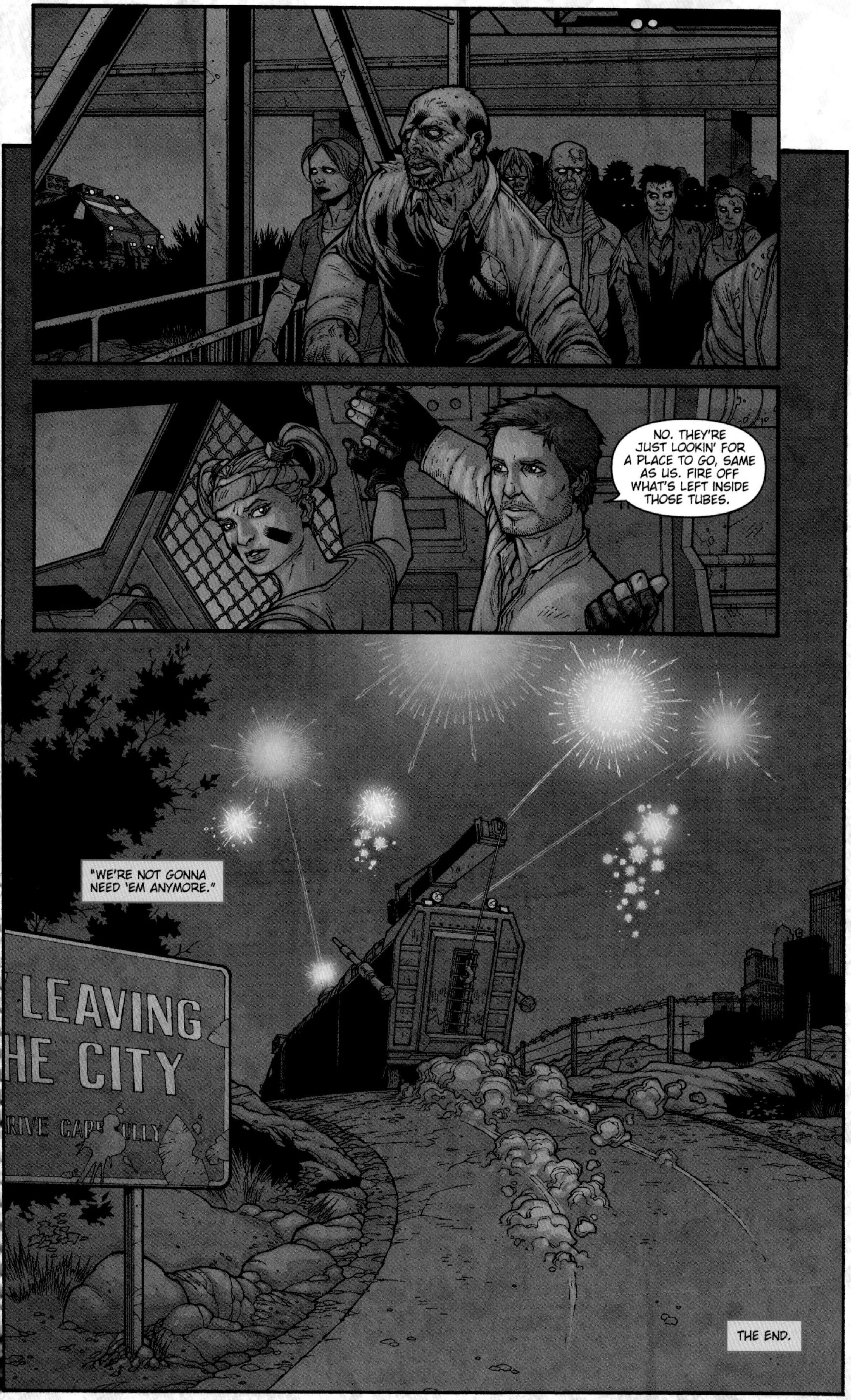
NO. THEY'RE JUST LOOKIN' FOR A PLACE TO GO, SAME AS US. FIRE OFF WHAT'S LEFT INSIDE THOSE TUBES.
"WE'RE NOT GONNA NEED 'EM ANYMORE."
LEAVING
CITY
THE END.

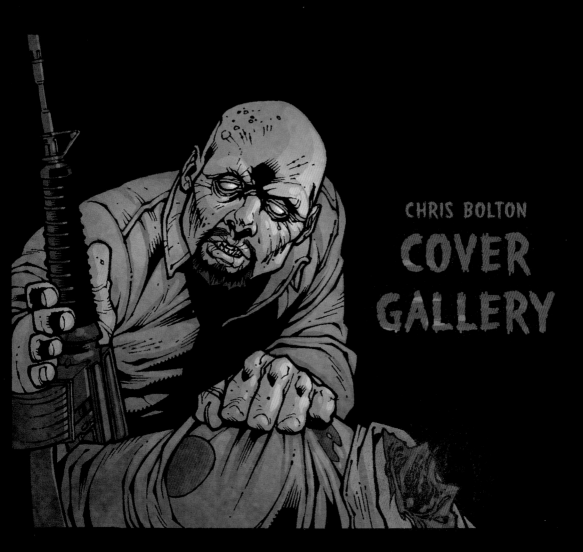

CHRIS BOLTON
COVER
GALLERY

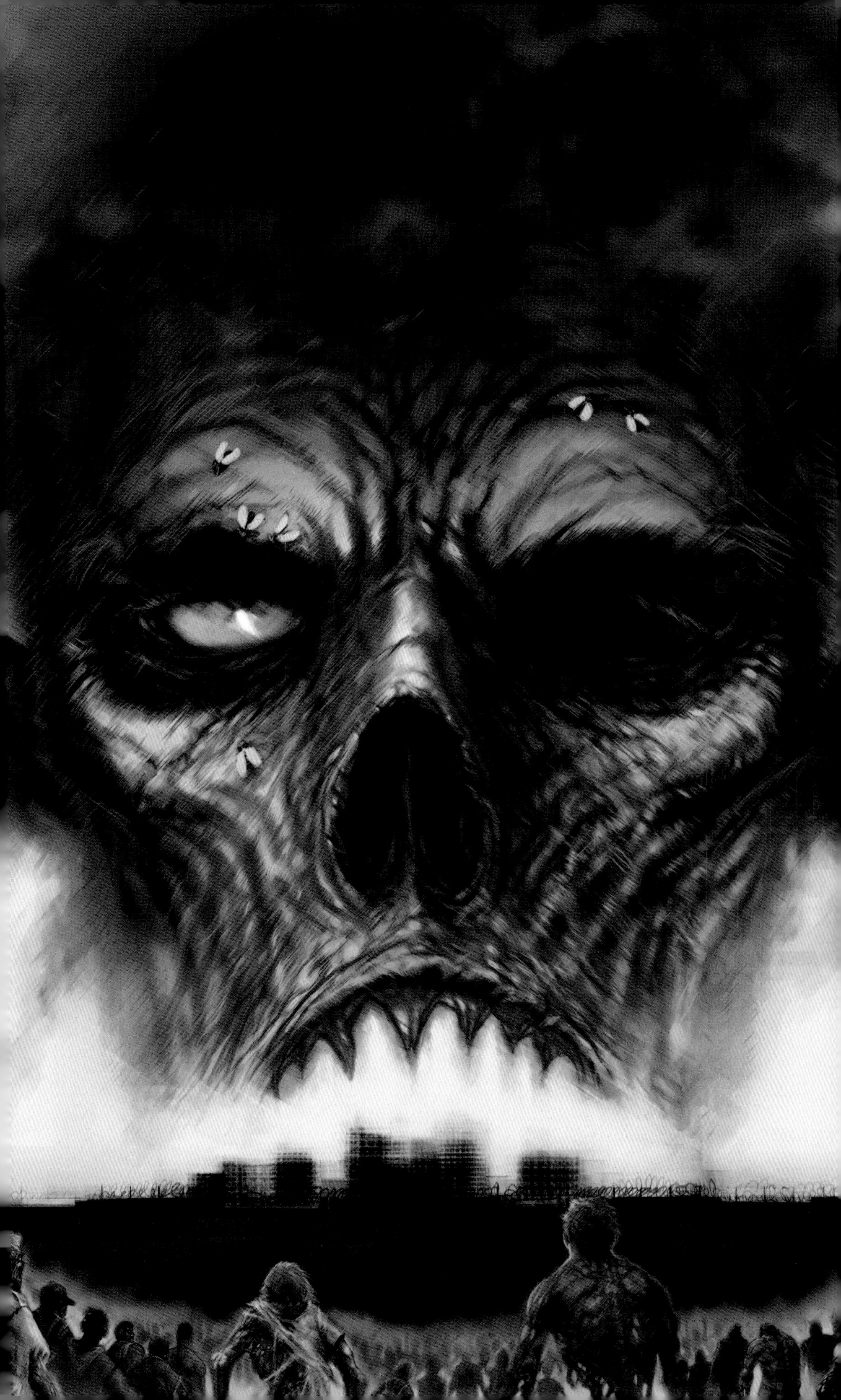

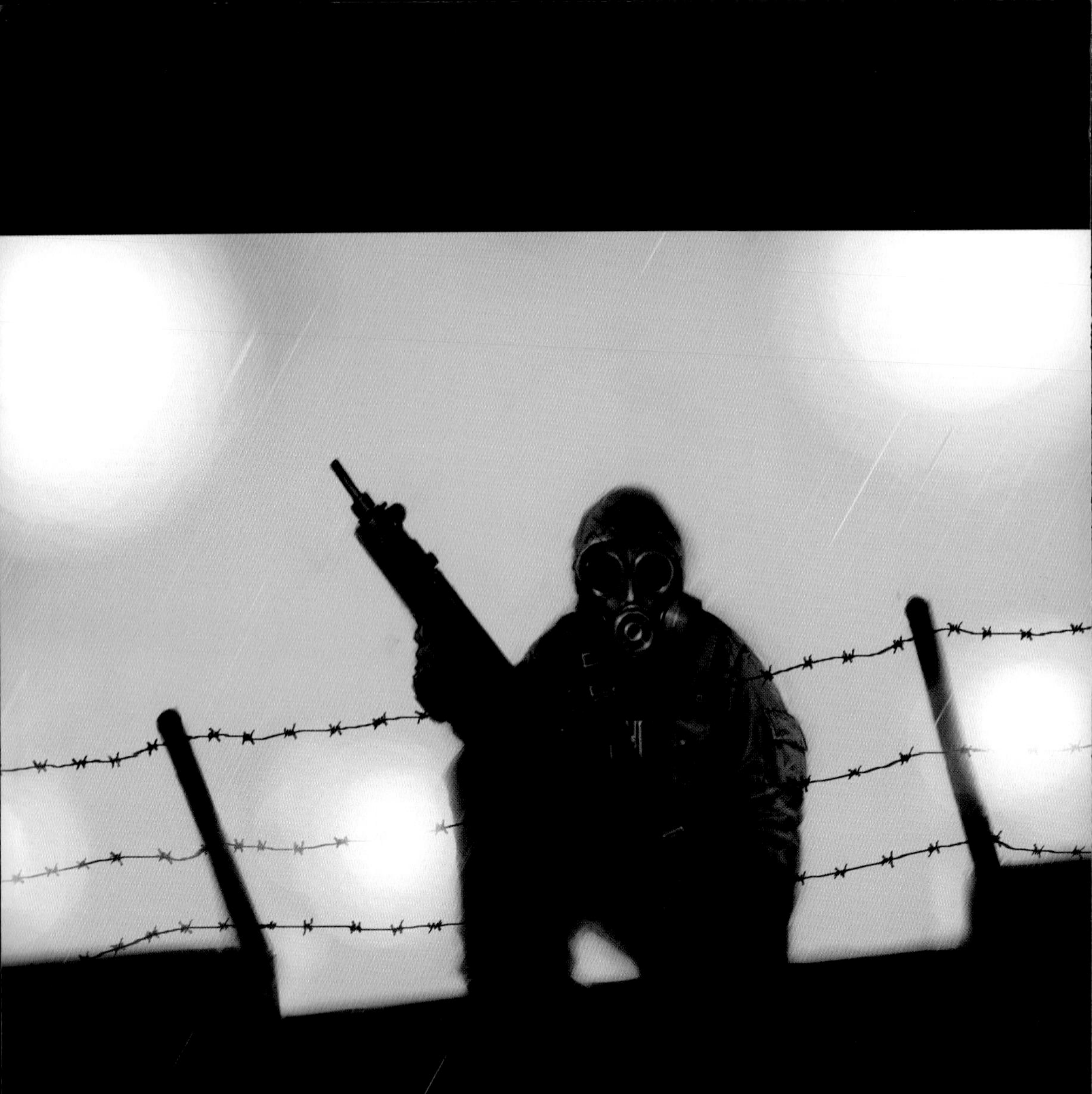

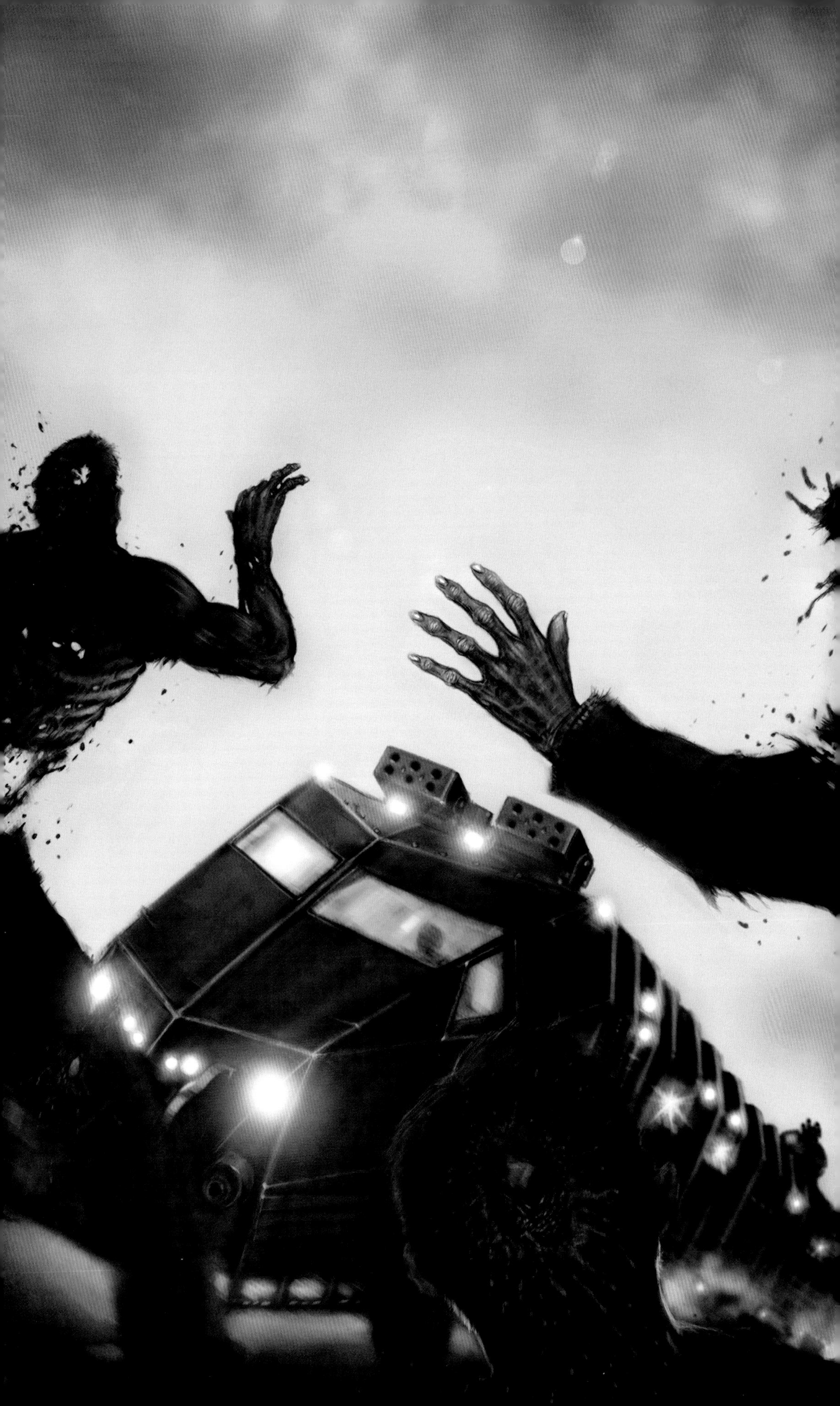

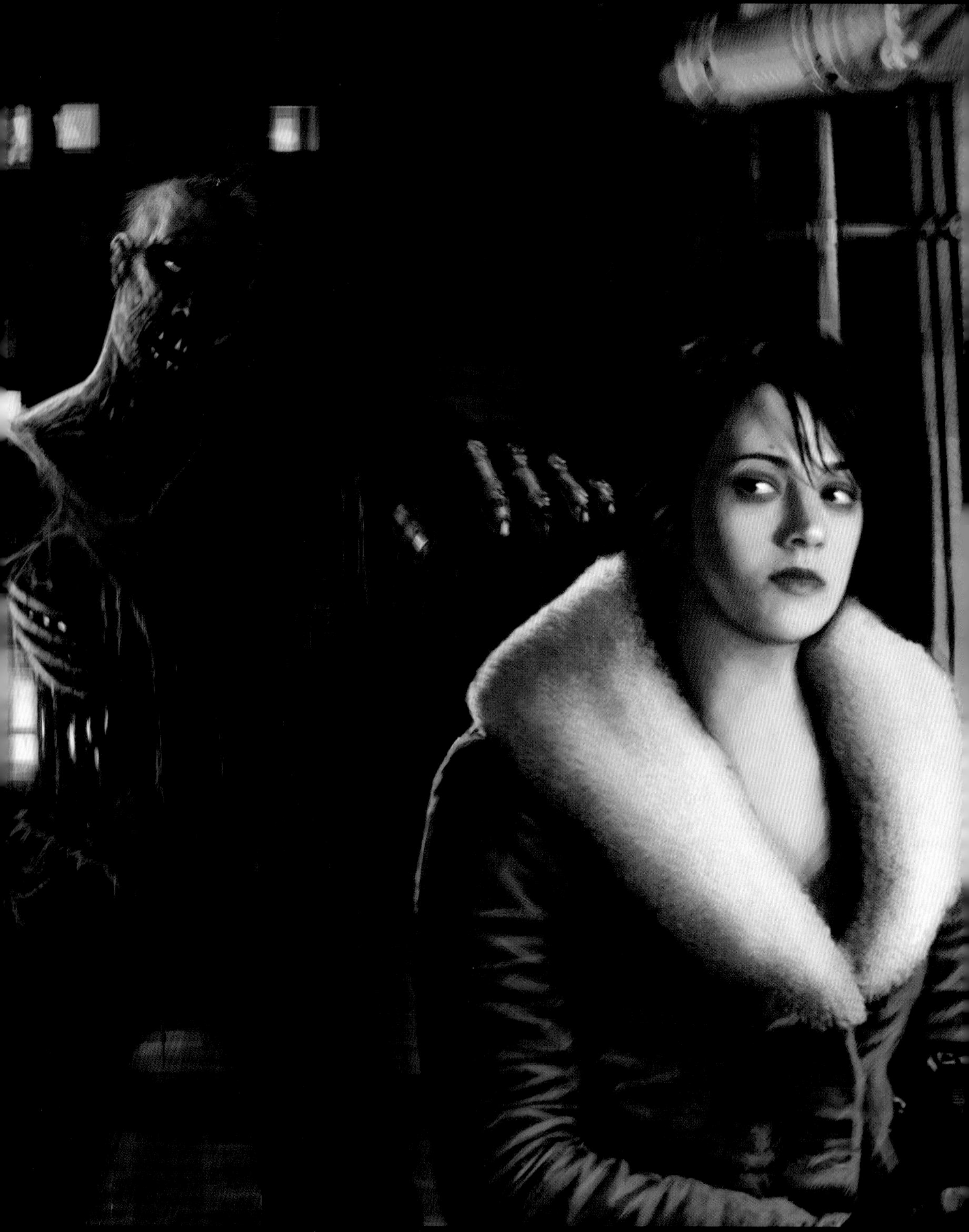

THIS PAGE : COVER ISSUE #4
NEXT PAGE : COVER ISSUE #5

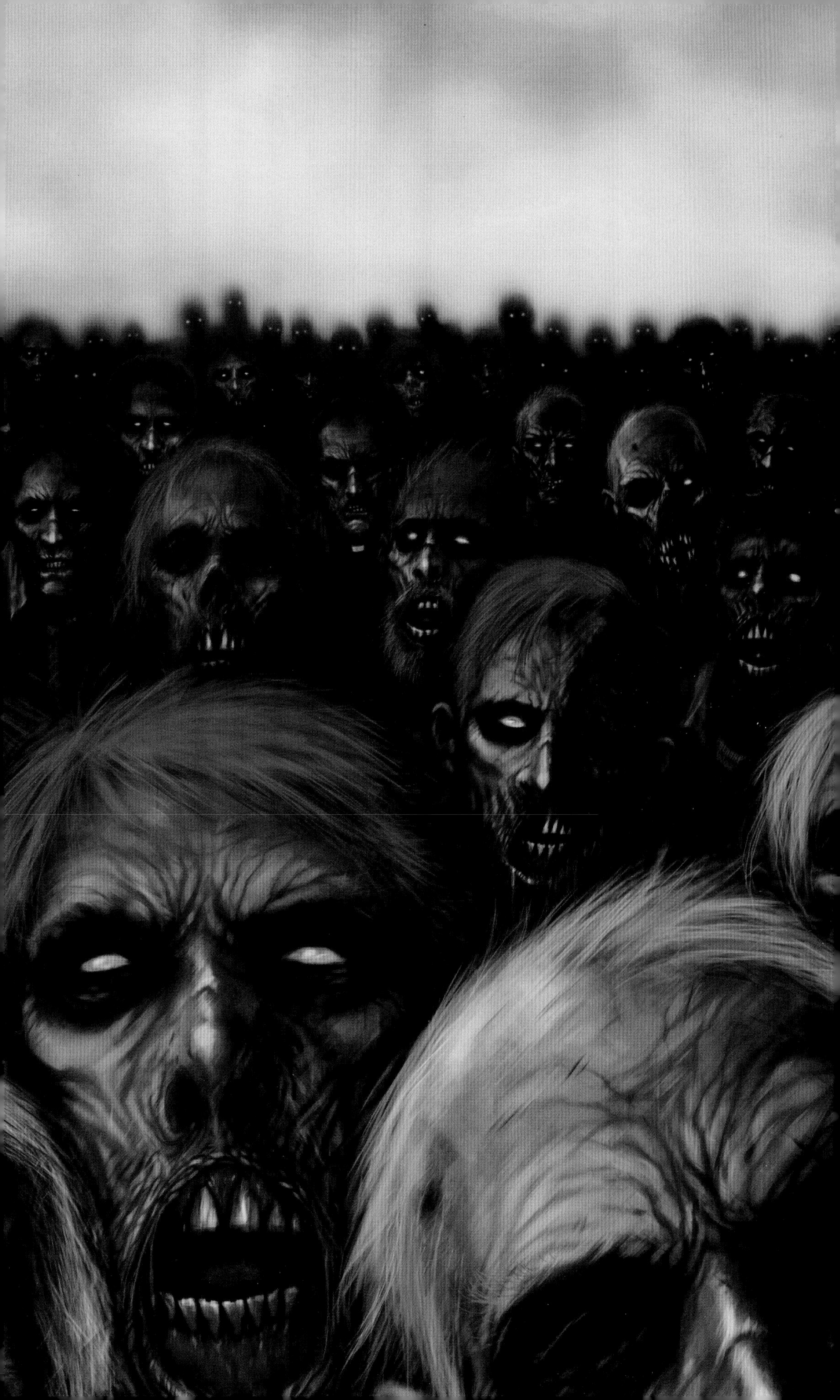

IDW Publishing.com